IMPRISONING A REVOLUTION

IMPRISONING A REVOLUTION

Writings from Egypt's Incarcerated

COLLECTIVE ANTIGONE

UNIVERSITY OF CALIFORNIA PRESS

University of California Press
Oakland, California

© 2025 by The Regents of the University of California

Library of Congress Cataloging-in-Publication Data

Names: Collective Antigone, editor.
Title: Imprisoning a revolution : writings from Egypt's incarcerated / Collective Antigone.
Description: Oakland, California : University of California Press, [2025] | Includes bibliographical references.
Identifiers: LCCN 2024013171 (print) | LCCN 2024013172 (ebook) | ISBN 9780520401365 (hardback) | ISBN 9780520401372 (paperback) | ISBN 9780520401389 (ebook)
Subjects: LCSH: Prisoners as authors—Egypt. | Prisoners in literature. | Revolutions—Egypt—History—21st century. | Egypt—History—Protests, 2011–2013. | Egypt—History—Protests, 2011–2013—In literature. | Egypt—Politics and government—21st century.
Classification: LCC PN494 .I47 2025 (print) | LCC PN494 (ebook) | DDC 892.7/0892069270962—dc23/eng/20240729
LC record available at https://lccn.loc.gov/2024013171
LC ebook record available at https://lccn.loc.gov/2024013172

33 32 31 30 29 28 27 26 25 24
10 9 8 7 6 5 4 3 2 1

Contents

List of Illustrations xi

Acknowledgments xiii

Note on Transliteration xvii

Foreword: Texts That Survived the Ashes, by Ahmed Naji xix

Introduction, by Collective Antigone 1

1. Anonymous 51
   A DIARY OF EVERYDAY LIFE IN PRISON 51

2. Alaa Abd El-Fattah 56
   TORA PRISON, CELL 1/6, WARD 4 58
   JAN. 25, 5 YEARS ON: THE ONLY WORDS I CAN WRITE ARE ABOUT LOSING MY WORDS 60

3. Anonymous 63
   FRAGMENTS OF A COPTIC PRISONER'S DIARY: ON THE MARGINS OF A BIBLE 64

4. Ayman Moussa 68
   "SCREAMS OF MY MIND" 69

5. Ahmed Abdallah 74
   TRUTH ABOUT GIULIO 74

6. Ahmed Gamal Ziada   76
   THE RECEPTION   78
   THE GIFT   82

7. Ahmed Douma   84
   "BEING AWAY HAS ITS IMPACT . . . AND OUR ABILITIES HAVE THEIR LIMITS"   85
   SEEKING REFUGE IN THE DARKNESS   86

8. Mohamed Morsi   90
   A MESSAGE FROM DR. MOHAMED MORSI TO THE PEOPLE OF EGYPT   92

9. Mohsen Mohamed   94
   TIME   95
   ON THE ROAD   95
   ON THE BURSH AFTER DINNER   98
   THE LIGHT ISN'T SURROUNDED BY GUARDS   100
   DISAPPEARANCE   103
   SERGEANT   105

10. Abdelrahman Tarek (Moka)   109
    THE "INTAKE"   110

11. Mohamed Nabil   112
    "HEAPS OF FLESH UNDER THEIR CONTROL"   113

12. Sarah Hegazy   114
    "AMIDST ALL THIS, ALL WE WISHED FOR . . . WAS A HUG BY OUR MOTHERS"   115
    A YEAR AFTER THE RAINBOW FLAG CONTROVERSY   116
    A DEDICATION   120
    FAREWELL   121

13. Yara Sallam   122
    "DID YOU SEE AYA IN QANATER PRISON?"   123
    HOW WE GOT USED TO THE SCREAMS OF THOSE ON DEATH ROW   125
    I LOST TRACK OF TIME IN EVERY SENSE OF THE WORD: ON COPING WITH PRISON AND ITS AFTERMATH   126

14. Ibrahim Ezz al-Din   128
    "BORED OF TORTURING YOU!"   129

15. Mostafa al-Aasar 132
    "WE ARE MUCH WEAKER THAN WE SEEM" 133
    "DESTINED FOR MISERY" 134
    RAMADAN NIGHTS IN PRISON 136

16. Sanaa Seif 139
    WHEN THE LAW IS NOT THE LAW ANYMORE 141
    DEATH'S CHILD 143
    ON THE VIGIL OF THE ARREST 146
    ABOUT PRISON, BOOKS, CHAOS OF THE MIND, AND THE STATE SECURITY OFFICER 148

17. Patrick George Zaki 151
    LETTER NUMBER 1 152
    LETTER NUMBER 2 152
    LETTER NUMBER 3 153

18. Malak al-Kashef 154
    A HUNDRED DAYS 155

19. Khaled Lotfi 158
    WHY AM I HERE? 159

20. Shady Abu Zaid 161
    FLOWER FOR A FRIEND 162
    TEXT ENGRAVED IN BOAT 164

21. Shady Habash 166
    "PRISON DOESN'T KILL, LONELINESS DOES" 167

22. Galal El-Behairy 168
    A LETTER FROM TORA PRISON 169

23. Walid Shawky 174
    SHADY HABASH: A TURNING POINT WHERE THE CIRCLE ENDS 175

24. Ramy Shaath 179
    DEAR FAMILY AND LOVED ONES 180
    DEAR LOVE 180

25. Haitham Mohamadin 184
    "DO YOU LISTEN TO UMM KULTHUM?" 185

26. Abdelrahman ElGendy 188
    AMMAD 189
    LUMOS 192

27. Anonymous 196
    A DAY IN THE LIFE . . . WE CREATED A DREAM NO POWER CAN ERASE 197
    "WE CANNOT HUG OUR CHILDREN": A DAY IN THE LIFE OF A MUSLIM BROTHERHOOD DETAINEE 197
    I AM AFRAID TO DIE IN PRISON 201
    AS IF PRISONS WERE DESIGNED TO KILL US 202

28. Islam Khalil 203
    FIVE BIRTHDAY CELEBRATIONS 204

29. Journalists in Prison 207
    SOLAFA MAGDY 208
    ESRAA ABDEL FATTAH 210
    SHEREEN BEKHEIT 211
    KARAM SABER 212
    HISHAM FUAD 213
    AHMED TAREK (ARNOUB) 214
    ANONYMOUS FEMALE JOURNALIST 215
    REEM QOTB GABARA 215
    HASSAN AL-BANNA MUBARAK 216

30. Mahienour El-Massry 218
    PRISON IS A MICROCOSM OF SOCIETY 219
    WE SHALL CONTINUE 222
    ABOUT GAZA DURING THE 2014 ATTACK 223
    ON THE ANNIVERSARY OF THE ASSASSINATION OF SHAIMA AL-SABBAGH 224

31. Mohamed Ramadan 227
    KNOWING YOUR TORTURER 228

32. Mohamed El-Baqer 230
    THE PANDEMIC IN PRISON 232

33. Collective Letters 234
    TO THE LEADERS OF THE MUSLIM BROTHERHOOD, FROM THE YOUTH OF THE MUSLIM BROTHERHOOD 234

FROM WOMEN PRISONERS 237
CRY FOR HELP FROM QANATER WOMEN'S PRISON 239
LETTER OF DISTRESS FROM DETAINEES AT SCORPION PRISON 240

34. Basma Refaat 242
    QANATER WOMEN'S PRISON 242

35. Mona Mahmoud Mohamed 244
    WHY AM I IN PRISON? 245

36. Israa Khaled Said 246
    I'M HERE BECAUSE YOU DID WELL, MOM 246

37. Ghada Abdel Aziz 248
    "FROM THE WORST PLACE" 248

38. Marwa Arafa 250
    DEAR BIG WAFAA 251

39. Essam Mohamed Atta 253
    LETTER 253

40. Anonymous 255
    LIFE ON DEATH ROW 255

41. Ibrahim Azab 258
    KISS MY COMBAT BOOT 258

42. Anonymous 261
    SOUNDS OF THE EXECUTION CHAMBER FROM
    THE ROOM NEXT DOOR 261

43. Anonymous 263
    I AM NOT A FAMOUS DETAINEE 263

44. Yassin 265
    YASSIN AND HIS PRISON PAINTINGS AND NOTES 265

45. Mahmoud Abu Zeid (Shawkan) 273
    INFORMANTS IN THE MORNING 277

46. Song of Submission 280

    Afterword: A Message to Egyptian Political Prisoners, Ngũgĩ wa Thiong'o in Conversation with Collective Antigone 283

    Selected Bibliography 297

Illustrations

1. Photo from "They are celebrating Eid in prison" campaign   27
2. Photo from "They are celebrating Eid in prison" campaign   28
3. Alaa Abd El-Fattah during Shura Council trials   61
4. Origami heart made by Ahmed Abdallah   75
5. Letter written by Abdelrahman Tarek (Moka)   110
6. Sarah Hegazy with rainbow flag   116
7. Sanaa Seif, Yara Sallam, and others ahead of a trial hearing   125
8. Graffiti celebrating Sanaa Seif   143
9. Portrait of Patrick Zaki   152
10. *Flower for a Friend* by Shady Abu Zaid   163
11. Small wooden boat sculpture by Shady Abu Zaid   165
12. Fragment of letter written by Ramy Shaath   182
13. Graffiti depicting Mahienour El-Massry   223

14. Letter written by Mohamed El-Baqer   231
15. Collective letter written by women prisoners   238
16. *Green Portrait* by Yassin   267
17. *Stick Figures* by Yassin   268
18. *Seated Figure in Corridor* by Yassin   270
19. *Rainbow Swing* by Yassin   271
20. Shawkan in prison   274
21. Screen capture from promotional video for Wadi Natrun Prison   281

Acknowledgments

JUST AS NO COLLECTION of prison writings can hope to include all the voices silenced by the Egyptian regime, we cannot hope to credit all the people without whom this volume would not have been created. Collective Antigone comprises both Egyptian and international scholars, journalists, lawyers, translators, and human rights and prisoners' rights advocates who have been working together for half a decade to collect, curate, and now publish the writing and artwork included in *Imprisoning a Revolution*. Our gratitude extends, first and foremost, to the prisoners themselves, whose writings and artwork epitomize speaking truth to power even when they cannot do so under their own names. Whether internationally renowned activists and intellectuals or ordinary people caught in Egypt's ever-expanding carceral web, just writing about their experiences and feelings in prison carried, and still carries, great risk. Not merely writing, but doing whatever was necessary to get their writing out of prison and into the public record constitutes courageous action that deserves our gratitude.

Most of the participants in this collective remain anonymous because their acknowledged or open participation in the creation of this volume would put their freedom, and potentially their lives, at risk. Beyond the prisoners, their families, lawyers, and local and national Egyptian NGOs not only provided many of the materials and art collected here but helped establish the reality of Egypt as one of the world's most intensely surveilled and imprisoned societies. Of the groups that provided help, advice, or letters and artwork and that can be mentioned, we would like to thank the *Mada Masr* collective; El-Nadeem, Center against Violence and Torture; the Freedom Initiative; the MENA Prison Forum; the Egyptian Commission for Rights and Freedoms; and the Egyptian Initiative for Personal Rights for their work collecting, archiving, and making available prisoners' testimonies. We owe a great debt to Amnesty International USA and Amnesty International Italia for supporting this project since its inception, and particularly to the former General Director of Amnesty Italia, Gianni Rufini, who was among the first colleagues with whom we shared the idea of this project and who sadly passed away during the curation of this book. As we prepare it for publication, his experience and enthusiasm continue to guide us.

We also express our sincerest gratitude to Ahmed Naji and Ngũgĩ wa Thiong'o for their powerful and inspiring contributions to this volume. We are grateful to the Italian and Egyptian artists who allowed us to use their works in this book, especially Gianluca Costantini, Yassin, and the creator of the cover design. We also thank those contributors who have died (including those who were executed or died as a result of their time in prison), and those we were personally unable to reach.

Special thanks to Laila Soueif, in conversation with whom we first conceived this book. The mother of a man who has been imprisoned by every Egyptian regime of this century, from Mubarak, to the SCAF, Morsi, and now Sisi, Professor Soueif continues to inspire human rights defenders worldwide. Her unique generosity invited us to look beyond the fate of her celebrated son and to unleash the voices of less well-known political prisoners: "There are a lot of young people who are writing in prison! You should look at their work!" This was the most powerful lesson we received about the meaning of being a human rights defender.

We thank our mentors and friends in Egypt, especially Ahdaf Soueif; the human rights lawyers Mahienour El-Massry, Sherif Azer, Ahmed Abdallah, Nasser Amin, and Hoda Abdelwahab, whose knowledge of the Egyptian legal system and profound commitment to human rights is a source of inspiration; and Lina Atallah, Sharif Abdul Quddus, Mona Seif, Wael Abdel-Fattah, and Gameela Ismail, whose knowledge of the cultural field in Egypt is always enlightening. These people and many others who prefer not to be named in this context are part of our elective family in Egypt, in whose company we always feel at home.

The manuscript also benefited from careful reading by many colleagues, including Edmund Burke III, Lisa Hajjar, Dwight Reynolds, and Zachary Lockman. We have no words to express our gratitude and we look to all of you as inspiration for what a scholar-activist should be in the twenty-first century. Equally important are the colleagues and comrades who lent their time and their expertise to help finalize the translations of numerous entries in the book.

Last but not least, we wish to thank our editorial team at UC Press, especially Niels Hooper and Nora Becker, as well as the art and production teams, for the enthusiasm with which they have welcomed this project, the competence and intelligence with which they helped us to give it shape, and the care with which they supported us to navigate all the complexities that a project such as this involves.

This book is dedicated to whoever in Egypt and in the world has paid with imprisonment the price for opposing authoritarianism, dictatorship, and military regimes. All royalties due Collective Antigone for *Imprisoning a Revolution* are being donated to Amnesty International for the direct support of prisoners, former prisoners, and their families.

Note on Transliteration

ARABIC TERMS IN THIS BOOK are transliterated according to a simplified version of the *International Journal of Middle East Studies*' style sheet, taking into consideration peculiarities of pronunciation of Egyptian Arabic or common English-language spellings in the Egyptian media. Whenever possible, the spelling of names of public figures (political and/or military leaders, journalists, lawyers, activists, academics, and public intellectuals) follows the English-language version of their names used in public documents, or the way these figures spell their names in publications or documents.

AHMED NAJI

Foreword

Texts That Survived the Ashes

I FIRST MET "Marcel Proust" in prison. On my first day in cell 2/4, a long row of notebooks next to his bunkbed caught my eye. On the second day, I noticed him engrossed in writing as I passed his bunk on my way to and from the bathroom. There were more than sixty prisoners with us in the cell, the majority of whom treated him with a sense of appreciation and respect. One of them explained to me that he was the first inmate in the cell, having been the one steady occupant for the last four years. On the third day, I exchanged greetings with him by nodding my head when we met for an hour of exercise. On the fourth day, I overcame my shyness, introduced myself, and asked him what he was writing.

He smiled and grew impassioned when he found out that I am a writer. He said he was writing his memoirs so that he would not forget even one day of the injustice he had lived through while in prison. Then he offered to let me read what he wrote. I opened the notebook and found each page beginning with a date and then recounting the most ordinary details of his day in prison: what time he got up, what breakfast he ate, what he did, who he talked to, whether he went outside for exercise. All his notebooks were filled with such small everyday details.

I gave him the nickname Marcel Proust after he explained to me that his motive for writing was to document and record the "lost time" of his life in prison. He was neither a writer nor a political prisoner, but rather an average employee accused in a corruption case of a crime of which he believed he was innocent; and for the last four years he had been in pre-trial detention, still waiting for his day in court.

Several months later, the court finally acquitted him, but only after he'd spent four years as a prisoner. While the process for his release was being finalized, the diary of his lost time was found by the guard, who handed it over to the investigative officer, who in turn examined it and read it, then told Proust that what he did was prohibited, because he had recorded details of the prison and its daily operations, and that he could not allow the diary to leave the prison. Legally, the officer did not have the authority to confiscate Proust's diary, but he gave him the choice of burning everything he wrote and completing the procedure for his release or staying in prison.

Proust clung to the memoirs of his lost time, but the officer collected the notebooks in front of him and placed a matchbox on top of them. Then he pointed to a metal barrel and told him: "There is no release . . . no freedom . . . until you burn all these notebooks."

In the end, Marcel Proust acquiesced, setting fire to the prison memoirs that he had written over the years, watching the flames devour his lost time, tears running down his cheek, on his way to freedom.

When I first arrived at Tora Prison, the investigative officer confiscated the books I had with me under the pretext of showing them to the State Security officer first, but he allowed me to keep my black journal and a blue pen. He said he knew that I was a writer, so he would leave me the journal, and that there were books in the prison library that he would allow me to borrow, on one condition: that I would not publish anything during my time in prison, otherwise he would deprive me of paper, pen, and books and turn my days in prison into a living hell.

After the Marcel Proust incident, I realized the trap. I couldn't publish anything while in prison, yet during my release anything I had written while here would be scrutinized, and I would likely be forced to burn it.

Over a succession of nights and days, I came to understand what Proust meant by documenting lost time. The days in prison resemble one another, and by repeating them they turn into one day, a slow, eternal waking moment.

Writing creates an identity and a footprint for each day, gives meaning to its passing, and turns lost time into history. Following in the footsteps of Proust, I began writing my memoirs, but this time I didn't record what was going on in prison, but rather recorded my dreams. Each page in my prison diary begins with today's date, then a narration of what I dreamt. If there was no dream or I didn't remember it, then I'd write a few lines about my state of health and mood.

During my time in prison (February 2016–December 2016), I left Tora twice to attend appeal hearings against the verdict. In one of the sessions, as I stood with other prisoners in a metal cage in the courtroom, my brother approached, confused, and said that he had run into Sonallah Ibrahim, who gave him a bag containing sets of ballpoint pens and reams of tracing paper and asked him to deliver the bag to me.

My brother, a cardiologist who comes from a world far removed from literature and politics, didn't understand the gift from Sonallah Ibrahim, who spent about five years in Al-Wahat prison in the 1960s, when he was imprisoned with thousands of leftists and communists jailed by Nasser. More than fifty years later, Sonallah explained to my brother, he thought about what a writer needs most in prison and decided to gift me pens and paper, which could be hidden and smuggled easily into prison so that I could write. I told Mohammed that I had enough pens and paper and asked him to convey my greetings to Sonallah for his gift, which I would not be able to accept, because my return to prison with that gift would raise suspicions.

I entered prison recalling the prison literature written by Sonallah Ibrahim, the writers of his generation, and various generations of Egyptian politicians and writers, all of whom considered and wrote about prison as a battlefield and a struggle against political authority. For the political activist, imprisonment is an extension of the battle, and therefore every action taken turns into an act of resistance. For political prisoners, writing is the highest form of resistance, because it is a declaration that their will has not been broken, and that they are capable of thinking, creating, and innovating, and as such it is also a crack in the prison walls. As the aim of the prison is to isolate the prisoner between the walls of oblivion, so the prison guard did not allow the release of Marcel Proust's memoirs, because their release and publication would have been a breach of the walls of the very prison he was charged with protecting.

This book is, in a way, a penetration into Egyptian prisons, a puncture in the wall, and a challenge to the authority of the warden.

To write in prison is to "present evidence" against the warden. The political prisoner, in particular, writes about the humiliation and torture endured in prison, so that the writing becomes a testimony and a documentation in its own right.

The role of prison literature as "testimony" has grown in recent decades with the proliferation of human rights organizations in the West and East, which rely on these testimonies in their legal and human rights actions against authoritarian states and repressive regimes. These organizations have teams of workers whose job is to reach victims/prisoners and record, document, and collect their testimonies.

While these testimonies have played a crucial political role in levying charges against the perpetrators and unmasking the brutal practices of torture and killing within prison walls, the methodology and linguistic mode employed in the collection and publication of these testimonies in recent decades have significantly undermined the humanistic and personal essence of prison testimonies and literature.

In the sphere of human rights testimony, there's no room for the prisoner's voice except as that of a victim speaking in the language of law and facts. Any expression of grief, anger, or desire is considered a violation of the artificial neutrality and objectivity of the language of human rights. Part of the significance of this book and other anthologies lies in the fact that the translated texts are not all legal testimonies, but instead include personal letters from prisoners to their families and literary texts, whether in the form of poems or prose. Anthologies of prison writing restore diversity to the voice of prisoners, bringing it out of the sphere of human rights testimony and into the space of literature that is capable of relaying a variety of emotions.

Prison literature presents itself as expressing a truth that is inaccessible to the ordinary reader. The writer introduces prison literature to the reader in order to demand reverence and submission: "I have come from hell, and I have no reason to lie; I am recording and writing here, being true to my cellmates and to experience." And since the experience presents itself as a sublime and sacred fruit, it has no need for any crafting or artistry. Some writers believe that artistry in prison literature contradicts the sincerity that the text should deliver, and that the charm of the text lies in its honesty.

The experiences in Egyptian prison literature are full of contradictions that raise doubts about the veracity of these narratives. One of the most widely read Egyptian prison books in recent years, for example, is the book *Mushaghib fi-l-mu'ataqal* [A rioter in detention] (Cairo: Dar al-Kanuz, 2016), by Sherif El-Serafi, a supporter of the Sisi regime who was arrested in 2013 and sentenced to a year in prison on charges of "disrupting the memorial" to the martyrs of the revolution. In his book, we do not see a single word of condemnation of the criminal system or of prisons in Egypt. Rather, Sherif glorifies himself and proves his patriotism by relating how he used to spy on his fellow prisoners from the Islamic currents, conveying their news and activities and planning to the prison administration, and then praising the prison system and the wisdom and greatness of President Sisi. Sherif's account of imprisonment contradicts that of most texts in this book.

Even in the 1960s, the prisons of Gamal Abdel Nasser contained prisoners from the Islamic and communist currents. Nevertheless, there appears to be a blatant contradiction between the writings of the two currents in their recording of the facts. The memoirs of the Islamists speak of daily torture parties, while the leftists talk about educational and study circles inside the prison, as well as literary and theatrical works written and performed inside. However, this contradiction may be an affirmation of the subjectivity of the prison experience, not its reality. There is no agreed upon truth, as every prisoner has political and class prejudices and unique experiences and pain.

The truth requires acceptance and agreement by all and proves itself through various forms of evidence, whereas the essence of prison literature is deeply rooted in the solitary soil of personal narratives. Every lie or contradiction can be interpreted to be a result of imprisonment and its psychological effects. Even if the facts clash and the portrait of truth is shaken, reality always remains on the side of the narrator, the writer. Every contradiction or error resulting from oversight or intention presents itself as an outcome of the prison experience and its pressures.

Then there is the ideological impact that spreads its shadow and exerts its weight on the text so long as prison literature is part of a political battle, just as prison in the political prisoner's consciousness is part of his struggle. The authors of most of the Arab prison literature I've read were imprisoned because of their political activities, and so imprisonment is a continuation of the political struggle. Prisoners keep their minds from going crazy, and their souls from rotting, for the sake of a better future they will make with their party or group when they get out. They write after their release from prison in order to record the experience of their political group on the wall of time, in order to make even a small scratch in the structure of the walls of power and its narration. And therefore what is important is not the artistry of what will be written about the experience, but rather the premise that the written testimony will carry, and its role within the unending struggle of the imprisoned writer/politician.

The prisoner's testimony seeks to clarify and educate the public. Literature is self-sufficient, its value is in its uniqueness, not in its clarity, and it is from literary work that writers learn their craft.

In a literary work, form is a core element, and form and content work towards the same goal—that is, both make up the significance of the literary work, whereas in prison documents and testimonies, the subject matter dominates and the artistic form is simply a vehicle for its expression.

Political detainees do not enter prison alone, and even if loneliness is their companion for the initial period of investigation and arrest, in their writing about prison, the moment always arrives when they meet their comrades in political work.

Prison writings differentiate between political and criminal prisoners and set a boundary between the two worlds. The writer even deliberately highlights the differences between himself or herself as a political prisoner and the criminal prisoner, even if the two share the same cell.

The prison experience is a melting pot for the political group; it tests the convictions of the members of the group and the bonds that exist between them, whether the bonds of brotherhood when tears fall at dawn prayer or when comrades tremble in ecstasy when someone hums a song by Sheikh Imam.*

Every writing about prison that I have known wasn't only about prison, but was rather the accumulated interpretations of the political conflict taking place at the moment it was written. In this regard, prison becomes one of the multiple arenas for this conflict, an arena that witnesses the defeat of the writer and the writer's multiple attempts at resistance.

Since my arrival in America, I have worked with a number of institutions and initiatives, all related to creative writing and prisoners in Amer-

---

* Imam Mohammad Ahmed Aissa (1918–1995) is a famous Egyptian composer and singer who for most of his career collaborated with poet Ahmed Fouad Negm, writing political songs about poor people and the working classes. See Andrew Simon, "An Ordinary Icon: Cassettes, Counternarratives, and Shaykh Imam," in *Social Voices: The Cultural Politics of Singers around the Globe*, ed. Levi S. Gibbs (Urbana: University of Illinois Press, 2023).

ican prisons. Some of them are projects to teach creative writing to prisoners, while others judge literary awards for prisoners. I participated in events and even had the honor of reading my work with former prisoners. In American prisons, there is no distinction between political and criminal prisoners, although the majority of prisoners are imprisoned for reasons deeply related to racial politics and economic inequality.

I worked with the American poet Jo O'Lone-Hahn to edit a number of issues of the journal *INTRA*, which is dedicated to publishing poetry by American prisoners, and while we read dozens of handwritten texts that arrived in the mail, I noticed the absence of any mention of the prison and its details and what goes on inside it, unlike the usual literature produced in Arab prisons. At that time, Jo alerted me that the magazine had sent several letters announcing the competition and its details to prisons in several states. Some prison administrators didn't respond at all. Some agreed and delivered the announcement to the prisoners, who in turn sent their work via mail, which is monitored by the prison administration. All we were reading were the writings of prisoners composed under the watchful eye of the jailer who, unlike the jailer in Egypt, has absolute power to confiscate what he does not like.

As for the writings of the Egyptian prisoners, it is writing that was smuggled out because of the jailer's negligence. The prisoners write, but they are keen to hide what they write. In my prison there were some prisoners who presented themselves as human safes. In the event of a search of the cell by the prison guards, prisoners rushed to these "safes" with papers that they did not want the prison administration to find. The human safes would fold them, put them in a plastic bag, and insert the bag inside their body, hiding in their orifices what their colleagues had written so that the jailer wouldn't find and confiscate it.

Since my adolescence I've written using a computer keyboard; most of us now write on a mobile screen. But such luxuries are not found in prison. Writing in prison begins first with the search for paper and pen, which are very expensive supplies, then finding a place in the middle of the narrow cell where you can sit and write away from the intrusion of those around you and at the same time not be deprived of light. Instead of the chair and the table on which we were trained to write, the prisoner writes on his body: the thigh becomes the desk over which you bend to write, the letters and words that come together to form sentences mix with the pain of hardened bones and joints, the humidity of the prison that penetrates the body in winter, and the drops of sweat that fall and wet the paper, dissolving the inked words.

When the order to release me from prison arrived in December 2016, all I feared was that Marcel Proust's fate would be repeated with me, especially as I had begun writing a draft of a new novel. The solution I resorted to was that I bought from another prisoner a copy of the magazine *Al-Itha'ah wa al-televiziun* [Radio and television], on the cover of which was a picture of the Lebanese singer Dominique Hourani in a short dress. I placed all my papers and the notebook that contained the draft of the novel in my bag, with the magazine on top of them. During my search at the prison gate, the officer this time opened the bag himself, and the first thing he saw was the magazine and its cover. He lifted it, laughed, and said, "Another woman? It's these women that will bring you to prison again."

I pretended to laugh at his silly joke, and the jailers and prisoners joined me in giggling, so he got high with joy. He put the magazine in the bag, pleased that everyone appreciated his wit, and ordered the door to be opened.

Since 2016, Egyptian prison conditions have changed for the worse. The number of prisoners has increased and overcrowding in inhumane prisons has increased. During the years of Trump's presidency, Sisi was given the title of "favorite dictator" and the United States turned a blind eye to all human rights violations committed by the Egyptian regime, so it became even more brutal in its abuse of prisoners.

My colleagues and brothers are in Egyptian prisons now; some of them have been deprived of books, and others have been deprived of paper, pens, and even the right to write letters to their families. For those who have been isolated from any light, and for those who have been left in the eternal darkness of Sisi's prisons, my wish is that this book contributes to breaking their siege, and that a day will come soon when we read it as a historical document of a bygone era, not as a record of crimes still being committed.

Ahmed Naji (born 1985) is an Egyptian journalist and literary novelist. He was born in Mansoura, Egypt. He has written three books: Rogers *(2007),* Seven Lessons Learned from Ahmed Makky *(2009), and* The Use of Life *(2014). Due to its sexual content and drug references,* The Use of Life *resulted in his being jailed in 2016 for "violating public modesty." Naji served almost 300 days in prison before being released. He was granted the PEN/Barbey Freedom to Write Award from PEN America. In 2018, Naji moved to Washington, DC, with his wife, Yasmin Hosam El Din. He completed a fellowship at Black Mountain Institute in Las Vegas, Nevada, where he now lives.*

COLLECTIVE ANTIGONE

INTRODUCTION

IMPRISONMENT, TORTURE, AND EXILE are the experiences that define the fate of dissidents across human history, from antiquity to the modern world. They generate long chains of stories whose main purpose is bearing witness; in so doing, they allow a deep connection between experiences that would otherwise be incommensurable.

When we first approached the testimonies of people who had been arrested and tortured for political reasons in Egypt since 2011, our minds called forth the many witnesses, such as the Austrian philosopher and resistance fighter Jean Améry (who was tortured by the Gestapo in both Auschwitz and Bergen-Belsen), who marked twentieth-century European history. As Améry described it, "Whoever was tortured, stays tortured.... Whoever has succumbed to torture can no longer feel at home in the world. The shame of destruction cannot be erased."[1] As the pages that follow make all too clear, Améry's words resonate with the writings of Egyptian political prisoners across the ages, and particularly today. Political incarceration and torture are experiences that have a beginning but seldom an end, and they contribute to shaping the entire lives of individuals and their families.

The book before you comprises letters and other writings by Egyptians imprisoned from the eruption of the January 25, 2011, uprising through the fall of 2023. Though with few exceptions they are not written by celebrated philosophers, activists, or public intellectuals of any sort, they nevertheless raise similarly profound questions about the nature of politics and governance today, in both authoritarian regimes and their "democratic" allies and patrons who enable and even support such violence. They offer few answers and even less consolation, but they do offer voices from behind prison walls that remind readers of our collective obligation to not look away and to not remain silent; to do what we can individually and collectively to help stop the rampant abuse and denial of the rights of our fellow human beings.

As we finish curating this volume, there are upwards of 100,000 people imprisoned in Egypt's sprawling and ever-growing carceral system, including, most recently, untold numbers imprisoned for protesting against the post–October 7, 2023, Israeli genocidal war on Gaza (a war itself rooted in Israel's unrelenting incarceration of thousands of Palestinians). That is not the world's highest incarceration rate, which belongs to the United States, although El Salvador, Rwanda, and Cuba also have claims to this ignominious distinction. Indeed, President Abdel Fattah El-Sisi promised Egyptians he would emulate the US with his massive prison expansion program. But political imprisonment in Egypt has had an outsized impact on the country's politics, and through that, its culture. How could it be otherwise when untold tens of thousands of people have been imprisoned for the "crime" of merely criticizing their government or otherwise expressing their anger and frustration at a system that fundamentally marginalizes and excludes them, or even for just "liking" a social media post?

The letters and other writings collected in this volume reveal, we argue, not only how the imprisonment of the revolutionary generation that was at the forefront of the 2011 uprising (and many whose activism runs years and even decades deeper) has functioned as a core component of the counterrevolutionary politics deployed by the Egyptian state since the demise of the Mubarak regime, but also how that mass imprisonment reflects its underlying rationale and horrifying costs: it was the only way to uproot a movement that had the potential to mark a fundamental turning point in Egyptian, regional, and even world history. This is why we have titled this collection *Imprisoning a Revolution*.

The Egyptian uprising of 2011 was not an extemporaneous upheaval. Rather, it expressed a well-rooted political culture that developed over two decades of both underground and open mobilization and protest by multiple social actors—students, workers, human rights and women activists, political parties, and civil society more broadly—against dictatorship, generalized corruption, police brutality, and the consequences of the intensification of liberalization policies that through the 1990s and early 2000s increased the precarity of life for an ever larger share of the population. As occurred in other Middle Eastern and North African Arab countries with regimes allied with the United States and Europe,[2] the 1990s saw a growing space for action by civil society movements in Egypt (although the space for politics and even simply criticism was highly constrained by the Mubarak government, particularly during the wave of violence by religious extremists in the latter half of the decade). For their part, the 2000s were punctuated by nearly half a dozen major events that pried opened new spaces for organization and protest by a rising generation of activists: first, the protests in support of Palestinians in the wake of the eruption of the al-Aqsa intifada beginning in September 2000; second, the mass protests against the US-led invasion of Iraq in 2003; third, the rise of the Kefaya movement in 2004, in which the brutal attack on women journalists in May 2005 was a pivotal moment of anger and organizing for women activists;[3] fourth, the wave of labor protests between late 2006 and April 2008 that led to the creation of the April 6 Youth Movement;[4] and fifth, the formation of the We Are All Khaled Said movement in the wake of the brutal arrest, torture, and murder of a young middle-class Alexandria man, Khaled Said, in June 2010.[5]

It was Said's murder that marked the decisive public shift in Egyptians' perceptions of police/state violence—how readily and brutally it could be deployed against literally anyone, anywhere, at any time. This realization produced the emotional wave of disdain that boiled over on National Police Day, January 25, 2011, initiating eighteen days of history-making protests followed by over two years of continuous mobilization and organization. Some 890 days later, the revolutionary period—tragically, as of now, an interregnum—ended with a military coup against Mohamed Morsi, Egypt's first nonmilitary president, who would himself die in a prison courthouse six years later.

In the interim, under the rule of the Supreme Council of the Armed Forces and then the Morsi presidency, thousands of Egyptians from all social classes and political backgrounds were arrested, jailed for long periods without trial, and prosecuted in military courts. During these labyrinthine legal proceedings, they were, as a rule, brutally mistreated, neglected, tortured, and occasionally murdered by police, security, military, and prison personnel. This situation was well known to international human rights organizations, which had long campaigned for Egyptian political prisoners. However, as often happens in international campaigns, they tended to focus on high-profile detainees who were young, urban, educated, and politically engaged. The names of Mahienour El-Massry, Alaa Abd El-Fattah, Esraa Abdel Fattah, Ahmed Douma, Ahmed Naji, Yara Sallam, Ahmed Samir Santawi, Ramy Shaath, and Patrick Zaki are well known to the international community of human rights defenders. Yet as most of these figures point out whenever given the chance, the large majority of incarcerated people are unknown and poor, with families who do not have the financial and social capital to gain them access to legal support or even clean clothes, medicine, or decent food (which are very much the exception rather than the rule for most prisoners), never mind international support. Their stories are documented only by local activists and organizations. Their writings, when they exist, are scattered, and the archives produced by activists who risk their own freedom to collect and document their imprisonment are all too ephemeral.

One of the aims of this book is to give visibility to these people, their stories, their fears and hopes, as well as the work that local organizations and networks in support of political prisoners are undertaking to help them. This task has become especially urgent today, as it has turned out that the suffering imposed upon political prisoners since 2011 was only a prelude to the wholesale brutality of the past decade. As we finish writing this introduction in December 2023, the National Elections Authority has announced for the third time (the first two were in 2014 and in 2018) that Sisi is the winner of the presidential election. His mandate will expire in 2030.[6]

FROM MASS POLITICS TO MASS INCARCERATION

No phenomenon has more powerfully, and negatively, defined Egyptian political life since the January 25, 2011, uprising that ended Hosni Mubarak's thirty-year reign than the mass incarceration of citizens by the three governments that have succeeded him: the Supreme Council of the Armed Forces (2011–2012), President Mohamed Morsi (2012–2013) and, most intensely of all, General-turned-President Abdel Fattah El-Sisi (2013–present). Indeed, no policy has done more to crush the dreams of contemporary Egyptians and to foreclose the possibility of a democratic future in Egypt.

For a moment, however, the efforts and creativity of the revolutionaries of Tahrir Square seemed to define a new global political imaginary for the twenty-first century, with Tahrir coming to symbolize a seemingly new mode of mass protest heralding successful freedom struggles the world over. Today, the dreams of that revolution have been replaced by prison bars, exile, and in thousands of cases, an early and sometimes unmarked grave. According to a 2020 Carnegie Endowment report, there are at least 65,000 Egyptians—and by some counts at least 100,000—imprisoned for political offenses. The scale of the current prison system is unprecedented: since 2012, the Sisi regime has built upwards of sixty prisons to handle the influx of political detainees, yet prisoners continue to suffer from unprecedented overcrowding. Conditions are atrocious: torture is widespread, as are other forms of abuse; medical attention, such as it exists, is rudimentary, and neglect the rule. It's not surprising that as many as a thousand prisoners have died in custody since 2011, including high-profile prisoners such as President Morsi and filmmaker Shady Habash. Many others, less well known, have simply disappeared, their deaths unrecorded even for their families. While no one disputes that in terms of sheer numbers Egypt is undergoing a prison crisis, a Kafkaesque legal system and a network of "dark" or "black" military sites and police jails make it difficult to determine exact figures.

Moreover, more than half of these prisoners are being held in "pretrial detention," a legal state of limbo that often extends far beyond the two-year limit on the detention of citizens held without charges. Similarly, some prisoners find that even when released from prison, they must still undergo years of "precautionary imprisonment," in which they are forced to spend half of every day—usually from 6:00 p.m. to 6:00 a.m.—in the jail cells of local police stations. These restrictions are all based on many of same emergency laws that ignited the 2011 protests in the first place.

THE LONG HISTORY OF THE EGYPTIAN CARCERAL STATE

The detention of political dissidents is not new to Egypt. Since its dawn in the nineteenth century, the modern Egyptian state has been a carceral state. Modern Egyptian governance and modern prisons evolved not merely together but through each other. This is in no way unique to Egypt. Imprisonment has been at the core of this relationship between modern states and political subjects since their emergence in the seventeenth century.[7] The very experience of modern subjectivity is inseparable from and profoundly shaped by the experience of prison, even for the majority of people who never enter one.

In the case of states built on the deliberate exclusion of large classes of people from any enjoyment of the rights of citizens—which would include almost every state in the modern world until quite recently—the goal of most governing authorities was, as a rule, to "criminalize and incapacitate" anyone those in power deemed to be a threat. In this process, entire classes of citizens were normalized as inherently criminal and threatening to the social order,[8] which meant they could be legitimately removed, en masse if and when necessary, from society.

Given this historical dynamic, it's not surprising that by the time the British occupied the country in 1882, Egypt's prison system was already among the world's largest, which can be understood in the context of the Egyptian government's long-term commitment to full-scale modernization beginning with Muhammad Ali (1805–1848) and continuing, with less success and greater indebtedness to Europe, with his son's and grandson's reigns.[9]

Modern states differ from their predecessors in the greater intensity and regularity of their extraction of wealth and labor from the people under their jurisdiction and/or control. The more modern a system, the more developed its carceral system, and the more people will be entrapped within it. Considered this way, Egypt was among the most modern of the early modern states on earth.

The carceral state began in Egypt in the aftermath of the 1829 reforms undertaken by Muhammad Ali; was strengthened with the onset of British rule in 1882; developed further during the post-1922 monarchy, when Egypt was formally independent but still under British control; intensified with the waves of arrests that accompanied the onset of World War II and then the Palestine War of 1948; and was reconstructed with the 1952 "revolution" and the establishment of the Egyptian republic led by the Free Officers regime. One of the most important continuities of the Nasser, Sadat, and Mubarak governments during the subsequent half century was the continual strengthening of the prison apparatus to control a population that, with the exception of the roughly two decades between the 1952 coup and the initiation of Sadat's *infitah* (economic opening) in 1974 (during which time an "authoritarian bargain" saw the state deliver unprecedented gains in health, education, and human development in return for broadly quiescent politics), had little incentive simply to accept near total control of politics and the economy by a small elite.

It is difficult to overstate just how deep the experience of imprisonment has run in Egyptian public life and popular memory ever since imprisonment became the main form of punishment in the mid-nineteenth century.[10] Whatever the period, from the start, Egypt's rulers have rarely if ever treated prisoners with anything less than brutality and contempt, a dynamic that became even more prevalent when the prisoners in question belonged to political opponents, whether Islamist, communist, or liberal. Even 200 years ago, during the reign of Muhammad Ali, a consular report described how "severe heavy-handed arrests and executions have quieted the capital which was on the verge of a rebellion. . . . The jails are full with people from all classes and religions. The population is terrorized."[11]

The writings, letters, court testimonies, and artistic and literary works produced in Egyptian prisons across two centuries reflect changing popular political aspirations and movements as well as the invariably consistent attempt by various governments to shut down this activity through incarceration. By the time of their arrival in Cairo in 1882, British officials found over a thousand political prisoners serving sentences for such offenses as "assisting the rebels" and "stirring up public feeling against the Khedive [vice-regent]."[12] Martial law was first introduced to Egypt with the effective takeover of governance in January 1882 by military officers led by Colonel Ahmed 'Urabi, and it was cemented with the British invasion, occupation, and imprisonment of 'Urabi five months later—and lasted, more or less without relief, right up to the January 25 uprising. The carceral state has long reflected the ethnic as well as political and class alienation of the country's elite from the majority of the population[13]—thus 'Urabi's cry of "Egypt for the Egyptians" (against the Turco-Circassian elite as well as the de facto political and economic control by Europe in the years before British rule), and the argument by young protesters almost 130 years later that Egypt was as occupied by the Mubarak regime as Palestinians were by Israel.[14]

> The terror of Tourah [Tora Prison] is now universal up and down Egypt.
> —SIR ARTHUR GRIFFITH, *Egypt's Prisons*, 1897

From the start of British rule, the number of prisoners increased while conditions deteriorated as the British implemented their infamous policy of a "just measure of pain." As early as 1884, the *British Medical Journal* declared that the country's prisons were "habitations of horrid cruelty," beset by "shocking" physical conditions, from filth collecting in the facilities to bare grounds, which were "constantly damp from infiltration from the Nile. . . . On this damp ground the prisoners had to sleep, without mats or boards. They were half starved, and imperfectly clothed."[15]

Plus ça change!

The use of coerced labor by prisoners was a source of cheap and reliable labor throughout the khedival and British rule. Indeed, as was recognized as early as 1897 in one review of Egyptian prisons at the start of British rule,[16] inmates were already part of the larger attempt to ensure Egypt's role as one of the world's most important cotton producers, largely for the benefit of the all-important British textile industry. Not coincidently, and quite relevantly, a similar process also occurred in the United States in the wake of slavery's end, as large numbers of African Americans were effectively reenslaved through imprisonment and put to work in the same cotton fields (and other jobs) that formerly imprisoned them as chattel.[17]

By the mid-1880s, according to Sir Arthur Griffiths, "An immense amount of good work [was] done by large detachments of convicts."[18] This use of captured or enslaved people for labor went back millennia in Egypt, but the use of convicts within a specifically penal system of incarceration reflected a core characteristic of modern carcerality—whether with unruly Egyptians or legally emancipated African Americans in the United States[19]—representing a new way both to justify incarcerating large numbers of troublesome and threatening populations and to make them "useful" and profitable to the state and its allies. On the other hand, while today Egyptian prisoners are not a source of free/coerced or cheap labor, a carceral economy has emerged in Egypt in which basic rights and privileges have been commoditized, with everyone from wardens and other senior officials to low-level guards demanding bribes or charging exorbitant markups for basic goods or to allow food and goods brought by families to be delivered to prisoners. The more prisoners, the more this economy grows.[20]

However profitable for those in control, Egyptian prisons contained horrors that needed to be brought to public light "for the sake of human beings," as Ahmed Hilmy Bey, one of Egypt's first journalists and its first political prisoner, declared in his memoir.[21] This would prove exceedingly difficult, as just one decade into the twentieth century the terms of public debate about British rule had been radically limited with the 1909 introduction of the Press and Publications Law, enacted to combat a rising tide of nationalist feeling. This led to the closing of newspapers, the imprisonment of dozens of nationalists for press and political offenses, routine censorship and, ultimately, a core justification for political imprisonment up to the present day.

In the wake of the Great War, the exile to Malta and then the Seychelles of the leadership of the *wafd* (the "delegation" headed by Saad Zaghloul that sought to participate in the Paris peace talks and that later morphed into the Wafd Party), and the consequent eruption of the 1919 uprising, the British deployed a broader array of carceral responses. The state of emergency put in place during World War I was renewed, hundreds of people were arrested, and the families of the exiled leadership were closely watched by British intelligence.

At the same time, unable to suppress the nationalist movement, in 1922 the British unilaterally declared Egypt "independent," although its independence was rather limited—foreign policy and most aspects of the economy remaining in British and European hands, especially through the maintenance of the Capitulations Law, while the new constitutional monarchy and parliament were responsible for internal security. As for who was actually responsible for this situation, when Huda Shaarawi (1879–1947), the founder of the Egyptian Feminist Union (1923–1956), felt compelled to complain about the conditions suffered by the husband of one of her friends while imprisoned, she wrote not to Egyptian officials but rather to High Commissioner Lord Allenby. As she explained in a September 1, 1922, letter, "He was three days kept in his cell after which he was removed to the infirmary on account of failure of health. . . . I am sure your Excellency can imagine the condition of this gentleman locked-up during 22 hours of the day in a two-metre cell in the Cairo August weather, both in light and in darkness undergoing all sorts of discomfort, ennui and indignity, sharing the private life and being in daily contact with criminals of the worst characters."[22]

Even as many nationalists were released in the wake of independence, within a year the newly installed Wafd government, which was in the process of assuming control over the prison administration, began a campaign of arrests of anarchists and members of the nascent Egyptian Communist Party—in so doing offering a vivid example of what decolonial philosophers would name the ongoing coloniality of power,[23] something that would define the dysfunctional relationships between ostensibly postcolonial governments like Egypt's and their citizens to the present day. A reformulated Press Law also facilitated fines and imprisonment for publishers, journalists, and writers.

By the 1930s, imprisonment had become a rite of passage for most political activists and intellectuals as the government engaged in several waves of arrests, building new prisons to accommodate all the prisoners. Not surprisingly, the prison memoir became a bedrock of the Egyptian literary canon.[24]

The formation of the Muslim Brotherhood in 1928, perceived as a direct threat to the still unsteady post-"independence" state, would ultimately generate more surveillance, repression, and imprisonment, especially as Brothers and nationalists joined the rising tide of nationalist sentiment across the region at the moment Britain and Europe were heading towards a new world war—which, not surprisingly, demanded even greater surveillance and increasing incarceration (including of thousands of "enemy" Europeans). With world war again looming, a new kind of martial law was introduced which, whatever the pretense of "constitutional government," saw more and more cases handled by military courts—the beginning of the system of parallel judicial systems of arrest, trial, and imprisonment that still defines Egyptian justice today.

As famed journalist and biographer 'Abbas Mahmoud al-'Aqqad explained of his experience of prison in this period, "I had to have my own Virgil to guide me as he did the Italian poet Dante in his journey to Hell, showing him the levels of Hell and the tortured souls."[25] Famed journalist Tahir 'Abd al-Hakim had a similar experience, explaining that "writing in prison, where the mere possession of a pen or paper was considered the crime of all crimes, was no easy feat."[26]

The end of seven years of world war was followed three years later by an equally shocking and politically devastating war over Palestine, in 1948, which led both to the flowering and repression of Islamist, communist, nationalist, and even feminist and working-class movements. For its part, the Brotherhood engaged in multiple acts of violence, including the attempted assassination of Nasser in 1954, which led to thousands of arrests. Prison was one of the few growth areas of the government as Egypt entered the new decade.

FOR PRISONERS, THE REVOLUTION CHANGES ~~EVERYTHING~~ LITTLE

The immediate cause of the July 1952 revolution was a British army massacre of Egyptian policemen in Ismailia in January of that year, after they refused to crack down on attacks by insurgents opposed to the continued British military presence in Egypt. The killings led to an all-out rebellion, along with looting and arson. A declaration of martial law temporarily quelled the situation, but the dissolution of the Wafdist government by King Farouq only increased instability. On July 23, the Free Officers launched their coup and within a week had forced Farouq's abdication. The monarchy was abolished in June of the next year; an agreement for the evacuation of the remaining British forces was completed in 1954 and implemented over the next two years. While the new government released "patriotic" political prisoners, it didn't release communists, who saw little change in their position, while colonial laws that criminalized forms of political activism, including writing, remained in place.

The structures of incarceration that solidified in the colonial era remained much as they were, even if they were now managed by local elites. While the post–July 23 Egyptian state developed a new legal infrastructure, language and practice of repression, trial procedures, and sentencing, practices often remained close if not identical to those under older versions of martial law, albeit under the guise of more appropriate names, such as "Revolutionary Tribunals," "The Revolution's Court," and later "The People's Court." For the convicted, a military tribunal was still more or less the same as it had been during the colonial period, right down to the cages in which the accused were kept, the torture they faced, the warning never to discuss their mistreatment in court, and issues of childcare for female detainees.

The Nasser Era

Inspired by the revolutionary example of the Free Officers and their declared aim of establishing "social justice," not long after the overthrow of the ancien régime in July 1952 thousands of workers at the Misr Fine Spinning and Weaving Company in Kafr al-Dawwar went on strike. But rather than address their grievances, the army crushed the strike, as the same demands that were previously applauded by nationalists were now a threat to social peace and their still incipient hold on power.[27] Thousands of workers were arrested, tried, imprisoned, and in two infamous cases, executed.[28] The Egyptian Revolutionary Socialist movement, one of the main organizers of the January 25 uprising, has sarcastically described the betrayal represented by the crushing of this strike by declaring, "This is how the Free Officers began their relationship with the working class."[29]

Despite the support received both from some communists and the Brotherhood, once in power, the Free Officers not only purged their ranks of both but moved to crush their organizations. Relations with the Brotherhood deteriorated even further after the removal of the figurehead of the coup, Muhammad Naguib, by Gamal Abdel Nasser and his more radical allies, as until then the Brotherhood had been allowed to continue to operate after political parties were banned because it was considered an "association" rather than a party.

In October 1954, the attempted assassination of Nasser in Alexandria by a Brotherhood militant led to a prolonged and intense crackdown against the organization, which the Brotherhood described as "the Ordeal" (*al-mihna*), recalling the persecution of religious scholars by the Abbasid caliph al-Ma'mun. The crackdown included thousands of arrests, detentions, trials, and dismissals from various positions.[30] Not surprisingly, torture was all too common, and it's here that what can be described as the "assembly line" of torture (as Human Rights Watch characterized it in a 2017 report)[31] that would define imprisonment in Egypt under the present regime first began. Interviews with former prisoners and archival documentation confirm that its roots can be traced back even further, to khedival and then British rule.

With the birth of the Non-Aligned Movement in 1955, led by Egypt along with India, Indonesia, and Yugoslavia, relations between the government and the communists improved briefly. On the other hand, the overthrow of the monarchy in Iraq three years later by a group of pan-Arab officers who were inspired by Egypt's Free Officers would, ironically, be perceived as a threat to the hegemony of Nasserism, which in turn led to a renewed crackdown on any form of leftist/socialist politics outside official control. Over the next decade the crackdown would remain more or less constant, with communists shipped off to concentration camps between 1958 and 1965 (when the party dissolved itself for most of the next decade). The crackdown on the Brotherhood was even harsher, as epitomized by the execution of Brotherhood ideologue Sayyid Qutb in 1966.

The situation became even more dire after the disastrous defeat of Egypt and four other Arab countries by Israel in the June 1967 war. Half a year later, workers, soon joined by students, began large-scale protests. This led to Nasser, and after him Sadat, placing increased power with the interior minister, who also took more active control over syndicates in order to ensure a wedge between students and workers.[32] The nonmilitary security services quickly grew to become a separate and rival power base within the broader Egyptian security system, one that would be regularly utilized by all Egyptian presidents from then on to ensure their own position by simultaneously strengthening and fragmenting security, intelligence, and policing in the country, using the hodgepodge of agencies in turn as a counterbalance to the military. This dynamic remained until the 2011 uprising, after which its high level of unpopularity among Egyptians, earned through decades of rampant abuse, led the Ministry of the Interior to re-forge closer ties to the military. This process synergized particularly well with the post-2013 Sisi government's focus on the army as the center of the security system.[33]

The Sadat Era

The death of Nasser in September 1970 was another turning point for Egypt, both for the country's politics and its prisons. Nasser's successor, Anwar Sadat, consolidated his grip in May 1971 with a "corrective revolution" (*harakat al-tashhih*) that reversed Nasser's national liberation rhetoric and removed Sadat's internal enemies. Just as important, land and labor reforms began to be rolled back, picking up pace in 1973 with the launching of the "Open Door Policy" (*infitah*) that encouraged foreign investment with incentives that would soon become the hallmarks of neoliberal policies across the Global South. Sadat reduced state subsidies on key commodities while opening up the economy to foreign investment in what is now recognized as one of the earliest examples of neoliberal reforms at the state level. As would occur in so many other places, these changes not only reversed what gains the poor had achieved under Nasser, they drastically and deleteriously impacted millions of Egyptians, workers and peasants alike. Not surprisingly, the *infitah* reforms were accompanied by Sadat's abandonment of Soviet sponsorship in favor of aligning with the US, once the surprise semi-victory of the October 1973 war with Israel gave him the cover to do so. Under the near total embrace of the West and conservative Arab regimes such as Saudi Arabia, the structural adjustment reforms that were implemented under International Monetary Fund tutelage would encourage greater corruption as the authoritarian bargain of Arab socialism broke down and many subsidies and other forms of social welfare began to disappear.

Even before Sadat's wholesale turn from Nasserism and Soviet patronage, his precarious position within the military-political establishment led him to reduce the military's power and privileges while, crucially, expanding that of the Ministry of the Interior. In a move that would reverberate to the present day, the ministry, along with its intelligence services and various police services, became primarily responsible for internal security, which naturally politicized the very concept of "intelligence" and "security"—in particular "national security"—even more than it was under the Nasserist regime. It is no surprise that the Central Security Forces (*al-qawwat al-'amn al-markazi*) were themselves established in the wake of the 1977 "Bread Intifada" (*intifada al-khubz*), also known as the "Revolution of Hunger" (*thawrat al-goa'*), and have been a central force of oppression right up to the "Intifada of Dignity" (*intifada al-karama*) in 2011 (not surprisingly, their role and power increased significantly after the assassination of Sadat by radical Islamist soldiers in 1981).[34]

It should be noted that like so many leaders who begin their time in power by critiquing the excesses of the previous regime or government, Sadat signaled his distance from Nasser by releasing some political prisoners, encouraging public critique of the torture that had occurred in Nasser's prisons, and promising a shift away from military tribunals and ostensibly towards the rule of civilian law. However, it quickly became clear that the new order would also rely on the old habits of the carceral state to stamp out political dissent, at least on the left. Many of Nasser's closest allies also soon found themselves incarcerated or exiled during these purges. In detention, they encountered the same leftist enemies they had so vigorously persecuted only a decade before. Former prisoners remember today that in women's prisons, Islamist women were for the first time housed together with leftists. Farida al-Naqqash, a high-profile journalist who was among the founders of the al-Tagammu' (Socialist)

Party in 1978 and since 1994 has been editor in chief of *Al-Adab wa al-Naqd*, the cultural journal of al-Tagammu', remembers that this was the first opportunity for Islamist and communist women to get to know each other: "They [the Islamist prisoners] were told we were *kafirun* (disbelievers), but they realized we were not. We were Muslim, yet leftists."[35]

Without minimizing the suffering and abuse, including torture, that many prisoners endured during this period, the words of journalist and theater critic Safinaz Kazem (who was also married to famed poet and political prisoner Ahmed Fouad Negm) indicate how different daily life was for many prisoners in 1973 compared with the present day: "Even though there were problems like in any other prison, we still had rights, we were in clean rooms, in beds with mattresses, and we were allowed to be visited by our families and our syndicates, and we were allowed to have lawyers, all the minimum rights we had there, which they don't have now."[36]

Shared opposition to Sadat's embrace of neoliberal capitalism led to a rapprochement between many on the Egyptian left and the Nasserists. The next half decade saw regular protests, particularly by university students, culminating in the 1977 bread riots mentioned earlier, against the costs of the *infitah*—especially the IMF-imposed end to bread subsidies—to ordinary Egyptians.

Following Sadat's assassination in October 1981, Hosni Mubarak was installed as president. For the next thirty years, he would rule Egypt under the same emergency laws that were invoked in the wake of Sadat's death. These laws gravely restricted all sorts of civil liberties—from the right to assemble to press freedoms—effectively stunting the growth and blunting the power of social and oppositional movements. While prison maintained its central governing function during the Mubarak years, from the late 1980s on, its focus was on jihadist activists and their sympathizers.

During the 1990s, Mubarak's main governance projects included painful economic reforms under the banner of IMF-imposed "structural adjustment policies," including privatizing public/state-owned companies (which, as in so many other developing countries, in practice meant turning them over to key members of the regime and the military/security system), cutting social services, loosening exchange rates, and lowering tariffs. Not surprisingly, this coincided with a "war on terror" against "radical Islamic" violence, an effort that involved a brutal counterinsurgency inspired by Algeria's war against the Islamic Salvation Front movement and then the Armed Islamic Group.

To offset widespread dissatisfaction, Mubarak compensated for his political crackdown by liberalizing the country's political system, albeit—similar to the process begun under Sadat—only on the surface. The regime allowed certain loyal opposition parties to operate, as well as a semi-independent press that still answered to a censor's office. By the early 2000s, a different political playing field had come into being. Dissidents had access to independent satellite broadcasters, nongovernmental press venues, and the internet. Similarly, a new generation of activists had emerged, some mobilized by solidarity with the second Palestinian Intifada and the US invasion of Iraq, others by critique of the corruptions of Mubarak's kleptocracy. Still others engaged in a new language of civil society and judicial independence in order to urge pro-democracy reforms, and some by all three developments.

Though illegal, public protests became increasingly common and were "managed" (funneled into side streets) as often as they were repressed. The growing repression even in the midst of a much ballyhooed liberalization program is exemplified by the experiences of famed sociologist Saad Eddin Ibrahim, who wound up visiting Tora Prison as a researcher in the 1970s and 1980s and then again as a human rights activist in the 1980s and early 1990s, only to find himself there once more, as an inmate, in the 2000s.[37] Another important example is former senator and presidential candidate Ayman Nour, who dared to run in the presidential election in 2005, when Mubarak opened the election to opposition candidates for the first time, only to be imprisoned for five years soon thereafter under false charges of forgery. Both of these well-known figures were badly mistreated in jail, suffering beatings and medical neglect; the headquarters of Ayman Nour's al-Ghad Party was the target of arson attacks in 2009 and 2013. Their families also suffered surveillance and bullying by security forces.

For the vast majority of prisoners with no visibility, the situation was far, far worse. And yet even this level of mistreatment allowed for contact and support that would no longer be available after the 2013 coup. As el-Dostour Party chairwoman Gameela Ismail, who was married to Ayman Nour during his imprisonment, explained in a 2022 interview with Collective Antigone, "When Ayman was in prison from 2005 to 2009, the situation was different. He could regularly write letters, not just home but to everyone—Obama, European leaders, various Egyptian officials. I could go see senior officials and they'd at least listen respectfully to my complaints about his treatment and even allowed me to do foreign television interviews. There's much less room for any negotiation with the government today."

NOT FIT FOR HUMANS: IMPRISONMENT IN THE POST-2011 ERA

As Egypt marks one hundred years since formal independence in 1922, little has changed regarding the epidemic of imprisonment. In 2010–2011, Amnesty International described Egypt's prisons as a "corrosive system of detention."[38] At the time, Human Rights Watch's 2010 country report on Egypt estimated that there were between 5,000 and 10,000 people being held in prison without charge, another 3,000–4,000 in pretrial detention, and a handful of journalists in jail. The number of security police required to manage this system of state violence and detention was over 100,000.

The situation a dozen years later is, literally, exponentially worse. Data from the World Prison Brief paints a grim picture: upwards of

119,000 prisoners, 31 percent of them pre-trial detainees, in upwards of 78 prisons.[39] Torture is a regular feature of this system, and Egypt remains the only UN member state to be the subject of two public inquiries by the United Nations Committee against Torture, which in a June 2019 report declared that the facts gathered by the committee "lead to the inescapable conclusion that torture is a systematic practice in Egypt."[40]

Though the orientation and composition of the modern Egyptian state has changed many times during the last two centuries, its carceral foundations have remained and indeed hardened. However, the 2011 revolution—and with it, the function of incarceration—marks both a continuity and a break with this past. While on the one hand it's important to foreground the continuity of carceralization over the broad sweep of modern Egyptian history, the scale, character, and viciousness of the Sisi regime's repression, even in comparison with the Nasser era, cannot be left unaccounted for. Clearly the broad popular nature of the January 25 uprising, its leadership by a younger generation largely outside its control and immune to its ideology, as well as the growing power of the Muslim Brotherhood in the following year, all meant that the military state, largely without a social base of its own, had to rely on pure and extreme repression to a far greater degree than its predecessors.

In some sense, the present moment is merely an extension of this longer history: now as before, imprisonment remains one of the main techniques of control, and thus rule. And yet, in terms of its scope and intensity, the present-day system marks a quantitative and qualitative break with these earlier eras—quantitative in the sheer numbers imprisoned; qualitative in the systematicity and even scientific application of torture, abuse, and neglect. Scholars today debate whether the Sisi regime marks an "upgraded" or "new" authoritarianism.[41]

Under the SCAF (Supreme Council of the Armed Forces) and Mohamed Morsi regimes, and subsequently under Sisi's, Egypt's prison population exploded to the highest number on record. While most of that jump occurred under Sisi, the foundation for post-Mubarak imprisonment was set with the policies of the first two governments, becoming supercharged after the renewed military regime murdered upwards of 1,000 Morsi/Brotherhood supporters engaged in a peaceful sit-in against the coup at the Rabaa al-Adawiya Mosque in August 2013. The massacre sparked an equally massive wave of arrests, with prisons becoming "a microcosm of the wider society," as an official with the Egyptian Initiative for Personal Rights put it in a 2015 interview. "At this point," one veteran activist remarked, "all Egypt's a prison with soldiers as guards."[42]

In such a situation, prison conditions were bound to deteriorate rapidly from their already risible inadequacy. As a result of the rapid increase in the number of prisoners, overcrowding became so dense that prisoners routinely complained of having to sleep standing up and not being able to breathe. But beyond overcrowding, large-scale violations of human rights occurred at "an astonishing rate" and with broad impunity during Sisi's first year in power.[43] What we argue in the context of this collection of prison writings is that the carceral violence of the post-2013 coup era has been used as much to restructure as to preserve Egypt's political power structure.

The large number of imprisoned Egyptians comprises many types of prisoners: arrestees and those held in investigative, or pre-trial, detention; those serving sentences of various kinds; those who have completed their sentences but have not been released; those who have been released into administrative house arrest; those who have (been) disappeared while in detention; those held incommunicado; and those unaccounted for and feared dead as a result of murder, torture, and/or lack of medical attention. While much of the focus of activists is on political prisoners, as with the case of TikTok stars Haneen Hossam and Mawada al-Adham (convicted multiple times of charges ranging from "using girls in acts contrary to the principles and values of Egyptian society with the aim of gaining material benefits" to even more troubling "human trafficking" charges), or novelist Ahmed Naji (sentenced to two years in 2016 for writing sexually explicit scenes in a novel, and currently living in exile in the United States), anyone publicly challenging the officially conservative morality sponsored by the government can also wind up spending years in prison.

If the number of prisoners is shocking, the conditions of imprisonment are even more so: torture and beatings are ubiquitous, beginning with the *tashrifa*, the collective beating new prisoners suffer before even getting to their cells. It has been refined to an art, with prison guards beginning a session with merely the flick of a cigarette. Overcrowding is rife and poses serious health risks; medical care is inhumanly inadequate. Together, they indicate a massive violation of international legal norms for detention and imprisonment, a violation taking place each and every day. In terms of scale and misery, notwithstanding the regime's propaganda about the new facilities allocated to jails, today's conditions are worse than at any time in Egypt's modern history (and likely long before that), a "slow death" that makes its current carceral regime among the most criminal in the world.[44]

The ongoing violence and repression also highlight the success of the Sisi regime's efforts: it has subdued a revolution, carried out a coup, immobilized millions of protesters and thousands of dissidents, and consolidated domestic and international support, power, and capital, all in the space of a decade. The direct relationship between the level of repression and success in remaining a full partner in the global strategic-military-security complex—evidenced equally by the ongoing success of countries like Israel, Saudi Arabia, and the UAE, among other regional powers—reminds us just how entrenched rationality, strategic expediency, and remunerative carceral political economies remain across the region a decade after millions risked everything to tear this system down.

FROM RADICAL HOPE TO NUMBING DESPAIR

The revolutionary era was born out of a similar level of despair, mixed with hope that a radically different future was possible. The initial spark for the January 25, 2011, uprising could be dated with some legitimacy to the June 6, 2010, arrest, torture, and murder of a young Alexandrian middle-class techie named Khaled Said. For some, Said's murder while in police custody exposed the atrocities of the Mubarak regime. For young middle-class Egyptians, Said's brutal murder distilled and clarified the brutality of everyday dealings with Egypt's police and security forces. It's thus not surprising that his murder accelerated the wave of mobilization that had been simmering under the surface since the early 1990s and that grew stronger after 2006, when social movements started to become organized among workers and students.[45]

The brutal assassination of Said, alongside worsening socioeconomic inequalities and corruption, sparked a wave of summer protests across the country and activated networks of activists who went on to play a leading role in the revolutionary social movements of 2011. Egyptian prisons would also play a pivotal role in the history of the January 25 uprising itself, beginning with the breakouts in which thousands escaped from state prisons during the first eighteen days of unrest. Indeed, a high-stakes prison break on January 30 freed some of the country's most high-profile political prisoners, including future president Mohamed Morsi and hundreds of other Muslim Brotherhood and Salafist cadres, along with numerous hardened criminals.

Despite the initial success represented by the removal of Hosni Mubarak from power after thirty years of near absolute rule, the transitional SCAF government that replaced him used imprisonment to corral pro-democracy protesters and contain the threat they posed to unchecked rule. Indeed, few developments are more relevant to the failure of the revolutionary era than the fact that military trials for civilian protesters, long abandoned under Mubarak, not only returned during SCAF's rule (February 2011–June 2012) but accelerated under Morsi's short-lived presidency (July 2012–July 2013).

From the outset, police singled out women activists for targeting. One infamous example of this occurred on March 9, 2011, when a group of eleven women was arrested during a protest against the attack on the International Women's Day march the day before. The women were subsequently detained in the basement of the Egyptian Museum, which had been retrofitted as a macabre theater of torture during the first days of the revolution, then subjected to so-called virginity tests. Activists observing the large-scale arrests and military trials of revolutionaries in the months that followed the January 25 uprising immediately grasped the danger: there was nothing sincere or benign about the military's claim to "safeguard" the revolution.[46] By March 2011, activists had created the "No Military Trials for Civilians" campaign to raise public awareness about the scale of arrests and the military's exercise of carceral power, and to pressure SCAF, then the Morsi government, to release the ever-increasing number of prisoners.

It is no coincidence that the campaign was led by women, in particular Mona and Laila Soueif, respectively the daughter and wife of Ahmed Seif al-Islam, a leader of the student movement in the 1970s who went on to become one of Egypt's most important human rights lawyers (and who himself was imprisoned multiple times by Mubarak), as women have long been at the forefront of struggles for human rights and prisoners' rights more specifically.[47] Seif's oldest and youngest children, Alaa Abd El-Fattah and Sanaa Seif, are among the most important human rights activists of the post-2011 era; their activism has led to multiple lengthy prison terms (see their letters in this volume). Alaa is today Egypt's most well-known political prisoner; he is also the author of the acclaimed *You Have Not Yet Been Defeated*, a collection of his prison writings.

Following the July 2013 coup d'état and the bloody massacres of upwards of a thousand unarmed civilian protesters that came in August, the government cracked down violently on all forms of protest. A new era of mass arrests was ushered in, along with military trials and long-term imprisonment that targeted not just Muslim Brotherhood members and supporters and activists of all stripes, but anyone who criticized or was suspected of criticizing the new-old regime. Since then, political activists have increasingly turned to artistic, often indirect forms of expression to denounce the crimes of the Sisi state and to deconstruct its master narratives. In October 2014 the streets of the central districts in Cairo were covered with posters portraying young activist detainees and emblazoned with one crystalline slogan, "They are celebrating Eid in prison."

The explosion of carcerality also led to the rapid expansion of prison-building in the decade and more since the 2011 uprising, to house the waves of political prisoners.[48] And whether in old or newly constructed jails, the sound of torture is ubiquitous. Inmates describe being "unable to tell from the screams" whether the victims are men, women, or children and whether they are being beaten, shocked, or raped.[49] It is not just political activists suffering incarceration: in 2020 the Committee to Protect Journalists rated Egypt the third-worst country in the world for journalists.

It should be evident by now that there is a carceral through-line from the colonial period to the post-independence period, from English administrator Cromer to Nasser, from Sadat to Mubarak and Sisi. All of them reproduced the same pronounced style of governance, what we would term a *carceralocracy*, and unabashedly developed it to fit their own ends.

In 1914, when the British first imposed martial law in Egypt to protect their commercial interests during World War I; in 1923, with the insertion of emergency legislation into the newly promulgated constitution; in 1948, with the declaration of martial law during the Palestine War; in 1958, when Nasser issued Emergency Law No. 162; and in 1981, when Mubarak extended the permanent state of emergency following Sadat's assassination (renewing it every two or three years until 2011),

Figure 1. Photo from the campaign "They are celebrating Eid in prison." Photo taken by Collective Antigone, Cairo, October 2014.

Figure 2. Photo from the campaign "They are celebrating Eid in prison." Photo taken by Collective Antigone, Cairo, October 2014.

Egyptian rulers have always relied on the prison and its attendant violence as their key tool of governance. After the uprising of January 25 through February 11, 2011, SCAF, Morsi, and Sisi continued these practices of intensively policing the population; indeed, thanks to the Emergency Law of 1958, since 1968 Egypt has been in a perpetual state of emergency for all but eighteen months in 1980 and 1981. While the law requires that police refer cases to a prosecutor and begin an investigation within twenty-four hours of an arrest and transfer detainees to one of forty-two registered institutions while awaiting trial, this is rarely what transpires, especially for political cases.

There is overwhelming evidence that military, security, and paramilitary police forces are operating parallel systems of detention outside official channels and outside the law, partly in order to deal with the sheer number of people arrested since the coup. Egypt has experienced a spike in the number of citizens in detention unlike any in its history. Sisi has waved away the data presented to him about the scale of mass incarceration under his rule. The official prisons do not, he claims, have the space to accommodate tens of thousands of people. He may be right. Yet imprisoned they have been. So where are they?

SOLIDARITY AND ARTISTIC CREATIVITY

In the 1997 documentary *Quatre femmes d'Égypte* [Four women of Egypt], four activists from different political fields—the communist literary critic Amina Rachid, the religiously grounded playwright and journalist Safinaz Kazem, the teachers' syndicate activist Widad Mitri, and the leader of the peasants' movement, Shahenda Maklad—remember the powerful bonds of friendship and solidarity they forged in prison: "Sadat made national unity in prison!" comments Rachid, remembering the diversity of social, political, and cultural backgrounds of the inmates.[50] They had been rounded up during Sadat's infamous September 1981 mass arrest of thousands of activists and journalists from across the political spectrum, from liberals to Marxists, from Muslim Brothers to a small group of the nascent jihadist organizations that had spread across the country in the preceding decade.

Militants from these latter groups would orchestrate Sadat's assassination the following month; others would go on to join the mujahedin in Afghanistan, paving the way for the increasingly global manifestations of radical Islamist mobilization. But successive waves of arrest and imprisonment didn't just beget more violence, they also produced artistic creativity. Indeed, throughout this history, Egyptian prisons were and remain today a space for both personal and artistic creation. For middle-class women especially, imprisonment meant facing charges of family dishonor both for challenging authority and for being put in jail with common criminals, including prostitutes, a situation that compelled women to reconcile their private experiences of prison with the public conceptualizations of women as students, wives, mothers, and respectable citizens.[51]

Three-quarters of a century later, repeatedly imprisoned human rights lawyer Mahienour El-Massry would explain that the desire for middle- and upper-class women, and particularly activists, to be separated from common criminals, and particularly prostitutes, was a tendency she had to regularly combat: "People would want to separate activists from the prostitutes. I had to explain that we are all victims of the same system."[52]

Prison was a formative experience of many of the country's most celebrated artists and authors, including Nawal al-Saadawi, Sonallah Ibrahim, Gamal al-Ghitani, and Ahmed Fouad Negm. Prisons were also spaces where inmates entertained themselves with popular culture. In an oral history interview we recorded with Safinaz Kazem, she remembers with amusement songs she composed to tease her fellow inmates in Qanater women's prison, when she was detained for the second time in 1981: "So anyway, in that jail we were close, and I used to sing and make everybody laugh.... I made a song for every one of them. Nawal's [al-Saadawi] song was 'Me, me me, me. My name is Nawal, I love myself, I adore myself.' About Amina Rachid: 'My name is Amina, I am wise, I love myself in secret.' And about Latifa al-Zayyat: 'I am a Marxist, if Marx lived, he would love me.'" With her characteristic sweetly tinged wit, she added: "Everyone loved the songs about themselves except Nawal."[53]

Among the artists who represented life in prison, the example of the communist and feminist painter Inji Aflatun, imprisoned along with other communists in 1959, is telling. In an excerpt from her memoirs, Aflatun talks about the effect that incarceration had on her painting style. The experience of detention was critical, a time for practice and study: "I was very interested in painting a tree close to the prison barbed wire. I used to draw it every season. This focus on a single subject taught me a lot. If I had been on the outside, I would have had many options and I would have painted more than a single tree. My cellmates named this tree after me. It's Inji's Tree."[54] Her illustrations of the everyday life of women and children in prison mark a wholly original turn in modern Egyptian art, to the point that, paradoxically, in the late years of her life, Aflatun was celebrated by the state and invited to represent Egypt at international exhibitions. Many of her works are today exhibited at the Museum of Modern Egyptian Art in Cairo.

Sixty years later, other artists continue this tradition, documenting the hard life of prison and meditating on carceral space, the natural world, and the possibility of freedom. One such artist is Yassin, who was imprisoned for four years following his participation in a protest in 2013. His work is also included in this collection. This carceral thread between Aflatun and Yassin is just one of many that connect five generations of political prisoners, some from within the same families, into a collective intergenerational and cross-political experience that continues to shape not only the experience of prison but how that experience is absorbed by Egyptian society more broadly. In the fall of 2014, writer/director Laila Hassan Soliman and historian Alia

Mosallam premiered a play titled *Hawa al-Horreya* [Whims of freedom] that linked the memories of the 1919 revolution to the revolution of 2011 through a collection that brings together the papers of the Milner Commission (sent by the British to ascertain Egypt's political aspirations in the wake of 1919), popular songs circulating at that time, and the letters of contemporary political prisoners, starting with Alaa Abd El-Fattah.

These are only a few examples of the thread that links the long history of political incarceration to the present day and shows the richness of prison writings at multiple levels: as a testimony allowing prisoners to write microhistories of their incarceration, and as works that, in many cases, have an aesthetic value per se.

PRISON WRITING IN THE CONTEMPORARY CARCERAL STATE

The current Egyptian regime has adopted a security-state model ostensibly necessitated by an open-ended war on "terrorism," whether against anyone who has ever had anything to do with the Muslim Brotherhood (which potentially includes tens of millions of Egyptians), against the majority of the population of the Sinai, or against any Egyptian who dares criticize the regime or violate "public morals." Sadly, none of these policies are unique to Egypt; most authoritarian regimes follow a similar pattern, particularly in the Middle East and North Africa. Equally important—and typical today—is the fact that the Sisi regime has strengthened its policies of simultaneous austerity (for the vast majority of nonelite citizens) through privatization and cuts to subsidies of basic goods, services, infrastructure, and other once-core elements of the now erstwhile "authoritarian bargain" on the one hand, and on the other, large increases in government building projects (from an extension of the Suez Canal to a massive new administrative capital) that will bring new revenues to the political/military and economic elite while safely isolating them further from the majority of citizens.

While the Mubarak regime often (but by no means generally) tolerated limited forms of protest (at least by young people) and the process of elections as a safety valve that helped head off broader unrest, this strategy clearly failed with the eruption of the 2011 uprising. No doubt hoping to avoid a similar fate, over the past decade the regime has instituted a total crackdown on any form of dissent, including on the part of students, who are now imprisoned at the slightest hint of unrest or even criticism. Not even holding a foreign passport or being part of the political or economic elite will protect anyone who is perceived as a threat or even a nuisance to the regime. Egyptians living outside the country, whether in the diaspora or exile, are regularly seeing their relatives harassed, threatened, and even kidnapped in an effort to force them into silence, and some are even returning to face "justice," turning the Egyptian diaspora into an exilic community.

Making the situation worse is that Egypt's allies in Europe and North America have maintained full-throttled support for the Sisi regime, including continued large-scale military and economic aid, which renders most criticism from civil society all but irrelevant in practice. Thus, for example, the United States continues to provide billions of dollars a year in military and economic aid, and the British and Italian governments didn't hesitate to strengthen bilateral ties, including arms sales and security cooperation, with Egypt even after Italian Cambridge University graduate student Giulio Regeni was tortured to death in police custody. Meanwhile, French president Emmanuel Macron awarded Sisi the Légion d'honneur in 2020 despite the murder of a French citizen, Eric Lang, in an Egyptian police station in 2013 and the long and harsh imprisonment of French-Egyptian-Palestinian activist Ramy Shaath. A system in which torture is so rampant that even the torturers complain of growing bored with the regimen (as architect Ibrahim Ezz al-Din explains in his letter) still can't find a way to curtail, never mind stop, the violence.

If weapons purchases and oil and gas concessions help grease the wheels of continued international support, there is little doubt that monetizing prisons—and prisoners—won't be far behind for Egypt's military and allied elite. A 2014 report by the Century Foundation explains, "With Egypt's military and security forces controlling so much of the economy, it is likely this prison build-up is partially based on financial incentives. Prisons, especially private ones, can be sites for lucrative business."[55]

As we explained above, there is a long history of using prisoners as corvée labor in Egypt. That has not been an important element during Sisi's reign (although soldiers have increasingly been called into factories to replace striking workers), for a telling reason: however exploitative, work would in fact be preferable to being stuck in a tiny, horribly overcrowded and filthy cell almost twenty-four hours a day. And that's why the government has no interest in having prisoners work—at least for now—since the goal of political imprisonment under Sisi is to break people completely, not rehabilitate them or profit off their labor.

This could change with the construction of new "American-style" prisons, videos for which depict prisoners at work in various types of factory labor. Indeed, as Sanaa Seif explained in a 2022 public forum celebrating the publication of her brother Alaa's collection of prison writings, "They showed us the infamous video for the giant new prison complex in Wadi Natrun and are basically using it as a carrot, telling us that the best-behaved prisoners will get transferred to the new prison with its larger and cleaner cells and so on."[56]

Indeed, the new American-style prisons point to the long-term danger of a carceral state when it comes to protecting the most basic rights of citizens. According to relatives of one prominent detainee, "From the standpoint of the family, the new prisons are better—there is parking, shade for those waiting outside, even an information booth where an officer will inform family members of the exact location where a loved one is being held in a large prison complex. But for prisoners, despite the improvement in cleanliness and overcrowding, there are many ways in which the situation is significantly worse."[57] Among the two most important are that prisoners are under continuous twenty-four-hour surveillance, and that smaller units with fewer people, while easing overcrowding, means that there's no real sense of community. Before, there was a kind of class division in the prisons, but at least poorer prisoners could earn money by doing odd jobs for those with more means. Some prisoners earned enough not only to ease their conditions inside but to support their families outside.

This is all gone now, at least for the moment. And the dynamic of making life a bit easier for families but even more isolating for prisoners points to a long-term future of American-style incarceration that is troubling in its implications. For women political prisoners, who are increasingly "subjected to severe physical and psychological abuse because of their work in the human rights field,"[58] the prohibition on cooking utensils means not only that they have to pay for expensive and less nutritious food at the prison cafeteria or canteen, but they also lose the ability to cook together, which had long been an important bonding activity. And if families have a somewhat easier time of it when they visit the new prisons, the fact that they are located far outside cities means traveling there is extremely expensive, with far fewer (if any) public or cheap private alternatives available.

Finally, in the newer prisons the ability to be physically next to loved ones has been greatly diminished if not eliminated. In Wadi Natrun, for example, visitations for political prisoners take place almost entirely with glass separations, to prevent any physical contact or even private communication. This was not the case under Mubarak. As Gameela Ismail explained, "Even with a high-profile prisoner like Ayman, [for] whom they wanted to force family visitations to occur in the officials' offices to better monitor them, we could whisper in each other's ears and he could pass me letters or notes surreptitiously until almost the end of his sentence."[59] All of these strategies to at least bend the system are rendered inoperative by the contemporary prison architecture, rules, and logic. Onetime student and long-term political prisoner Ayman Moussa expressed it best in his letter in this volume in describing the all-enveloping nature of imprisonment in Egypt today: "I exhale darkness . . . I inhale darkness . . . then I look at my watch . . . it is 3:08 a.m."

THE IMPORTANCE OF THIS COLLECTION

In the context of a century of largely brutal imprisonment, where violence and violations of prisoners' most basic human rights has always been the norm, what can letters from Egyptian political prisoners jailed since the eruption of the eighteen-day uprising of January and February 2011 tell us that we don't already know? What testimony can they offer that we don't already have, besides a testimony to the horrors of the "state of exception" and "bare life" that have long been the plight of political prisoners the world over?[60]

First and foremost, this collection is an act of collective witnessing and solidarity. It's one thing to be aware of the suffering endured by hundreds of thousands of Egyptians during the last dozen years; it's quite another to be confronted with the bald realities of imprisonment. These letters and other writings need to be read, circulated, and acted upon precisely because detainees risked so much—more torture, abuse, and worse—to write and get them smuggled from prison. And they need to be read because they represent an irrepressible desire to tell one's story, regardless of the cost. The prisoners' courage bears witness both to the cruelty of successive Egyptian governments and to the generative power of collective resistance. Each generation of prisoners has, in a way, bequeathed its writing as a warning, or invitation, to push future generations to continue the struggle no matter how slim the chance of victory.

While this collection focuses on the experience of Egypt's political prisoners in the past dozen years, its content will resonate all along

Egyptian modern history and across national borders. The writings collected here not only impart crucial information about the history and the present of the Egyptian state but also speak to global questions of governance, citizenship, and the colonial/postcolonial promise, as yet unfulfilled, of democratic self-rule. Our collection can thus be read in continuity with the broad corpus of global prison literature and/or literature produced in jail by political activists from the Italian anti-fascists to Nobel laureate Bertrand Russell, jailed during the World War I for conscientious objection to the British war effort, to Wole Soyinka, sentenced to prison, then to death, then forced into exile by the military dictatorship of Sani Abacha in Nigeria, through to the late Luis Sepúlveda, imprisoned and tortured by the Chilean military dictatorship in the 1970s—to name just a few well-known examples.[61] The long-lasting political effects and increasing global salience of this literary canon, which Barbara Harlow aptly termed "resistance literature" in her seminal work of the same title, is not least illustrated by Antonio Gramsci's *Prison Notebooks,* in which the Italian anti-fascist intellectual narrated his experience of detention while also delineating a new philosophy of history that has become the cornerstone of much contemporary critical and postcolonial thought. To quote Ahmed Naji's words in his foreword to this volume, such literature is like a "puncture in the wall" not only of the prison, but of the entire carceral state. Or as famed Kenyan author and critic Ngũgĩ wa Thiong'o—himself a political prisoner in the late 1970s—described it to us as we prepared to interview him for the afterword, such writings are like the proverbial bird resting on a ledge outside the bars of a prison window before flying away to freedom.[62]

This book takes inspiration from this global corpus, illuminating the human, political, cultural, and economic costs of Egypt's prison system through letters, testimony, prose fiction, poetry, and artwork created by prisoners, whether in their cells or following release. Many of these texts are artifacts of prison contraband, smuggled out at great personal risk. Some of the prisoners represented in this collection are well-known figures, spending their second, third, or fourth stint in prison, while many are not. Some are ideologically engaged, either from religious and/or political motivations—Muslim Brotherhood members or communists, for example. Many are ordinary people who dared not to respond deferentially to interactions with corrupt police and security officials and found themselves imprisoned alongside professional activists. Still others are those who happened to be in the wrong place at the wrong time and who, upon entering Egypt's labyrinthine justice system, got lost in the maze.

In recent years, affecting this sense of "lostness" and unpredictability has increasingly become the organizing praxis and purpose of Egyptian law. In the words of a human rights lawyer we interviewed in January 2020, "There is simply no rule of law. You go to court, and you don't know what the outcome is going to be, because rules are not followed anymore."

Yet even this indictment does not describe the bleak realities of those thousands upon thousands whose fate has been to languish behind bars for months or years without ever having their day in court. This book is a collection of voices—perforce neither exhaustive nor fully representative—of those whose freedoms to speak, to move, and to *live* have been brutally proscribed. These voices offer a historically and politically broad if not precise representation of the most important groups and voices imprisoned by various regimes.

In most of the selections, the translated letter or writing is introduced by a member of the curatorial team, providing a short biography of the author and the specific circumstances of their imprisonment, when they are known. Many scholars, activists, human rights practitioners, and organizations from around the world have contributed to making this work possible; the names of those who felt comfortable being identified are indicated in the acknowledgments, the table of contents, and the entries they curated for this volume.

"WE DON'T LIKE PRISONS, BUT WE ARE NOT AFRAID OF THEM"

The collection is multigenerational and includes women and men of multiple social classes and ideological and political points of view. We have included not only letters from prisoners describing the conditions of their imprisonment or their political views as shaped by prison, but also their literary, artistic, and everyday intellectual and cultural production, including artwork. As noted in the individual entries, two groups in particular, *Mada Masr* and El-Nadeem Center against Violence and Torture, have played a crucial role in documenting, collecting, and publishing the writings of post-2011 political prisoners, well known and unknown alike, as have anonymous groups of activists who have archived and collated websites, Facebook pages, and other social media locations where such letters, artwork, and reflections have been initially shared by friends and family of prisoners. More recently, the MENA Prison Forum has emerged as a collective that aims at documenting prison conditions across the region.

Even with the large and widely sourced number of entries and an explicit commitment to including a diverse range of voices and experiences that would reflect and represent a cross section of the political prison population in the post-2011 period, there are several gaps in our coverage that keep it from being as comprehensive as we would have liked. Chief among the gaps is the overall underrepresentation (compared to their numbers in prison) of Muslim Brotherhood members and other Islamists, and to a lesser extent of members of two of the most important groups during the revolutionary era: the Revolutionary Socialists (the most important revolutionary left-wing political movement in Egypt) and the Ultras (the organized soccer fan clubs associated with Egyptian Premier League teams, who had been battling Egyptian security services in football stadiums and the streets for years before the eruption of the uprising, and who were crucial to taking and holding Tahrir and other major squares during the eighteen days and subsequent occupations).

In fact, all three groups are crucial to the overall narrative of the last decade, and the Muslim Brotherhood in particular is over-represented in the prison population. However, because of the nature of imprisonment under the post-2013 coup regime, it has become very difficult for detainees from these groups get any writings out of prison, or to even risk being caught trying to do so, and what does escape tends to be broadly descriptive, formulaic, and repetitive. Nonetheless, we have included individuals from all three groups as part of a broad corpus of narratives, not only about prison conditions but also about the political visions and aspirations that circulated and cohered there.

At the same time, there are relatively fewer letters in this book from the first two years—between 2011 and 2013—of the post-uprising period. This represents a comparatively smaller body of letters for this period in general, which, according to several activists who were working directly on imprisonment issues during SCAF and Morsi's rule, most likely resulted from several factors, ranging from the relative lack of literacy of people imprisoned during those two years (when the military/security services were more interested in reasserting control over the streets than over the political system, which meant that far more nonpolitical, poor, and working-class Egyptians were arrested for offenses like violating curfews, compared with after 2013), to the fact most arrested people did not believe they would remain in jail for a long period of time, or were able to be visited regularly, and thus there was less need to engage in regular correspondence with family or friends. The fact that civil society organizations like El-Nadeem and No Military Trials for Civilians were very active also meant that prison conditions were being documented in other ways.

It should be noted here that while we have included many of the most prominent prisoners of the "revolutionary generation," such as blogger and political activist Alaa Abd El-Fattah, his sister Sanaa Seif, and human rights lawyers Mahienour El-Massry and Yara Sallam, our main focus is on less well-known and even anonymous voices, precisely to illustrate both the similarities across conditions, gender, and reasons for and location of imprisonment, and the myriad unique ways in which the imprisoned have responded to and narrated their experiences.

These voices stand out as among the most creative and powerfully evocative narratives of everyday life in prison, bringing to a new level and from the narrow space of the cells the reflections about freedom, dignity, and social justice that were begun in the square during the uprising. The styles of the letters in this volume vary. Some are lyrical, others could be sociological essays, others are scattered messages to family and friends. Conflicting views and emotions are in these letters, ranging from pain to compassion, fear, hope, and despair. As beautifully expressed in one of Mahienour El-Massry's Facebook posts shortly before a 2014 court hearing, "We don't like prisons, but we are not afraid of them."[63] While both men and women activists are often equally eloquent about the broader political dynamics surrounding their imprisonment and their vision for a different and more just order, among the many ordinary Egyptians whose letters we've included, a distinct difference emerges between women and men, with the former offering a more hopeful and tenacious desire to remain steadfast and resilient in the face of long-term confinement. This relatively more positive—but by no means universal—attitude could be attributed to many factors. Sadly, there is plenty of evidence of sexual abuse and rape of women in prison,[64] which negates the theory that they are held under less torturous conditions than men. The reality is that women have a historically rooted experience with having their bodies subject to both family and state surveillance, control, and violence.

Days pass in unending routine inside Egypt's women's prisons; girls become women, and some lose hope of ever leaving. After former president Mohamed Morsi was removed from power in July 2013, dozens of women were arrested for political reasons. They come from different backgrounds and have differing political beliefs and stories, but most have deep psychological scars from their time in prison, their souls deeply injured from an ingrained sense of literally "falling into nothingness" day in and day out, as the already cramped space of an overcrowded prison cell closes further in on you with each passing day, as Ahmed Tarek, Sanaa Seif, and an anonymous female detainee describe in the pages that follow.

Some prisoners are beaten until they lose their hearing. Others, like Sanaa Seif, only heard the beating of women in adjacent cells. "Don't be fooled by the deterioration in conditions you already see. Their plans are for much worse," explains Seif. Indeed, since Sisi's assumption of power, conditions have worsened significantly in two important ways. First, overcrowding has increased appreciably; the number of new prisoners continues to outpace construction of new cells to hold them, even with the prison building boom of the last decade. Where one cell used to be split in half, each half containing two prisoners, now it is split into sixths, each sixth containing up to eight prisoners—the math might be hard to calculate, but the effect is easy to imagine. Second, the dreaded State Security services, which used to be restricted from entering prisons, now have offices right next to cell blocks so they can continuously monitor prisoners. The normal prison guards no longer have any authority, heightening the level of abuse. Women political prisoners tell of sexual harassment and assault, of long periods without being allowed to bathe or have family visits, of being put in cells with hardened criminals—what imprisoned activist Solafa Magdy terms in one letter the "criminal prisoner bogeyman"—or kept in solitary confinement, where abuse can occur without anyone seeing it.[65] Perhaps worse, women are increasingly kidnapped, disappeared, or held arbitrarily for years not merely because of their activities, but to punish or coerce male relatives who are either themselves in custody or who are outside the country.

If there was a moratorium on executions at the end of the Mubarak era, as of 2023 there can be fifty or more per month, with prisoners given little warning as to when their execution is to be carried out; nor are their families informed in a timely manner. According to feminist human rights activist Yara Sallam, jailed for fifteen months in 2014, death row—the Makhsous ward—in the women's prison emptied and filled up again during her imprisonment; there were enough executions that she could no longer "remember when it was that I got used to the screams of the women in al-Makhsous."[66] And even the most high-profile prisoners, like Rami Shaath, Alaa Abd El-Fattah, and even Westerners, routinely suffer physical abuse, from the *tashrifa* or "welcome parties" received at the hands of guards when they first arrive to vicious assaults and torture in their cells. Additionally, and against Egyptian law, reading and writing materials are kept from prisoners and no outdoor time is allowed.

Broadly speaking, the government has "ratcheted up denial of most basic rights . . . in every way the situation is worse," according to Sanaa Seif. The hierarchies of abuse—which used to mean common prisoners were abused far more than high-profile prisoners—are dissolving to the point that no one is safe. As Seif explains, "The goal is to break you, to leave no hope by making an example of you, especially if you're someone with a name. . . . They want to create an Egypt that is in much worse shape than it is even now, which is necessary because unlike Mubarak, who had a massive party and patronage system—the National Democratic Party—to secure a basic level of public and political support, Sisi has no party, only a small coterie of allies to maintain control of a sprawling system with many competing power centers."[67]

This is very different than the Mubarak era, during which time there was an elite of opposition that was cohesive but small. Today there is far more popular anger, although the heightened level of state violence has kept it in check. As Egyptian as well as foreign scholars, activists, and policymakers debate how stable or brittle the current regime remains, we point out that what is clear is that the power of the Sisi regime might be brittle and unstable, but even an unstable system can last a very long time, and a massive prison system is almost always a crucial element of its durability. Indeed, if Alaa has courageously reminded us that we—that is, the rest of us outside Egypt's prison walls—have "not yet been defeated," on the inside, as journalist Mostafa al-Aasar put it in a frank letter about prison life, there is a great risk that "we are much weaker than we seem."

Time passes slowly in prison, for women as for men, although it seems to move at different speeds and with different intensities for everyone. But the scars remain. Many women form attachments to the objects that sustained them inside, like Salwa Mehres, who still drinks her coffee from the contraband Nescafé glass that she hid in her cell. Others find it hard to forget the experience of sleeping on the ground at night and flitting between boredom and trauma during the day. They know what they looked like before entering prison but are often surprised on release, because mirrors mostly aren't permitted. If and when life can begin again, it's never the same.

"I THANK GOD FOR THE DEATH OF MY MOTHER"

The documents comprising this collection can and should be read at once as historical sources and as works with significant literary and even philosophical merit and impact, if not intention. In other words, they are unique testimonies of a moment, but they also bear a more universal meaning when they address the nostalgia of the detainee for their beloved, the fear of being forgotten, and anxiety about loneliness and isolation. Some of the letters included here address both Egypt and the human condition more broadly, and this is what makes them pieces of literature: they restore humanity to an inhuman condition.

In his final message before his death, filmmaker Shady Habash laid bare the difficulty of resisting in prison without destroying at least part of what makes one human: existing in relation to other human beings and being remembered. He iconically wrote that "prison doesn't kill, loneliness does" (see chapter 21). And loneliness is made even worse when one's days are passed ping-ponging between electrocutions, mock executions, and promised pardons that turn into even more sadistic forms of revenge, as several writers document in the pages that follow.

Loneliness is even harder to bear when the universe surrounding you is devoid of beauty. As one female prisoner wrote in response to her worsening situation, "The destruction inflicted upon us" by the prison authorities is so great that "everything around me kills everything beautiful inside of me." Sometimes the pain is so great that inmates thank God their loved ones are not alive to witness their suffering. Another woman, imprisoned in the infamous Qanater Prison wrote, "For the first time in my life, I thank God for the death of my mother."

These writings offer a unique opportunity to rethink and reframe the global discussion about human rights, democracy, and citizenship. It is our hope that the letters, poetry, and art that readers encounter in the pages that follow will inspire them to shine a light on the ongoing and unending misery of the 100,000 people presently in the grip of the Egypt's all-encompassing carceral system and lead to a commitment to press the international community to do more to compel the Egyptian government to live up to its international obligations and to its responsibility to treat its own citizens with the modicum of decency and respect guaranteed to every human being under international law. Indeed, more than seventy years after the proclamation of the Universal Declaration of Human Rights, it is evident that human rights cannot belong only to some people; they only exist insofar as they are accorded to all human beings regardless of race, gender, ethnicity, religion, class, and political views.

The experience of political imprisonment in Egypt during the last decade, as in too many other Arab countries and societies across the

Middle East, but also in Africa, China, Brazil, Russia, India, and indeed in their racialized counterparts in the United States, Australia, and other countries with large numbers of incarcerated minorities, Indigenous communities, and/or migrants, demonstrates just how pervasive carceral systems are to modern political systems, "liberal democratic" as well as authoritarian. Whether these systems are used as a tool to quarantine and even profit from citizens deemed disposable or undisciplinable owing to racialized neoliberal policies, or to silence opponents to dictatorial regimes, confining, marking, and even destroying the bodies of millions of people have become core survival practices of states across the world. This surely accounts for one reason why Western governments are not just unmoved by the large-scale and systemic human rights violations in these countries but are complicit with them.

When it comes to Egypt in particular, as the second-largest recipient of US military aid and with close economic, security, and strategic relations with most of the major European powers despite harassing, imprisoning, torturing, and murdering their citizens as well as its own, there is little doubt that Western countries remain complicit in the ongoing regime of political and penal terror, or that their citizens have the right and indeed obligation to press for their governments to end their support for this and every other regime that steals the lives of so many of its children. In the end, as with climate change, the COVID-19 pandemic, and other global disasters, the impact of mass political imprisonment, torture, and repression cannot be cordoned off; these practices eventually infect every country and constitute a violation of everyone's rights as much as of those of their most direct victims.

In this book, we have tried first and foremost to include writings or artworks that have historical significance because of the author or the event being described, or because they have aesthetic/literary value. Whenever possible, we have chosen documents that exemplify both qualities. We have also chosen letters that describe not only the brutality but the mundanity of prison life, its rhythms, accents, and daily grind.

Our second goal was to provide a broad cross section of imprisoned Egyptians: women and men, young and elderly, rich and poor, urban and (far too infrequently) rural, Muslim Brotherhood and communist, liberal and Ultra, professional and laborer, Muslim and Christian—there is no group that we consciously excluded or whose presence we deliberately underrepresented vis-à-vis its share of the population. Nevertheless, as explained above, this is not a sociological or ethnographic study, and it was not possible to include a proportionate amount of contributions from all the social groups represented in the prison population. What the enclosed do offer, however, is a historically and politically broad if not precise representation of the most important groups and voices imprisoned by various regimes, voices whose descriptions and recollections offer a powerful testament to the indignities and horrors of imprisonment and the resilience of so many of those forced to undergo the experience.

Whichever period one considers, our primary goal has been to put the disappeared, absent, and all too often forgotten at the center of our narrative, to name them and in so doing to reaffirm their existence, their specific stories of detention, and their ongoing resistance. We also aim to shed light on the intellectual contribution offered by many imprisoned Egyptians to cutting-edge artistic, aesthetic, and political debates within Egypt and on the global scale. In other words, what brings together the essays, artworks, and documents that compose this anthology is not only the experience of prison, but also the aesthetic value of the writing and art and its capacity to envision a new episteme of freedom for the prisoners, for Egypt, and for readers wherever they may be.

In Turi, the small village in southern Italy where Antonio Gramsci was imprisoned from 1926 until 1937, the prison where he was detained still stands. On the façade of the main building, at the top, to the left of the large entrance door, is a plaque placed there on April 27, 1955. It reads, "In questo carcere visse in prigionia Antonio Gramsci. Maestro liberatore martire, che ai carnefici stolti annuncio' la rovina, alla nazione morente la salvazione, al popolo lavoratore la vittoria" ("In this jail Antonio Gramsci was imprisoned. Teacher, liberator, martyr, who announced to his foolish executioners their ruin, to a dying nation its salvation, to the working class victory.") Our deepest wish is, sometime soon, to read a similar sentence on the gates of Tora, Qanater, and all the other Egyptian prisons where today the bravest among the Egyptian people are paying the highest price for having dared to dream of a better world.

NOTES

1. Améry, *At the Mind's Limits*, 34, 40.
2. These countries include Morocco, Tunisia, and Jordan. See Norton, *Civil Society in the Middle East*, vols. 1 and 2.
3. Sorbera, "Body Politics and Legitimacy."
4. Beinin, "Egyptian Workers and January 25th."
5. Stacher, *Watermelon Democracy*, 33–35; El Amrani, "The Murder of Khaled Said."
6. Mamdouh and Hindy, "President Abdel Fattah al-Sisi Re-elected until 2030."
7. Epstein, *The Birth of the State*, 2.
8. Echebiri, "The Carceral State and White Supremacy, One and the Same."
9. Daly, *The Cambridge History of Egypt*, vol. 2.
10. Peters, "Egypt and the Age of the Triumphant Prison."
11. Cattaui, *Le regne de Mohamed Aly*, 312.
12. Royle, *The Egyptian Campaigns, 1882–1885*, 201.
13. Cole, *Colonialism and Revolution in the Middle East*.
14. LeVine, *We'll Play till We Die*, 2.
15. July 5, 1884, bulletin, quoted in Shaker, "Cannot Be Contained."
16. Griffiths, "Egyptian Prisons."
17. Blackmon, *Slavery by Another Name*.
18. Griffiths, "Egyptian Prisons," 282–83.

19. Dikötter and Brown, *Cultures of Confinement.*
20. Walsh, "Shareholders in Repression."
21. Hilmy, *al-Sijun al-misriya fi 'ahd al-ihtilal al-'inglizi*, 4.
22. Public Records Office, UK, FO/141/511/5, letter by Huda Shaarawi to Sir Lord Allenby, September 1, 1922.
23. For the original discussion of the "coloniality of power," see Quijano, "Coloniality of Power, Eurocentrism, and Latin America."
24. Booth, "Women's Prison Memoirs in Egypt and Elsewhere"; Benigni, *Il carcere come spazio letterario.*
25. al-'Aqqad, *'Alam al-Sudud wa al-Qiyud*, 15.
26. 'Abd al-Hakim, *al-Aqdam al-ariyya*, 6.
27. Beinin, "Labor, Capital, and the State in Nasserist Egypt, 1952–1961."
28. Lockman, "Notes on Egyptian Workers' History," 6–8.
29. Revolutionary Socialist Movement, *Rayat al-idrab fi sama' misr*, chap. 3.
30. Al-Arian, *Answering the Call.*
31. Human Rights Watch, "'We Do Unreasonable Things Here.'"
32. Bianchi, "The Corporatization of the Egyptian Labor Movement," 437–41; interview with senior member of student movement and Communist Party in the early 1970s, December 2022, Cairo.
33. Alsharif and Saleh, "Special Report."
34. *Al Jazeera*, "Qawwat al-'amn al-masriyya."
35. Ghiglia, "Journalistes en quête d'eux-mêmes," 114; interview with Farida al-Naqqash, December 16, 2022, Cairo.
36. Interview by Collective Antigone, January 2020, Cairo.
37. Ibrahim, "Saad Eddin Ibrahim."
38. Amnesty International, "Time for Justice."
39. World Prison Brief, "2022 Egypt Report."
40. The report is detailed in Cairo Institute for Human Rights Studies, "Egypt: Systematic Torture."
41. Stacher, *Watermelon Democracy*, 109; Awad, "Egypt's New Authoritarianism from an Institutionalist Perspective"; Armbrust, "Trickster Defeats the Revolution"; Rutherford, "Egypt's New Authoritarianism under Sisi."
42. Stevenson, "Sisi's Way."
43. Amnesty International, "Egypt."
44. Yee, "'A Slow Death.'"
45. Abdelrahman, *Egypt's Long Revolution*; Hopkins, *Political and Social Protest in Egypt.*

46. Hafez, "Bodies That Protest"; Hafez, "The Revolution Shall Not Pass through Women's Bodies"; Hafez, *Women of the Midan*.

47. Sorbera, "Gender: Still a Useful Category to Analyse Middle East History?"

48. Yee, McCann, and Holder, "Egypt's Revolving Jailhouse Door."

49. Sanders, "Egypt's Prisons."

50. *Quatre femmes d'Égypte*, Tahani Rached, dir., 1997.

51. Elsisi, "'They Threw Her in with the Prostitutes!'"

52. Personal communication with Collective Antigone, Cairo, 2022; see her letters in this volume.

53. Interview by Collective Antigone, January 2020, Cairo.

54. Aflatun, *Mudhakkirat Inji Aflatun*.

55. Khalil, "The Rise of Egypt's Prison Industrial Complex."

56. Sanaa Seif, from "Book Talk with Sharif Abdel Kouddous, Sanaa Seif, and Aslı Ü. Bâli" for the release of Alaa Abd El-Fattah's book *You Have Not Yet Been Defeated*, UCLA Center for Near Eastern Studies, Los Angeles, May 9, 2022.

57. Interview with former political prisoner, London, November 2023.

58. Magdy, "Women in Egypt's Prisons."

59. Gameela Ismail, interview with Collective Antigone, January 2022, Cairo.

60. See Giorgio Agamben's two generative monographs on these concepts, *Homo Sacer* and *The State of Exception*.

61. For these writings, see Ippolito and Gonnella, *Bisogna aver visto*; Taurasi, *Le nostre prigioni*; Russell, *Autobiography*; Thiong'o, *Devil on the Cross* and *Wrestling with the Devil*; Sepúlveda, *La frontiera scomparsa*; and Soyinka, *The Man Died*.

62. Ngũgĩ wa Thiong'o, interview with Collective Antigone, May 2023, Irvine, California.

63. From a Facebook post Mahienour El-Massry wrote before appearing in court in May 2014. Personal communication.

64. Middle East Eye staff, "Egypt."

65. Magdy, "Women in Egypt's Prisons."

66. Sallam, "How We Got Used to the Screams of Those on Death Row."

67. "Book Talk with Sharif Abdel Kouddous, Sanaa Seif, and Aslı Ü. Bâli" for the release of Alaa Abd El-Fattah's book *You Have Not Yet Been Defeated*, UCLA Center for Near Eastern Studies, Los Angeles, May 9, 2022.

1

ANONYMOUS

A DIARY OF EVERYDAY LIFE IN PRISON

1—The Reception

When we arrived at the prison gates, we were left in the transfer vans for about an hour. We were handcuffed and surrounded by a large number of bags and blankets in the heat. Then finally the van was opened for us. We heard screams and abuse and swearing. We climbed down as fast as we could despite our handcuffs and our heavy belongings. We found two rows of soldiers, informers, and sergeants who came down on us with kicks, slaps, and beatings with sticks, hoses, and chains. We ran as fast as we could. We were unable to protect ourselves from any of the strikes because of the handcuffs and bags. Before we reached the gate, a soldier beat one of us, an elderly man. He beat him brutally with a hose on his back. The marks of that hose remained on his back for weeks after that. The beating and the slaps continued, mixed with cursing and insults. Then we were seated like prisoners of war, on the ground, our eyes looking down. Whoever dared to look up was met with kicks. They checked our personal information, comparing it with the information in their files. Then they took us to be searched. They took off our clothes, tore them, and searched us in a humiliating way. They took all the bags and shoes. They confiscated almost everything, leaving us nothing but a blanket and some underwear. Everything else, the food, the water, the clothes, the shoes, the medicines, even extra blankets, was taken away and distributed among the informers. They then made us stand face to the wall amid kicks and slaps delivered by the officer himself and the informers. They took us to the ward and divided us in two rooms, twenty-five in each room, and nine of us were taken to other cells.

2—Room and Crowding

The size of the cell is 4.5 × 3.5 square meters. One toilet. No sun at all. It has a small window close to the ceiling and a smaller window in the door. It has a fan that does not work. The maximum capacity of the room is fifteen people. But we were twenty-five. The number can reach twenty-seven in some rooms. We sit crammed together. Each of us has 35 square centimeters where we live, eat, drink, and sleep. You cannot extend your legs. We take turns sleeping. No more than one blanket is allowed per person. It is as if you are sleeping directly on the floor. The overcrowding is very dangerous, especially in summer. The heat, the difficulty showering because of the overcrowding and the fact that there is only one bathroom, leads to the spread of skin diseases. The lighting is very dim. They ban lightbulbs, even if brought by family members.

3—Time in Open Air

They open the cells for one single hour per day* in the morning, although the prison regulations state that a prisoner is entitled to a minimum of two hours outside the cell. The yard is not big enough for all of us. Overhead are iron bars that allow very little sun in. Criminal inmates are allowed two hours. The restrictions apply only to political prisoners.

4—Cell Inspection

The rooms are inspected and searched periodically, especially those where political prisoners are held. The search is very humiliating and inhuman. An informer bangs the door open with his foot at 7:00 a.m. and is followed by many other informers who swear and insult us while kicking us awake and then pushing us outside the cells using slaps and beatings. Outside the room, the officer is waiting. He orders us to stand face to the wall and to raise our arms. Then they strip off our clothes and do a body search, among insults and humiliations, most of which are political. They have a conviction that all political prisoners are members of the Muslim Brotherhood. Then the officer and informers enter the cell and with pocketknives cut through any ropes, plastic bags, and other bags. They turn all the bags inside out and empty them of clothes and food, mixing everything together. They take anything they like or anything of value. They don't search for anything. Their only aim is to humiliate and disturb us.

5—The Treatment

They do not treat us as political prisoners, but more like criminals. Upon entry into prison, they order political prisoners to take off their

---

* Some prisoners, most infamously Alaa Abd El-Fattah, have been prevented from leaving their cells for years at a time.

clothes, squat, and empty their bowels like criminal prisoners, although there are engineers, doctors, and other respectable people among us, and they know very well that we do not do the tricks done by criminal prisoners who smuggle drugs in their stomachs. They scream, "Sit and shit, you son of a bitch!" Whoever refuses is beaten until close to death. When we say we are political prisoners, they say there is no such thing as a political prisoner, we are all criminals. But when we ask for any right enjoyed by criminal prisoners, such as two hours outside the cell or access to TV or newspapers, they say those things are prohibited to political prisoners. The treatment always involves humiliation, degradation, insults, and beatings, at any time and without reason. Sometimes they choose a prisoner to beat and insult just for fun.

6—Medical Care

The level of medical care is very low. There is a small clinic where most of the time there is no doctor. When there is one, he is a general practitioner. He is usually not willing to examine anyone, so as to be spared any effort and be able to go home early. They take us to the clinic once every two weeks; sometimes they do not take us at all. When they do, they take two people from each cell, irrespective of the number of the sick. If someone is taken to the clinic and he is not dying of his sickness, they accuse him of faking illness and beat him up and take him to disciplinary detention. If somebody gets ill at night and needs to go to the clinic, we have to bang at the door. They take hours to come, during which the ill person may die if he is seriously ill. When they do come, they beat the patient and whoever banged at the door. One time they almost beat one of us to death because he needed the clinic. Whoever is lucky to get to the clinic safely is treated by the doctor in a most humiliating way.

7—Visits

Visits are very difficult in this prison. Visiting day is a sad day. The visits are once every fifteen days. Families usually come from far away. We are allowed to see them for only fifteen minutes maximum. It is too short to talk about anything; really—just exchange hellos and make sure everybody is alright. They prevent us from moving or standing or eating or even touching the things our families brought. During the visit we are surrounded by informers, who wait for their money so as not to insult us in front of our families. Then they pull us from their midst and push us back inside. For the most part, they refuse to allow us to keep the things our families bring. They steal a lot of the food and the sweets. While they are searching what our families bring, they take us into a room where they shave our heads completely, then make us take off our clothes and search our bodies. Then they take us to a room where we collect the things our families brought from the floor, usually destroyed, and take them to our cells. The informers take whatever they wish. Also, the prison regulations do not mention anything about shaving every visit. We may get infected in the process because they use the same razor on all of us. It is painful for our families to see us like this. They must have forgotten how we looked before.

Letter sent in August 2015 by an anonymous prisoner in Wadi Natrun Prison to El-Nadeem, Center against Violence and Torture. Courtesy of the Archives of El-Nadeem, Center against Violence and Torture.

2

ALAA ABD EL-FATTAH

ALAA ABD EL-FATTAH is among the most well-known political prisoners not only in Egypt, but in the world today. The son of one of the country's pioneer human rights campaigners, Ahmed Seif al-Islam (co-founder of the Hisham Mubarak Law Center in Cairo) and Laila Soueif, the equally well-known professor of mathematics at Cairo University, human rights defender, and co-founder of the March 9, 2004, movement for the democratization of Egyptian universities, Alaa first came to international notice along with his then wife Manal Bahey El-Din Hassan as one of the Arab world's first professional internet coders. His activism as an Egyptian internet pioneer and human rights campaigner earned him well over half a million followers on Facebook and Twitter.

Alaa was first arrested in May 2006, spending over a month and a half in prison. He was next imprisoned in late October 2011 while reporting on the massacre of Coptic protesters by Egyptian security forces* and spent another month and a half in prison. His third arrest occurred in March 2013, while Mohamed Morsi was still in power, and his fourth occurred in November of that year, after the military coup that put Abdel Fattah El-Sisi in power. That arrest and trial led to a five-year sentence in February 2015. He was released after four years but placed under onerous probation conditions that forced him to spend from 6:00 p.m. to 6:00 a.m. every day back in prison. He was rearrested in September 2019 as he was leaving the Dokki police station for his daily release.

He spent the worst of the COVID-19 crisis in the maximum security Tora Prison, where conditions were bad enough to prompt him to undertake several hunger strikes. His situation became so intolerable that in September 2021, in a court interview with the judge reviewing his pre-trial detention, he explained that "I'm in terrible conditions . . . I can't carry on like this. Tell Laila Soueif to accept condolences for me" (*takhid e'azaya*), clearly indicating that he was suicidal or otherwise expected to die soon. However, in a subsequent letter to his sister after his words were made public, he apologized for worrying his family, explaining that he was struggling with the conditions of his detention but that he would do his best to withstand them.

In late 2021 a collection of Alaa's writings was published by Fitzcarraldo Editions (UK) and Seven Stories Press (US) by a collective of translators. Titled *You Have Not Yet Been Defeated: Selected Works, 2011–2021*, it was named one of the most influential books of the year by the *Los Angeles Review of Books*. It was published in Arabic soon thereafter. In December of that year, Alaa, his attorney Mohammed El-Baqer, and blogger Mohammed "Oxygen" Ibrahim were convicted of "spreading false news." Alaa was sentenced to five years and his comrades to four, not including time served.

---

* His reporting on the massacre was originally published on October 20, 2011, in *Al-Shourouk* magazine. The English translation is in Alaa Abd El-Fattah, *You Have Not Yet Been Defeated*.

Soon after, he was confined to one of the most notorious areas of Tora Prison, in more or less solitary confinement, without access to reading or writing materials or music, or even sunlight or clean water, and under consistently harsh conditions. This led him to begin an increasingly severe hunger strike on April 2, 2022, that would continue for well over 200 days. In May he was transferred to Wadi Natrun Prison without any significant improvement in his conditions of confinement. An international campaign surrounding both his book and the hunger strike raised Alaa's profile further; his continued imprisonment became a diplomatic issue, one heightened by his family's taking UK citizenship (through his mother), his hunger strike, and Egypt's hosting of the COP27 global climate summit in Sharm el-Sheikh. Alaa ceased drinking water on the summit's opening day, November 6, and only ended close to his birthday on November 18, with a note to his family to bring a cake to celebrate his birthday with him and with cellmates.

No doubt part of the reason for Alaa's despair was that he was beaten, along with other new detainees, when he arrived at Tora in September 2019 and engaged in a multiweek hunger strike to protest the brutal conditions, conditions made worse by the COVID-19 crisis. Despite his numerous and harsh imprisonments, Alaa has written several open letters and personal letters to family addressing several issues, from the development of the revolutionary movement, to the prisoners' conditions, to his personal life in relation to politics. As of summer 2024 Alaa remains in Wadi Natrun, serving a sentence that will continue until 2027.

TORA PRISON, CELL 1/6, WARD 4

What you are celebrating has a taste of cowardice. When we met to make this decision, I did not have the courage to listen to the opinion of Manal, whom I shall leave alone during the final days of her pregnancy, whom I shall leave her alone to supervise the workers preparing Khaled's room. Manal, whom I shall leave while in prison to face all the hardships of looking after my needs and livelihood in prison, as well as the visit permits and the campaign for my release. I left her in a fix and made a decision in a meeting in which I listened to the colleagues of the revolution and didn't listen to my wife, believing that she would definitely support whatever decision I made.

Still, I am proud. True, I am not the macho Nawara thinks I am, but neither am I a coward. I was offered a bargain by an important personality in the revolution, a bargain that secured my release provided I didn't insult the field marshal.[†] Just that. A very simple concession, and I refused. How would I have faced my family if I had accepted?

Let us start from the beginning: How are you? I am Alaa. A member of the infantries of the revolution. Many have sacrificed much more than I have. Many were much more courageous than I am. Many had a much greater role to play.

I am Alaa, and I am very proud that I am doing what I can, and sometimes I surprise myself by what I can do. I know myself and know what I cannot do. I try never to be late and I try to always conquer my fear and I try to always be on the front lines. If you think I am courageous, chivalrous, and brave, then you should know that I learned this from my mother and my younger sisters and my wife (who being separated from is the most difficult thing in prison).

November 3, 2011. Accessed via the blog Letters from the Darkness *in August 2023. Courtesy of Alaa's family.*

[†] Field Marshal Mohamed Hussein Tantawi.

JAN. 25, 5 YEARS ON: THE ONLY WORDS I CAN WRITE ARE ABOUT LOSING MY WORDS

People talk of a barrier of fear but to me it always felt like a barrier of despair and, once removed, even fear, massacres and prisons couldn't bring it back. I did all the silly things over-optimistic revolutionaries do: I moved back to Egypt permanently, had a child, founded a start-up, engaged in a series of progressive initiatives aiming at more popular, decentralized and participatory democracy, broke every draconian law and outdated taboo, walked into prison smiling and walked out of it triumphant.

In 2013, we started to lose the battle for narrative to a poisonous polarization between a rabidly militarized pseudo-secular statism and a viciously sectarian-paranoid form of Islamism. All I remember about 2013 is how shrill I sounded screaming "A plague on both your houses," how whiny and melodramatic it felt to complain about the curse of Cassandra warning of an all-consuming fire when no one would listen. As the streets were taken over by rallies that raised the photos of policemen instead of their victims, sit-ins were filled with chants against the Shia, and Coptic conspiracies flourished, my words lost any power and yet they continued to pour out of me. I still had a voice, even if only a handful would listen.

But then the state decided to end the conflict by committing the first crime against humanity in the history of the republic. The barriers of fear and despair would return after the Rabea al-Adaweya massacre. Another battle of narrative would start: getting non-Islamists to accept that a massacre had happened at all, to reject the violence committed in their name.

Three months after the massacre I was back in prison, and my prose took on a strange new role: to call on revolutionaries to admit defeat. To give up the optimism that had become dangerous in its encouragement to choose sides: a military triumphalism or an unpopular and

Figure 3. Alaa Abd El-Fattah during the Shura Council trials at the Cairo Police Academy, November 11, 2014.

impractical insistence on complete regime change. What we needed was all the strength we could muster to maintain some basic defense of human rights.

I narrated defeat because the very language of revolution was lost to us, replaced by a dangerous cocktail of nationalist, nativist, collectivist and post-colonialist language, appropriated by both sides of the conflict and used to spin convoluted conspiracy theories and spread paranoia.

I spent most of 2014 in prison yet I still had lots of words. My audience was much diminished, my message not one of hope, and yet it felt important to remind people that even after admitting defeat we can still resist; that going back to the margins we fought from during Mubarak's time was acceptable as long as we continued to fight for basic human rights. But by early 2015, as I heard my sentence, I had nothing left to say to any public. I could only write personal letters. The revolution and, indeed Egypt itself, would slowly fade out even from those letters, and by fall 2015, even my personal words dried up. It's been months since I wrote a letter and more than a year since I've written an article.

I have nothing to say: no hopes, no dreams, no fears, no warnings, no insights, nothing, absolutely nothing. Like a child showing signs of autism, I am regressing and losing my words, my ability to imagine an audience and mentally model the impact of my words on them.

. . .

Now tomorrow will be exactly like today and yesterday and all the days preceding and all the days following. I have no influence over anything.

Excerpt from a longer letter published in The Guardian *and* Mada Masr, *January 14, 2016. Also in* You Have Not Yet Been Defeated, *255–62. Courtesy of Alaa's family.*

3

ANONYMOUS

ON OCTOBER 9, 2011, thousands of peaceful protesters marched towards the Maspero building, the headquarters of the Egyptian Radio and Television Union, to demonstrate against the demolition of St. George Church in Edfu, Aswan. Footage showed security forces attacking the demonstrators, while official state media were reporting about "Coptic[s] attacking" the military and were inciting "honorable citizens" to defend them. Twenty-four people were killed and about 300 injured. The fact-finding committees nominated by SCAF, and later by President Morsi, never published the results of their inquiries.* Instead, more than thirty civilians (including Alaa Abd El-Fattah) were investigated and arrested for being present at Maspero, inciting

---

* Tahrir Institute for Middle East Policy, *Fact Sheet: The Maspero Massacre, Seven Years On*, October 10, 2018, https://timep.org/transitional-justice-project/fact-sheet-the-maspero-massacre-seven-years-on, last consulted April 7, 2021.

sectarian strife, disturbing public security, and attacking security forces. Ten years later, no high-ranking government, military, or police official has been held accountable for the massacre.

The anonymous author is a Coptic Christian who was imprisoned following the Maspero massacre. He was captured in front of the Egyptian state television building and accused of causing public agitation and disorder. He spent four months in jail and was released around Orthodox Christmas, on January 7, 2012. Finding it impossible to reintegrate into his neighborhood parish or make sense of his experiences with friends and family members, the author left Egypt for a European country in 2017, got married, and has two children. The following selection is drawn from notes and comments he wrote in the margins of his Bible during his imprisonment. The many margin notes challenge the theology and politics of the Coptic Church and its alliance with the Egyptian state. Moreover, the notes question the meanings of the punishment and discipline practiced by God, the Church, and the Egyptian state. Last but not least, the author interrupts aspects of repentance and confession that he learned in particular via the biblical parable of the Prodigal Son.

FRAGMENTS OF A COPTIC PRISONER'S DIARY:
ON THE MARGINS OF A BIBLE

"But during the night an angel of the Lord opened the doors of the jail and brought them out" (Acts 5:19).

Commentary: Who can bring me out? The Egyptian prisons seem more resistant to miracles than the Roman ones during the first days of Christianity. Is it because the Egyptian military allies with the Church? I do not know if Jesus is confused about whether I should be rescued and released like the apostles, or if the Egyptian security forces are more powerful than him.

"But the Lord was with Joseph in the prison and showed him his faithful love. And the Lord made Joseph a favorite with the prison warden" (Genesis 39:21).

Commentary: Joseph was innocent, or so we learned at Sunday school. God put him into jail because he had a better plan for him. This is what we learned at Sunday school. But I do not know God's plan for me!! Maybe Joseph also did not know God's plan, as I do not know mine. I won't be a prime minister like him because I am a Coptic Christian. I will also be an ex-prisoner in a few months (or maybe years???). Jesus, my prison warden is so wicked. Why did not I get one like the one that Joseph had?

"From inside the fish Jonah prayed to the Lord his God. He said: 'In my distress I called to the Lord, and he answered me. From deep in the realm of the dead I called for help, and you listened to my cry. You hurled me into the depths, into the very heart of the seas, and the currents swirled about me; all your waves and breakers swept over me'" (Jonah 2:1–3).

Commentary: Did Jonah pray to get released from inside the fish? Or did he pray to be forgiven for escaping God's plan? God asked Jonah to ask sinful people to repent, and Jonah did not execute this plan. Was my participation in Maspero against his plan? What is his plan from the beginning? I want to know so I do not feel that he is punishing me like he did Jonah. God was speaking directly to Jonah, but I cannot hear his voice. I think Jonah was quite sure that God would listen to him because he was already speaking to Him. But now, God speaks to us through the Church and its priests and pope. How can I know what God wants to tell me if the Church is in alliance with the military that killed us?

"The soldiers led Jesus away into the courtyard of the palace known as the governor's headquarters, and they called together the whole company of soldiers. They dressed him up in a purple robe and twisted together a crown of thorns and put it on him. They saluted him, "Hey! King of the Jews!" Again, and again, they struck his head with a stick. They spit on him and knelt before him to honour him. When they finished mocking him, they stripped him of the purple robe and put his own clothes back on him. Then they led him out to crucify him" (Mark 15:16–20).

Commentary: Jesus himself was imprisoned. His imprisonment preceded his crucifixion. I think this was an important part of his salvation plan. He died for our sins, but this came after he was tortured in the prison. Will my imprisonment precede a better future, like Jesus's resurrection? I do not know when I will be released. I have been here for two months. Jesus was just imprisoned for one night, and they killed him the following day. I think Jesus was lucky that his imprisonment was short and that it was quickly followed by the most splendid event in the history of the whole world. But here in this prison everything is stagnant and time does not move. Nothing better seems to come. I am afraid. No resurrection would happen in this dark cell.

"Then the King will say to those on his right, 'Come, you who are blessed by my Father; take your inheritance, the kingdom prepared for you since the creation of the world. For I was hungry and you gave me something to eat, I was thirsty and you gave me something to drink, I was a stranger and you invited me in, I needed clothes and you clothed me, I was sick and you looked after me, I was in prison and you came to visit me'" (Matthew 25:34–37).

Commentary: I am happy with the Church's service devoted to taking care of prisoners. They visit us here once a week on Sunday to confess and to receive communion. I am happy that I can still pray in prison, but the priest treats me as the prodigal son who returned to his father after losing his money due to his wrongdoings. What did I do wrong? I was protesting against the demolition and burning of churches, the houses of God. I am confused. I feel lost. What is right and wrong? I really do not know. For what should I repent? For what I should be forgiven? Lord have mercy.

Curated and translated by Mina Ibrahim.

4

AYMAN MOUSSA

AYMAN MOUSSA WAS A NINETEEN-YEAR-OLD student of engineering at the British University in Cairo and a diving trainer at Heliopolis Sporting Club when he was arrested at a protest on October 6, 2013, during a nationwide military crackdown on any visible opposition to the renewed military regime. In a mass military trial in October 2014, Ayman and sixty-eight other protesters were sentenced to fifteen years' imprisonment, a 20,000-pound fine, and five years' probation. Ayman's appeal was rejected on March 9, 2016, at which time he wrote, "I once believed that I could fly, so they locked me up in this cage. I once believed that I'm alive, so they buried me in this grave." Since then, Ayman has been held in several prisons and was refused permission to attend his father's funeral. Despite a concerted campaign by family and friends, as of summer 2024 he is being held in Tora Prison in conditions that supporters decry as "injustice beyond imagination."

"SCREAMS OF MY MIND"

"The screams of my mind are driving me crazy!"

Time is frozen . . . I am surrounded by silence . . . the screams in my mind annoy me!

I walk in an empty space . . . I am walking among the still-breathing dead!

I stop . . . I look at my watch . . . I see 3:02 a.m. shining at my face.

I hold my head to stop the screaming . . . No use . . . I ignore it and continue walking to and fro over bodies strewn on the ground . . . I walk uselessly . . . aimlessly . . . I only want to exhaust my body so that my mind stops thinking . . . stops screaming . . . No use!

I lie down in the space allocated for my sleep . . . I squeeze myself between two sleeping corpses . . .

I listen to the screams of my mind. "Where is privacy?!" I hear it say, reminding me of past situations . . . it reminds me of my sleep here and how it destroys every rule of privacy!

How bodies of those next to me collided with me during my sleep . . . how many times I woke up to find the foot of one of them in my face or a knee hitting my back . . . how many times I turned to find myself sleeping on top of the man next to me!

I close my eyes to avoid all those memories from haunting my brain . . . my mind recalls another scene where I was studying, or trying to study. At the time I was squeezed between the same two, sitting in a very uncomfortable position, in front of me a file in which I failed to understand what I was reading!

In the middle of my lack of concentration and lack of understanding, I saw a head slowly emerge until it rested between me and my file.

I heard his voice saying, "What is this? Are you studying?!"

I remained silent for a while and did not answer him. But my strong wish not to study, my lack of understanding when I did and my forgetfulness of how to study—I haven't studied for three years—made me decide to chat with him.

"No, I am eating watermelon." That is what I did not say. "Yes, I am studying," that is what I said, followed by an obviously fake smile. I saw his confusion when he realized how fake it was. I didn't move a muscle in my face until he—embarrassed—said, "OK . . . God be with you." Then he left me with the file in which I understood nothing.

Where are the riddles? The equations? Engineering? My mind was screaming.

Economy and political sciences?!! How did I get to be in this faculty?!

How did I get to be in prison . . . again, how did I get to be in prison . . . in this narrow grave . . . this exile away from home . . .

My home? I forgot its details . . . I hoped to return home . . . so I did and wished I hadn't . . . I returned and lost a part of me . . . I returned and my father passed away . . . the soul of the house departed . . . I returned for a few minutes to receive condolences, but I didn't meet him!!

Amid the memory of my house and the armored vehicle that took me from prison to my house and from my home to prison . . . amid the memory of the sound of sirens and seeing officers and soldiers armed with weapons . . . and the exaggerated and pointless wishes . . . I remembered what happened to me a few days earlier.

I remembered sitting in another prison . . . in a grave slightly wider than this. I was reading a novel after giving up on studying, and we heard a voice from outside the cell saying "Listen!! Transfer is tomorrow!" And he started calling names. Nineteen names are returning to the exile that I had been waiting to return to four months ago after completing my exams. Nineteen names, and my name was not one of them . . . I breathed a sigh of relief and sat down writing letters to the young people there.

The next day came and as usual I was awake early in the morning to drink coffee and sit down to study, or to read another book that has nothing to do with studying, as the situation usually settles . . .

I woke up early while people slept so I might get some privacy for a few hours, but today is a different day, today there is a "transfer" . . .

Unusually and fortunately for us, the news had come to us one day early, nineteen names and my name was not among them.

Nineteen names from the same case . . . nineteen names are now being called. "Get ready for transfer." I sighed again, my name was not called, sometimes late names "drop" as they call it here.

I helped the youths prepare their bags and "brush the mattress" and wished them a happy transfer.

Then I heard a voice calling from afar, "Ayman Ali Ibrahim Moussa . . . transfer"!

My eyes widened, my heart accelerated, my mind stopped working completely, silence prevailed in the dungeon [i.e., cell], along with pitiful looks at me!

I hate these looks . . . and suddenly my mind returned to working again. "How come I am transfered!! I have an exam here in fifteen days!!!"

These words fled my lips and I searched for the schedule of exams that the administration gave me a copy of a week ago, and I gathered my stuff, helped by my colleagues, and I avoided looking at them so that I would not see that "look" on their faces.

I looked at my books and my belongings and asked how I could carry them while I was tied to another person who was loaded with his belongings!

The transfer comes suddenly . . . just like death!!

I carried my belongings and got out to wait for the transfer. . . . Some of the students preceded me to the officer to tell him that we would be returning after a few days here to take exams, so why transfer us now?!!

But he said something about a fax that did not come, and that it was instructions, and such talk . . . words that reminded me of the officer in the movie *Zawaj biqarar jumhuri* [Marriage by republican decree] when he repeated "Forbidden." I smiled sarcastically and decided not to argue. Why argue?! Argue about being in prison?!

Here it's a little better but I do not have the energy to argue. . . . Carrying those loads while shackled, climbing into the transfer van, sitting in it squeezed together, the unpleasant smell, enduring the bumps on a painful metal bench, the red grooves in my hands from the handcuffs, leaving the van, waiting in the sun, the search of our belongings, taking some things from them, entering a new room, laying out the mattresses, hanging luggage, getting used to people and place, preparing psychologically for studying, and when I qualify psychologically, the transfer order comes and takes me back here again, and so on again and again . . . All of this is easier for me than arguing.

. . .

I see myself lying in the midst of bright white, in endless rest, wearing most of the clothes I traveled with, which the cold still pierces! My feet are attached to a snowboard, and a Norwegian girl—a few years older than me—is standing beside me, laughing at me after I lost my balance, not for the first time, while I was snowboarding. She and others were responsible for helping us—we are the diving team from the Heliopolis Sports Club—after competing in the championship in Norway.

"Hey, stand up," she said in accented English while laughing. I was barely fourteen then. I blushed out of shame. I smile remembering these days . . . I smile despite the darkness of the place—now—and its narrowness. But I still hold a beautiful memory.

Why are you still awake?! I am interrupted by a rattle at my side . . . I look at him and I say to him in the dark, "I can't sleep, you know that. . . . You sleep, just don't mind."

I see his ghost shaking his head, then he sleeps. I envy him for the speed of his mind's response to sleep . . . and I blame my mind for losing this talent.

I exhale darkness . . . I inhale darkness . . . then I look at my watch . . . it is 3:08 a.m.

Letter written December 23, 2016, in Wadi Natrun Prison. Courtesy of the Archives of El-Nadeem, Center against Violence and Torture.

5

AHMED ABDALLAH

TRUTH ABOUT GIULIO

Ahmed Abdallah is a human rights lawyer and one of the founders and trustees of the Egyptian Commission for Rights and Freedoms. The organization campaigns for human rights and against the systematic use of enforced disappearance in Egypt. He was arrested on April 25, 2015, in the context of the crackdown against the human rights community that followed the protests against the government's decision to give the islands of Tinar and Sanafir to the Kingdom of Saudi Arabia.

Ahmad Abdallah is part of the team of lawyers representing the family of Giulio Regeni, the Italian graduate student from Cambridge University who was kidnapped and tortured to death by officials of the Egyptian State Security in January 2016. During his detention, Ahmad Abdallah produced an origami with the script "Al-Haqiqa li-Giulio" (Truth about Giulio).

Figure 4. Origami heart made in prison by Ahmed Abdallah in solidarity with the campaign Truth about Giulio Regeni, the Italian student from the University of Cambridge who was kidnapped and tortured to death by Egyptian security in 2016. Courtesy of Ahmed Abdallah.

Upon his release in September 2016, he posted a photo of the origami on his Facebook cover, and it is still there today: "I don't think I will ever change my cover on FB as long as the case is open."

6

AHMED GAMAL ZIADA

AHMED GAMAL ZIADA, a journalist and human rights activist, was born in 1988. He studied history and cultural studies at al-Azhar University and political science and international relations at the Free University of Brussels. Like many others of his generation, he was part of the 2011 revolutionary movement. He had already participated in demonstrations organized in solidarity with the second Palestinian Intifada, as well as in previous events against the policies of the Egyptian regime, but his anger erupted after the torture and murder of Khaled Said and Sayyid Bilal in 2010. Capturing the experience of an entire generation, he'd later write in his memoirs that "I lost part of myself in Tahrir Square, and the other part in prison."

Ahmed joined every political event happening at the time and witnessed the tragic end of the extensive protests aimed at creating change in the middle of 2013. Many of his friends in the Egyptian opposition were killed by the regime. He was deeply moved and frustrated by these deaths, and this led him to stop working for a while. He had previously worked for several human rights organizations, including El-Nadeem, in addition to his career in journalism. It was only a short time before he went back to work, around the end of 2013, to cover political events on the streets of Cairo. On December 28, Ahmed covered the students' protests near al-Azhar University in Madinet Nasr. He documented, in photos and videos, the arrest of two students who were on their way to their exams and did not even join the demonstrations. The two students were later sentenced to seven years in prison. One of the arresting officers saw Ahmed filming, stopped him, checked his camera, destroyed its chip, and then hit and arrested him. Like thousands of young people at the time, he was detained without trial, spending around 500 days in the Liman Abou Zabal 2 prison. Since the beginning of Ahmed's journalistic and photojournalistic career, his desire has been to write and report more. His painful experience in prison motivated him to write more intensively; he secretly wrote on cigarette papers during his imprisonment, and succeeded in smuggling many of his writings to friends outside. They in turn managed to publish, on social media and other platforms and in newspapers, his texts and letters describing his dreadful solitary confinement, the torture to which he was subjected, and his desire to not see "history . . . written by the victors."

After his release on May 5, 2015, Ahmed published numerous articles, reports, and blogs. He also published a long and detailed report on Egyptian prisons with a human rights lawyer, Gamal Eid, and began to collect his own prison notes and memoirs in preparation for a book about his experience in prison. Despite threats of torture, he exposed the violations occurring in that prison and showed the committee traces of the atrocities committed on his body, all in the presence of the prison's director and officers.

Ahmed's prison notes are rich and reflective, illustrating how prisoners attempt to find their own world, in his case by isolating himself from other people by making a tent out of bedsheets and "not leaving unless it was absolutely necessary. I read a lot of books there, and I wrote about everything, even things which were not worthy of being written about."

THE RECEPTION

When I first entered the prison, shackled in steel and hope, and saw the faces of the soldiers who follow their officers' orders, the idea came over me that the first to ever erect a prison was Egyptian. I had no evidence for this, except that this nasty place called Abu Zaa'bal Prison left me with a strong feeling that prisons are intimately connected to Egypt.

They are all idiots, they all hate prisoners and wish for their death. For the prisoners, of course, the feeling is mutual. They order prisoners to curse themselves as whores, and my advice to those who find themselves in this position is to refuse, because they won't escape their destiny anyway. An hour or so and it [the beating] will pass. If the prisoner kisses an officer's foot or says that they hate the revolution and the revolutionaries and love Mubarak and Sisi, they will not escape the beating, as they will have fallen into the trap. They want nothing but to break the prisoner, and as they say, "He's dead dead anyway." This is why prisoners should not humiliate themselves, and should receive the blows with the greatest measure of fortitude.

He signaled with his cigarette and the *tashrifa* [reception] began. They burned our clothes and we stood in our underwear. The obligatory shave reminded me of the primary school punishments for when we had not copied the lesson ten times; no matter how much I tried to run away, I would always end up submitting to the shaver. The sound of the shaver was making my body shake and tremble uncontrollably. Something surely died or broke inside me in that shaving session. The compulsory shave was the line that demarcated my life before prison and a new life that would go on for an unknown period. Afterwards, I imagined that I must have looked like a terrorist on his way to be executed.

They beat me with a baton for no reason. Anyway, the sound of batons is cause for celebration, because it means that the *tashrifa* is nearing its end. We changed into the white uniforms [for the accused], and our lives took on the color of black. Each of us received two blankets, and they stored us somewhere called the "incoming cell." Yes, they stored us like incoming goods.

We could not find anything to store our food in, so one of the prisoners donated a plastic bag to put the rice and lentils in, together. We ate with our hands, as if it were a famine. We ate like the first primitive people, everyone sticking their hands into the plastic bag, closing their eyes to block the depressing sight.

I was pressed with thirty other students into one truck, and they placed eight girls in the section reserved for soldiers, which was theoretically designed for three. Though it was winter, the roof of the truck was dripping with our sweat. I need not describe what the truck is like in the summer heat, to say nothing of the plastic bottle that everyone was relieving themselves into over the course of the long journey. The scent in the truck gave me the feeling that I had fallen into a sewer with no hope of escape. We had with us someone who suffered diarrhea, a disaster both for us and for him. He had to empty the plastic bottles on the truck's floor, only to refill them himself. The truck is effectively a magically sealed box, with tiny metal openings that themselves are covered in several layers of wire and metal grilles—all of this combined to ensure that it was impossible for air to enter. The oddest thing of all was how the girls' voices mingled and mixed with the scent of sweat and urine; they were singing Sheikh Imam's songs, as if they looked forward to prison.

I conducted my first phone call in prison. The phone had just come fresh out of a criminal prisoner's anus and gone straight to my ear. I put the phone to my ear, not bothering about its travel itinerary. It was a small phone, manufactured in China; its size implied that China had manufactured it with the intended market of prisoners' anuses in Egypt. Everything is calculated in Chinese manufacture, believe me. I made a two-minute phone call in return for two packs of cigarettes. I spoke to my mother and cried afterwards, I missed her. I cried from the scent of shit.

Write about everything, no matter how odd. Write about the blanket and the search; about the food, good and bad; about the metal and the bars and the walls; write about all that happens in your life in great detail; don't worry about your prose or grammar mistakes; just write. Write so that history is not written by your oppressors. Learn to play chess too, they will forbid its entry sometimes, but you will find those who sculpt the prison soap into chess pieces. Learn to sculpt, and regard yourself a rich and celebrated artist. Listen to those who sing, for the prison transforms into a theater at night. Depending on your luck, it may be low theater or high art; laugh at the former until you tire of laughter and enjoy the fine variety, but do not miss the theater in any case.

Egyptian prisons have their own bogeyman myth: the "criminal prisoner" bogeyman. "Do not approach the criminals or they will tear you apart, rape you and rob you. They will make your life a living hell and make you sleep in the toilet. They will chop off your dick." These are all myths with little to no truth to them. In reality, criminal prisoners are not all criminals. Among them are many innocents, and many who were imprisoned for trivialities like "stealing electricity current." Like everyone, I too used to look at the criminals as bogeymen to avoid, bogeymen the MOI [Ministry of the Interior] officers routinely threatened us with. The criminal for me was essentially a stigmatized creature, his whole body covered in tattoos, his lover's name on one shoulder and his former lover's name, disfigured, on the other. The criminal of myths is waiting to devour you, but this is incorrect. Rather, we can say that if you make an enemy out of them you will suffer, but they, like us, love, and respect, and understand, and fear, and look forward to life, and commit crimes. Let me tell you that the only real difference between criminal and political prisoners is that if a criminal prisoner were tortured to death, no one would take notice. . . . My letters were smuggled out by a criminal prisoner, my pens and paper and books were obtained thanks to a criminal prisoner, my radio was regularly fixed by a criminal prisoner. This does not mean one should trust every criminal prisoner, for many among them worked as informants, as did political prisoners.

I have a surprising story for you, I think you'll like it. The surprise was that one day they took three prisoners out of other cells and chucked them in my cell, which barely has room for one. We were all squatting, with our legs drawn up to our chests, held tight with our arms and our heads buried between our knees. This was the new position we had to take, and if we tired, we stood up. Torture is not only to be whipped on the back with batons while screaming for help, or for the jailer to put electric wires to sensitive parts of the body. No, in fact, being placed in the disciplinary cell is considered the most severe form of torture, which leaves no mark on the body. The prison authority regularly tortures prisoners officially, and with official paperwork, under false pretexts. Well, under a single false pretext that never changes and is always entered into the prisoner's logbook: "refusal to enter the cell." If you ever see this noted in a prisoner's logbook, then you can know that one of the security agencies has given orders for that prisoner to be disciplined and tortured without leaving any bodily traces. They also discipline those who try to smuggle out letters exposing violations in prison, or those who incite prisoners to protest undignified body searches, or those to incite prisoners not to oblige when officers order them to squat and look at the floor like prisoners of war.

On the morning of the 28th of Ramadan, I was in a deep slumber after around twenty-three attempts to fall asleep. I woke up then to find that my trousers were wet; it seems that a beauty had visited me in my sleep. I woke up from the most beautiful dream to the ugliest voice I have heard since the day I was born: the jailer's voice (he is an angry, big-bodied imbecile).

Yesterday, a group of big-bodied, small-minded men, all masked and in black, broke into our cell, weapons and batons in hand. They ordered us to sit on the floor, facing the wall with out hands over our heads, like prisoners of war. They then beat us incessantly for no reason. They beat us as if we had murdered their children and ruined their lives. They beat us with a vengeance I have never known. We protested, so the beating became more violent and cruel. They called us sons of bitches. They were all wearing balaclavas, possibly because they were afraid because they know that one never forgets the face of one's torturer, no matter how many years have passed. Maybe it was just to scare us. They didn't leave anything behind, they stole everything (winter clothes, water heaters, the elderly's chairs, cigarettes, watches, blankets). As for the things they had no use for, these they just destroyed: they tore all my papers and books.

November 29, 2014. Courtesy of the Archives of El-Nadeem, Center against Violence and Torture. Curated by Atef Botros.

THE GIFT

The usual morning search routine. Insults and property theft, followed by a lewd insult by the warden (Officer Ahmad Amr) directed at one of the students. The student objected, but there is no room for objections in prison; even if they put a stick up your ass, you are to stay silent if you wish to live in their cells. The officer ordered the student taken to the disciplinary (and torture) cell. So we all objected, and they promised us they would pardon him. We awaited the pardon, but we received revenge instead. As the saying here goes: revenge, not pardon, upon ability! The prison director, his deputy, and the national security police declared war on their prisoners of war. They took twelve students to the graveyard of cells below (the disciplinary), blindfolded them, then gave them a beating they would never forget. They sent one student from each cell in the ward to disciplinary, each to serve an example for their cellmates. Ali 'Aqud sustained the worst injuries; the marks are still clear on his body.

Letter written March 18, 2015. Courtesy of the Archives of El-Nadeem, Center against Violence and Torture.

I was acutely depressed, and in the next cell there was a criminal prisoner who was about to be released, along with his lighter. I have no idea how he got it in. So I asked him for it, and he slipped it to me under the door, expertly I should add, as it stopped exactly where my hand was extended. He thought that I needed it to smoke a cigarette, but I used it to burn a plastic plate and water bottle. The sight of them used to depress me. The prisoner started calling to me as he could smell the smoke. I didn't respond; I only laughed. He thought I was burning myself, yelling, "Don't do it! You'll die a non-believer!" I lost consciousness then. I was very pleased to have lost consciousness, it allowed me to feel nothing. I have no idea how or when I came to; I felt like I had seen death. I woke to the voice of the doctor explaining my case, and learned that I was not okay. The doctor told the warden, "He needs an inhaler; he has trouble breathing." He told me to use it when I can't breathe . . . and asked me, "Why aren't you eating!?" I told him I was no dog waiting for their servings of disgusting food. They threw me back in the graveyard and closed the disciplinary cell's door on me, with my new inhaler!!

Letter written March 24, 2015. Courtesy of the Archives of El-Nadeem, Center against Violence and Torture.

7

AHMED DOUMA

AHMED DOUMA IS A LONGTIME activist and one of the founders of both the Kefaya (Enough) movement in 2004 and the April 6 Youth Movement in 2008. He was imprisoned twenty times under Mubarak, SCAF, and then Morsi. In the wake of the January 25 uprising he was involved in a three-week sit-in outside the Cairo cabinet offices in November and December 2011, a protest against the decision by the Supreme Council of the Armed Forces to appoint Kamal Al Ganzouri as prime minister and a call for a civilian government during the post-revolution transition period. After clashes between military forces and protestors led to the killing of eighteen protestors and the injuring of more than 1,900 others, Douma and 268 others were charged with numerous offenses. On December 22, 2013, a Cairo misdemeanor court convicted Douma, along with two other political activists and founding members of the April 6 Youth Movement, Ahmed Maher and Mohamed Adel, in another case in which they were accused of "illegally organizing a protest" under Law No. 107 of 2013 on the Right to Public Meetings, Processions, and Peaceful Demonstrations. They were sentenced to three years' imprisonment and fined 50,000 Egyptian pounds (US$7,239) each.

On January 4, 2015, an Egyptian court sentenced Douma to life in prison. When the judge read his verdict, Douma laughed and clapped from his courtroom cage. The judge then threatened to jail him for another three years for insulting the court. In January 2019 his sentence was reduced to fifteen years. After that conviction Douma was placed in solitary confinement and allowed minimal time outside his cell. He contracted COVID in 2020, with his family sending out alarms that his health was in serious jeopardy.

While known internationally as a political prisoner, Ahmed Douma is a well-known poet, and his *diwan* (collection of poems) *Sotak tali'* [Your voice is rising] is widely acknowledged among Arab poetry scholars for its significance. Douma was released from prison after a presidential pardon on August 20, 2023, after more than a decade of concerted efforts by his legal team and the lobbying of high-profile members of the civil society in the National Dialogue.

The first letter that follows was shared online by his then wife, Nourhan Hefzy, in a post surrounded by photos of him and calling on people to show solidarity by attending his court session.

"BEING AWAY HAS ITS IMPACT . . . AND OUR ABILITIES HAVE THEIR LIMITS"

The result of our bet, alone, with love and justice to win against ugliness, prohibitions, and the prisoner was unfortunately not in our favor.

Maybe it is a logical reflection of the defeat—even if temporary—in the January 25 battle of our life. We were euphoric at a moment of victory that did not last; then we broke with its successive defeats . . . something in us is no longer the same . . . as if we have become more liable to loss . . . the cruelty of the experience changed our personalities, which had met and fallen in love . . . the long waiting and the crowded details suppressed the emotions and suffocated even the passion which could have kept our hopes alive . . . the piling up of concerns and fears blocked our perception of reality and our view of a future, so we stopped trying and surrendered to the loss.

We are sorry that the story which at one time you considered to be an inspiration is concluding—because of all of the above—with a separation.

Today we separate with all the love and respect, and with all the hope. May the future bring us a freedom that will revive our spirit and a coming together that defeats a separation.

Written in Tora Prison. Courtesy of the Archives of El-Nadeem, Center against Violence and Torture.

SEEKING REFUGE IN THE DARKNESS

He asked me something, so I answered him—while burying my face under the covers: Would I manage to escape the light only to go back to it again?! "I am not coming out!"

My response was shocking to both of us. Since when had light come to represent the bogeyman, such that I began to take refuge in the darkness?[*]

One of the characteristics of authority—any form of authority—is its ability to upend the beliefs of its opponents and objectors and to shake their self-perception, such that any potential movement—

---

[*] In the newly built prisons in Egypt, Badr and Wadi Natrun, the lights in the cells are kept on 24/7 and can only be operated from outside the cells. When prisoners asked that they be turned off, they were told that the lights are necessary for the surveillance cameras.

emanating from my sense of necessity—is shaped internally within oneself before it translates into physical activity.

And realizing this, authority therefore seeks not to suppress activity once it occurs, by suppressing bodies with its abundant tools such as weapons and prisons, among other things, but rather seeks preventatively to crush the driving will and to destroy the psychological soil that incubates any [new] ideas, no matter how unlikely, in its opponent.

This is an old colonial practice—with different tools for different eras—whose purpose is to maintain control over a hostile society and to redirect its energy (after having distorted the values and meanings in its mind) to whatever serves the colonialist's plan to spare him the dangers of resistance or the rebellion that arises from it.

With this purpose, authority does not reconfigure space and redistribute these bodies within it solely in order to monitor, anticipate, and control the bodies of those forcibly crammed into this space (modeled after Jeremy Bentham's panopticon).

(We must not forget that targeting these human beings and pushing them to act is itself part of "the plan," an effort to instill a permanent feeling of being watched and completely exposed, and that there is therefore no escape from the paths drawn out for them in advance by this authority.)

And so this authority is not satisfied with just capturing bodies (and controlling them), or destroying them (through assault and weakening and torture and disrespect . . .), or even getting rid of them through killing. This is not enough.

Rather, it expands by targeting its crimes toward the masses, as if it were forced to avoid physical abuse as much as possible—even if only temporarily—for several reasons, perhaps the most important of which is the inability to hide direct evidence or to guarantee its consequences, especially when it dons a mask claiming innocence of such actions, particularly in its international stance.

And therefore—instead of or alongside—it turns to another form of abuse, with perhaps a more lasting effect, easier to deny and a better fit with the state of pretense it adopts across all issues.

Authority establishes this new abuse as part of the [larger] order and legitimizes it, then punishes those who reject it or attempt to rebel against it in any form. And in all of this, it sets out to reshape meaning in our minds, distorting the established connotations of words, repurposing words with new meanings often contrary to those firmly established in the mind and the language, to be recalled when these words are then used, and to consequently change the feelings associated with them.

We are up against not only a crime of torture (although it is certainly that), not merely a disruption, for an extended period of time, of the personalities of those targeted, but rather—this time—a blow to what is deeper and more complex . . . the demolition of concepts as old as humanity:

As it was with the ancient Egyptians, Abraham in search of his God, Prometheus's rebellion out of sympathy for the human condition . . . Electra, all the way to Tesla to Edison and their companions:

Even those returning from the dead gathered to see him at the end of the tunnel they visited: The Light

This intuitive meaning, across cultures and tongues, with its embedded connotation that has filled the literature of all those seeking goodness, righteousness, justice, and freedom.

All of this and more falls apart and its structures collapse under the consecutive blows to our nervous system at the hands of this Light directed at us for months uninterrupted: depriving us of sleep, of any stillness—even temporary—and keeping us naked. Enforced nakedness and exposure to another, with the surveillance camera fixed inside the cells.

Wasted efforts all day to create a darkness to calm the soul, if only a little. Searching for a blind spot to vent your emotions and allow your face freedom of expression (or even to cry unwatched). The nightmares that abandon their usual self-inflicting tools (assaults, bullets, gas, vans . . .) and are now fully satisfied with "Light" as their sole tool of abuse. The negative-like neurological map that burns out with every eye shut, and the body tremors—as if electrified—with every attempt to relax or sleep.

> *Is that how butterflies die in their graves of light?*
> *Or is their choice of death significant in a way we did not grasp?*
> *Sing for the darkness please*
> *Wish it for us*
> *Sing for freedom*

AHMED DOUMA
January 2023—Badr Prison

Private correspondence passed on to Collective Antigone through an intermediary.

8

MOHAMED MORSI

MOHAMED MORSI (August 8, 1951–June 17, 2019) was the fifth president of Egypt and the first one democratically elected in the country's long history, serving from June 30, 2012, to July 3, 2013, when, after an oceanic political campaign and series of demonstrations to oust him, he was deposed by a popular military coup led by his defense minister, Abdel Fattah El-Sisi. A metallurgical engineer by training, he received degrees from Cairo University and then the University of California before serving as a professor at California State University Northridge in the early 1980s. In 1985 he returned to Cairo to teach at Zagazig University. A longtime member of the Muslim Brotherhood, he was elected to parliament in 2000 as an independent candidate and served until 2005, after which he became a member of the Guidance Office of the Muslim Brotherhood until 2011.

Morsi was arrested by the Mubarak regime during the uprising on the Day of Anger, January 28, 2011. He escaped from prison two days later, during the infamous Wadi Natrun prison break. His escape, allegedly facilitated by armed gangs, would ultimately come back to haunt him after he was deposed by Sisi, as the crimes for which he was prosecuted and convicted included an illegal escape from prison.

After Mubarak's removal, Morsi became leader of the Muslim Brotherhood's newly created Freedom and Justice Party. He was elected president after a second-round runoff in 2012, but his tenure was met with extreme controversy and opposition from the start, particularly from so-called liberals and remnants (*felool*) of the old regime. The general public began to turn against him after he issued a temporary constitutional declaration in November 2012 granting him close to unlimited powers. His increasing though not brutally authoritarian style led most of the liberals and revolutionary forces, who already distrusted the Brotherhood for many reasons, to turn against him before the end of 2012. Large protests occurred in Tahrir Square and at the presidential palace towards the end of 2012 and into 2013, which saw the Morsi government, Muslim Brotherhood, and security forces join together to attack protesters. In response, the Tamarod (Rebel) movement was formed in the spring of 2013. After tens of millions of signatures demanding Morsi's removal from power were collected, mass nationwide protests (which were ultimately revealed to have been at least partially organized by the military) began, leading by the late spring to a crisis of confidence in the government that ultimately precipitated the coup after a June 30th deadline for Morsi's resignation passed and he continued to refuse to step down.

Morsi's treatment in prison, particularly in consideration of his ill health, was brutal even by Egyptian standards. Suffering under conditions that a commission of foreign dignitaries who reviewed his detention described as "cruel, inhuman and degrading" and that met the threshold for torture according to both Egyptian and international law, the former president suffered a heart attack after addressing the court at a hearing at the infamous Tora prison complex, where he was imprisoned and died on June 17, 2019.

The following letter was smuggled out to his supporters and published on his official Facebook page during his imprisonment.

A MESSAGE FROM DR. MOHAMED MORSI TO THE PEOPLE OF EGYPT

O proud rebel people!

God decreed for our blessed revolution—the January 25 revolution—to meet a difficult end, but He created . . . male and female revolutionaries that Egypt and the rest of the nations would be proud of.

O free revolutionaries!

Walk on the path of your peaceful and bloodless revolution as steadfast as mountains and with determination like thunder, so your revolution will soon be visible—this is my certainty in God. Behind you an overwhelming majority of the people are waiting for you to prepare the revolution for them, to hear its thunderous roar after the world heard rumbling silence at the inauguration of the coup leader. Ignorant people slapped them consciously and humiliated them in their forgiveness. So gather, do not disperse, do not quarrel, otherwise you will fail and your strength will disappear.

God bears witness that I have spared no effort in resisting corruption and criminality, once and by revolutionary measures, so I have been right and I've been wrong, but I have not betrayed your trust and I will not do so.

O youth of Egypt, the revolution!

You have dazzled the world by completing your revolution: you are today, tomorrow, the present and the future, you are the homeland . . . and the revolution is based on your will. I trust that you will raise its banner and proclaim its glory. Revolution is revolution and patience is patience, you extraordinary people. I swear to God my proposal is that I see generations to come telling your children how you were patient and were victorious. You were clear and your revolution prevailed.

All free peoples have not recognized this criminal coup regime because of the continuation of the Egyptian revolution and their support of its creative peace, and no free person in the whole world will recognize the falsehood built on this falsehood.

Last but not least, I say to my pioneering people, keep your eyes on your revolution and its lofty goals and the blood of the martyrs will not be wasted, nor the grief of the wounded and the injured. The sacrifices of the detainees will never be in vain as long as the revolution has men who carry forward its purpose and raise its banner and believe in its principles and line up behind it in order to fully achieve its goals. I know that the road is difficult, but I believe in the nobility of your principles and I trust God Almighty to help you. God bless you on behalf of your country and your nation, and may you always be revolutionaries.

Letter written June 4, 2014, from prison and published posthumously on the Facebook page of Mohamed Morsi on June 23, 2019. Last accessed September 2023.

9

MOHSEN MOHAMED

MOHSEN MOHAMED IS AN AWARD-WINNING poet whose work has been featured in *Poetry Magazine, Cordite, Media Part*, and other publications. He is an Arabic in translation editor at *Rowayat*. In 2014, Mohsen was arrested on the fringes of a protest at Mansoura University, where he was a first-year student. Although he had no involvement with the protest, Mohsen spent five years in prison. During his time inside, he completed his university degree and wrote his first poetry collection, *Mafeesh raqam birudd (No One Is on the Line)*, which despite his imprisonment won the Sawiris Cultural Award and the Cairo International Book Fair Prize for vernacular poetry under the auspices of the Ministry of Culture. He is currently working on another collection of poems around the theme of identity and exile.

TIME

In
at twenty
out
at twenty.

You ask,
"But
how many
years inside?"
Sigh—
"A lifetime confined."

In
at twenty
out
at twenty,
with
new notions of time.

ON THE ROAD

On this road in a blue uniform
I walked,
and on that road over there,
I was taken away.

On that road,
I laughed till I wept,
tenderness tasered away—dazed.
On that road,
I saw home,
like an instant caught on tape,

stuck on repeat,
as you run on asphalt.

The transport van
a cancer,
gnawing at the roads.
The city is a body,
drowned in sleep,
that suddenly contains
a prison on wheels.
If you happen to ride in it,
you'll see
all walks of life
walking about.
An incredible feat in itself,
if only you knew.*

Or if you once happen to ride
the international highway to Natroun,†
you'll take in the sights,
the people, listen to the sounds,
all the while, you are the alien—
voiceless, invisible,
screaming like the dead.
But no one will hear you
from now till doomsday.

If you spot your home through the wire mesh,
look away.

---

* From the Quran verse 56:76: "and this, if only you knew, is indeed a great oath"—seeing things is of great consequence, especially while going through forced disappearance.

† A reference to Natroun prison, located in Wadi El Natroun, which is a valley with several alkaline lakes, natron-rich salt deposits (used historically in mummification), salt marshes, and freshwater marshes.

Your eye is no more than a memory,
like an instant caught on tape,
stuck on repeat,
as you run on asphalt.

On this road in a blue uniform,
I walked,
and on that road over there,
I was taken away.

Roads like memories are hazy.
In seconds,
they shape things that you forgot,
they startle
with something memory erased.
Me and my feelings
battered each other
when I recognized from the yard,
the home of my loved ones,
on a road
known to me only by its smell,
my hands cuffed behind me,
my eyes blindfolded.

On this road
I went,
on this road
I came.
On this road
I dreamt and yearned,
and so often on this road
I circled,
but never ever in the end
did I arrive.

On this road,
now,
I walk alone.
I call out in regret:
"If only our friends could stand with me
here on the asphalt."

ON THE BURSH AFTER DINNER

Farewell to the prison bars and walls.
Farewell to friends and our nighttime talks,
when the moonlight was divvied up among us.
The moon in the sky—bewildered, lonely, shivering—
chanced upon you all, so you kept him company
and warmed his light with your coat.
Farewell to windows of wire mesh that thwart hands
from escaping—
while the morning dew seeps in to seek your smile.
Farewell to the stranger you will long for.
Farewell to one you loved and missed—even before you left.
When you're out there, living in the light, look up
to see how many stars are missing from the prison's night.
Farewell to your friends and remember, while you might
be outside,
there are people in here who never forget the ones who've left.
Your fellow inmates still gather on the bursh‡ after
dinner—and talk.
They bring you up in conversation,
and your image enlivens the chatter—

---

‡ *Bursh* is the Arabic word for the prison-sanctioned bedding rolled out on the floor like mats, which are given to inmates.

But even before we start,
your name is still here in your handwriting
on the wall across from the door
next to all of ours.
We follow the same order, filing from ward to ward
as every door opens, into every absence of
sun in the exercise yard.
We collect and distribute books, with monthly rations
of medicine,
steal moments of happiness like overgrown children,
as if we play hide-and-seek with the guards—
slipping beneath the bedsheet while one passes.
We take risks, give things a try—
the phone wrapped up, smuggled in during visiting hours,
then caught at the last minute during inspection,
when a guard grazes it by chance.
Farewell to cell phones caught during lights-out,
and to ones caught from carelessness.
Farewell to the Mixed Courts,[§]
where we came together,
glanced at each other as we were brought in,
and died laughing at the judge
and the lawyers.
Farewell to prison walls and cells.
But the end of your ordeal is still in motion.
Your role still needs to be played out—
Still empty handcuffs await the hands of one who hasn't come.
Still the inmate's uniform will hang on the washing line.

[§] The Mixed Courts of Egypt (Al-Maḥākim al-Mukhṭaliṭah) is a colonial legacy, an autonomous institution administered by European judges to streamline legal issues between Egyptians and foreigners.

Your empty place is unfilled next to me—
and the things you left behind are here,
with memories, if you recall them, like fingerprints
on the walls—greetings to those who've left.
Your fellow prisoners still gather together
on the bursh after dinner—and talk—
so don't forget us.

THE LIGHT ISN'T SURROUNDED BY GUARDS

I am the son of my father and Uncle Amir,
I am the son of the soil and of the plow,
a sum total in one single heart
flowing into the wounds of the people.
The throes of my agonies are in
the pulse of this land.
I am the son of my father and Uncle Amir
who taught me to be a sculptor,
to sculpt from the darkness of the night
a luminous horse with my chisel.
I am the son of my father and Uncle Amir,
my friend, my companion—a colleague
because he lent me his glasses.
He dissolved me in his sorrows
and warmed me in the circle of his arms
on internment's cold nights.
His gaze was a duvet of love atop the sleepers
and on those sharing
their blankets on the floor.
There is still goodness in this life, he says,
as long as there's charity—

among the poor, for the poor—
enriching both the giver and the receiver.¶
My son, he says, bitterness is for the past.
There is only what's left.
His sweet laughter reflects on his cheeks.
Hey, you know what, Uncle Amir, my friend?
I am like Egypt in chains, I make pennies
and live on a gulp of air when starved,
when the change is scarce.
When their palms wrung our necks,
and our souls were suffocated by a hundred chokes,
we relaxed and stretched out—
an inch or a handspan in her prison.
Happy and sad by turns like me,
she cries in the muteness of night and together
we laugh when someone asks . . .
with God's grace we get by, we say.
I am like Egypt in chains.
I look like my father in the photo,
with his worries and suffering.
Our hopes walked slowly at first,
but now they've stopped in their tracks.
They see that pain remains as long as there's life on earth.
But we two are different from each other
in our suffering and in its significance.
My father hasn't shed a tear.
He abandons life—when it wrongs him,
and returns to it—when it's fair.

¶ Almsgiving (Zakat) is one of the pillars of Islam. Muslims believe that giving to others purifies their own wealth, augments its value, and prompts us to recognize that everything we have is a trust from God.

He said, "Life upturns or balances the meaning of our
 existence.
The world is unjust
even when it's fair."
Even if a child holds back a tear,
it's unable to change the lies of this world.
When his laughter vanishes and reappears,
before my eyes can adjust, there it is again,
all at once, like a dawning sun.
He would rise alone,
hum the melody of his moans
to the rhythm of his pain.
His violin strings trilled.
In his love of birds, he was Sufi,
and he echoed its spiritual soliloquies,
but he neither walked nor reposed at night.
On a stairway he danced
between hope and helplessness
didn't waver on the bridge or give up,
he crossed over.
And he inherited my grandfather's stoop,
along with the spirit of a toddler
delighted by his own first steps,
which he would imitate with his cane.
Hey, Amir, prince of princes, I also limp along,
except I glimpse from afar certain traits
of a star or moon, so I've hobbled along on hope,
even hopped on one foot,
but made it all the way to the end.
I never said that turning back would be easier—
my despair sidetracked me, so I'm delayed.

I am in no hurry with you all.
Hey Amir, I'm being patient.
We will sculpt the horse with bells that ring in
the dawn and reverberate with song.
We will still lean on hope and, behind
our moon in a cell, push on.
We will sculpt the mare with feeling,
our heartbeats pounding with life,
despite poverty and want,
mouthfuls scraped from the bowl.
As I pass by each of you
I'll share my smile equally,
my poetry to the people.
Amir, tell my father Fouad[**]
I'll sing and be sure to say: Hey guys,
"Rays of light aren't surrounded by guards."

DISAPPEARANCE

I was hidden away
but I'd not disappeared.
my strong presence here
made my absence there more intense.
It's not a problem:
I have a small room,
a window, a garden beneath the moon
a mass of examples—
from life, human beings,

[**] Fouad Haddad, father of all the poets, and the poetic father of the author. The title and the final line allude to the inspiration of his poetry.

prison . . . and laborers,
each one silently growing in the world;
my heart is the closest example
of all the time I spent
in exile.
Most hearts know the meaning
of nostalgia and longing;
hearts deprived win lofty titles,
and taste experience,
while those satiated have forgone their presence
at the table.
If the dust were lifted
from the surface of those absent,
the purest in attendance
would be the ones that permeated.
The looks of inmates when they leave,
hidden glances behind the wires—
eyes that have roamed the city most,
the most seeing of eyes,
while blindness is brazenly routine
and unmasked,
and those who act for reality
are the merchants of usury,
the ones who joined the ranks
who push forward their image;
these are the fakest among us.
Glory be to the one left behind
glory to the jewel,
to shining inside (and outside the city)
on a lonely, extinguished night;
glory be to the one present here
who has disappeared there.

SERGEANT

Sergeant,
lemme go.
I left a window open upstairs,
and the boy will catch a cold from the wind.
Basha!
Excuse me,
can we talk?
Sergeant, hey Sarge
The boy's mother ain't returning tonight,
the cold wind's banging on the shutters,
who's gonna give him his medicine?
Days, months have passed.
Basha, I don't know how that happened!
No one tells me
what's coming,
or how much time is left to come
or when I'll return to my life.
How did it happen that you invaded my stories
against my will, brought me pain
made me sing,
made me speak about you
every time I speak about myself.
Basha,
let someone explain it to me.
Oh Sergeant,
lemme go!
Years have passed,
and time is incomprehensible,
how it comes and how it goes.
I found a window

from which the soul can escape
to fly into the stillness of the night,
and I found out how to live.
Oh Sergeant,
can't you just loosen my handcuffs,
so tight in deportation?
And if possible, allow a book to slip in?
I'm surprised
that I'm well-disposed to laughter, joy and love,
to adorning my cell
on festive nights,
that I'm inclined to fight away futile sorrow,
that is like an infection
spreading among prisoners old and new.
Oh Sergeant,
fifty-nine months
the age of a being in survival mode
no creature exempted
or granted victory
save for bowing down
and praying for the sandstorm to pass.
Fifty-nine months
a flowing river
of wonders and tales
a land cleft for him in the south,
nights in the eastern delta
on his way he shares time with hearts
within the terrain
a whirlpool extended
to the Mediterranean.
Sergeant
Do you want to leave Egypt?

Fifty-nine months, done.
Oh Sergeant,
I'm heading off and leaving you
with the keys you dangle from your belt loop.
But promise you'll tell the guard,
the officer, the policeman and the warden
and all your siblings and loved ones
not to raise the wire any higher on the fence
and when they smash the lightbulb—
let them do it gently
because I've left my shadow
inside with them.
Oh Basha,
I'm walking in the street
without your hand against mine,
neither handcuffed nor afraid of getting lost.
I'm looking for something
that was somewhere here;
lost to me is a picture that resembled me
in the city
in my home
in inhabited areas
and deserted ones
after you changed me?
My body is now part of what is visible
after I used to see the world from a window!
Is this what freedom is?
I'll tell you
what I can see now, Basha,
People of all races and ages
wearing all the colors
and friends behind bars

displayed as if on a screen!
A son abandoned by his mother
left to live as he pleases,
is soon lost
between his longing for her embrace
and his journey through life.
And your longing means
that freedom is much smaller than itself
that the image is always the most
sublime of material meanings.
Freedom will always be led,
as you in all your shackles, dream of it
as you grow, and your longing for it grows.
Oh Sergeant!
Won't you understand me?
When does prison begin,
And where does it end?
I am asking from the outside,
after leaving the continent,
and everyone keeps saying
"Come on now, forget it, just live.
The world is wide open before you."
But I am asking you, Sergeant,
if you can understand me,
if this time you'll really let me
go home?

Originally published in the collection Mafeesh raqam birudd *(Cairo: Dar al-Merayya for Cultural Productions, 2020), and translated by Sherine Elbanhawy in* No One Is on the Line *(Chapel Hill, NC: Laertes, 2023). Courtesy of the poet and translator.*

10

ABDELRAHMAN TAREK (MOKA)

ABDELRAHMAN TAREK, KNOWN TO FELLOW protesters and revolutionaries as Moka, is a political activist who has been imprisoned repeatedly since 2013. His last arrest took place in April 2019 while he was completing his daily twelve-hour probation at Qasr al-Aini police station in Cairo. The court ordered his release twice but he was not freed. Instead, after a period of illegal detention and despite the court order, State Security would open a new case against him using the same charges, in a repetitive process that has come to be called "recycling" of detainees. He never faced trial. In early December 2020 Moka started a hunger strike protesting his seventy-nine days of illegal detention. He was ultimately released in early June 2022 as part of a general pardon of 986 inmates by President Sisi. He was expelled from the university during his imprisonment in 2017 due to the authorities' intransigence against him while taking his exams. After his release from prison, the university administration was

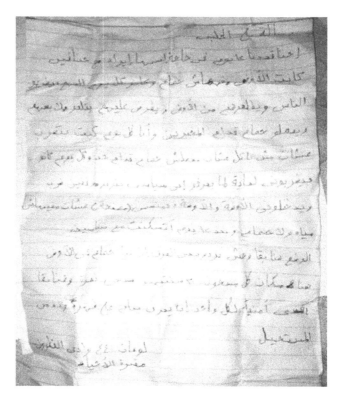

Figure 5. Handwritten letter by Abdelrahman Tarek (Moka), July 2016. Courtesy of the Archives of El-Nadeem, Center against Violence and Torture.

unwilling to allow him to return to complete his studies because of his previous activity demanding students' rights.

Moka wrote this letter in July 2016 from Wadi Natrun Prison, which he described as a "graveyard of the living."

THE "INTAKE"

We remained for twelve days in a place called the "intake" with criminal prisoners. The room had no toilet. Every morning they would beat us and take us out of the room and force us to strip naked and to defecate in front of the informers. Every day I was beaten because I did not eat so that I would not need to pass stool in front of them. They would beat me until they realized that I was a political prisoner, then they would take me back to the room. This room is called the "tank" because it does not have any water or toilet. After twelve days I was transfered to a cell with political prisoners. The situation here is also bad, but the difference is that the rooms have a toilet. Each of us has a space of 30 cm in which to sleep; it is called a pit. Here, your utmost hope is to sleep on your back. But this is impossible.

Excerpt of letter written in July 2016 in Wadi Natrun Prison. Courtesy of the Archives of El-Nadeem, Center against Violence and Torture, and Abdelrahman Tarek (Moka).

11

MOHAMED NABIL

MOHAMED NABIL WAS A MEMBER of the April 6 Youth Movement in solidarity with a workers' strike that was forbidden by the state authorities. A cross-ideological alliance, together with the We Are All Khaled Said movement, it became one of the engines of the 2011 revolution. The April 6 Movement was declared illegal by the post-coup government in 2013, and most of its leadership was arrested. Nabil wrote this letter on February 20, 2019, while in Giza Central Prison, a transit jail from which detainees are moved to other prisons when it gets too overcrowded. After his release, Nabil went into exile.

"HEAPS OF FLESH UNDER THEIR CONTROL"

In the 10.5 km detention center* they put us in the room they call health quarantine. It is next to the room of the investigation officers on the first floor. Every midnight we would smell hash coming from the officers' room and then the sounds of torture "parties," electricity [electric shocks], and the screams of prisoners in the nearby cells. They did not do this because they were questioning them or trying to get any information, because the torture room was on the ground floor. They did this for recreation, to entertain themselves with an evening of hash and heaps of flesh under their control to which they could do whatever they wanted. And then in court the judge would say, "But you have confessed!!" God bless those who have perished here.

Excerpt of letter written February 20, 2019, from Giza Central Prison. Courtesy of the Archives of El-Nadeem, Center against Violence and Torture.

---

* The detention center is presumably so named because it is 10.5 kilometers from Cairo.

12

SARAH HEGAZY

SARAH HEGAZY WAS BORN in 1989 and started blogging in 2012. A queer activist, on May 17, 2017, the International Day against Homophobia, she created a social media event titled "Support Love." At the beginning of October of that year she was arrested in the "rainbow flag case," so known because in September 2017 she was captured in a photo raising a rainbow flag during a concert by the popular Lebanese indie rock band Mashrou' Leila, whose lead singer, Hamed Sinno, is considered the first performer in the Arab world to come out as gay. Sarah was officially charged with "promoting debauchery and joining an illegal organization that threatens public and societal peace." Mashrou' Leila was banned from performing in Egypt, and later in their native Lebanon, and broke up in 2022 after years of harassment.

Sarah saw her mission as critiquing "the conservative majority of society." If the immediate aftermath of the January 25 uprising saw greater public discussion of issues related to sexual and gender equality and justice, and greater openness in questioning long-standing public societal norms more broadly, the anti-LGBTQ+ backlash, as well as violence against women, was swift and increasingly severe. In this context, public outcry and a campaign of dehumanization led to Sarah's imprisonment for three months in 2017, which reflected the more general support for the return of military authoritarianism and social conservatism.

In her writings Sarah denounced the torture and sexual harassment she endured in prison, as well as the sense of alienation from her family and discrimination she faced in her community for being a gay woman. After her release from prison, Sarah fled to exile in Canada, uprooted from her family, her community, and her country, which she deeply loved, and she never returned, not even when her mother died. She remained engaged with events in Egypt, however, wrestling with the intersections of class struggle and LGBTQ+ issues. Tragically, she committed suicide in Canada on June 14, 2020. In an Instagram post the day before she died, under a photo of her lying on the grass with a blue sky above and a smile on her face, Sarah wrote, "The sky is sweeter than the earth! And I want the sky, not the earth." Her death caused a global wave of grief among Egypt's exiled queer and broader revolutionary communities.

"AMIDST ALL THIS, ALL WE WISHED FOR . . . WAS A HUG BY OUR MOTHERS"

Between the walls of a prison and in the midst of the cruelty of the attacks by a homeland and the inevitability of the struggle for ourselves, for the sake of two people unable to see the sun. Amidst all this, all we wished for, Ahmed Alaa and I, was a hug by our mothers. Despite our presence in prison, and the state that passes naked in front of me

Figure 6. An image shared widely over social media shows Sarah Hegazy with a rainbow flag at a 2017 concert of the group Mashrou' Leila in Cairo.

inside this prison because of its failure to accept and respect the other, despite disappointments and failures, we continue to live.

November 14, 2017

A YEAR AFTER THE RAINBOW FLAG CONTROVERSY

Islamists and the state compete in extremism, ignorance and hate, just as they do in violence and harm. Islamists punish those who differ from them with death, and the ruling regime punishes those who differ from it with prison.

This could be described as a race for religiosity. I am speaking of religion not just as a set of practices, but as pride and a sense of superiority that comes simply from belonging to a certain religion or for carrying out certain rituals.

The regime uses its tools—such as the media, and mosques—to tell Egyptian society, which is understood to be "religious by nature": We too protect religion and social morality, so there is no need for Islamists to compete with us!

The state, and the ruling regime in particular, is puritanical. As I was being arrested from my home, in front of my family, an officer asked me about my religion, about why I had taken off the veil, and whether or not I was a virgin.

The officer blindfolded me in the car that took me to a place I could not know. I was led down a stairway, not knowing where it would take me. Just the sound of a man's voice saying "Take her to al basha," and a disgusting smell, and the sounds of people moaning in pain. I was sitting on a chair, my hands tied, and a piece of cloth in my mouth for reasons I could not understand. I could not see anyone, and no one spoke to me. A short while later, my body convulsed and I lost consciousness for I don't know how long.

It was electricity. I was tortured with electricity. They threatened to harm my mother if I spoke about it to anyone—my mother who died later, after I left.

Electrocuting me was not enough. The men of the Sayeda Zeinab police station also incited the women being held there to sexually assault me, physically and verbally.

The torture didn't end there. It continued in Qanater women's prison, where I was held in solitary confinement for days and days, before being moved into a cell with two other women, whom I was prohibited from speaking with.

I was prevented from walking in the sunlight for the entirety of my time in jail. I lost the ability to make eye contact with people.

The interrogation that took place at State Security Prosecution was a demonstration in ignorance. My interrogator asked me to provide evidence that the World Health Organization does not consider homosexuality to be a disease. My lawyer Mohamed Fouad actually did contact the WHO, who produced a memo stating that homosexuality is not a disease. My lawyer Hoda Nasrallah contacted the United Nations, who also produced a memo stating that respect for sexual preference is considered a human right.

Ahmed Alaa and I discussed all of this at the State Security Prosecution.

My interrogator's questions were naive—he asked me whether communism was the same as homosexuality. He asked me, sarcastically, what was keeping homosexuals from having sex with children and animals.

He did not know that sex with children is a crime, and that sex with animals is also a crime.

It is not surprising that his thinking is so limited. He probably considers Mohamed Shaarawy a great sheikh, Mostafa Mahmoud a fine legal scholar. He probably thinks the world is conspiring against Egypt, and that homosexuality is a religion we invite people to. He has no sources of thought, other than his family, religious men, school and media.

After

I became afraid of everyone. Even after my release, I was still afraid of everyone, of my family and of friends and of the street. Fear took the lead.

I was struck with severe depression and post-traumatic stress disorder, and I developed severe anxiety and panic attacks. These were treated with ECT [electroconvulsive therapy], which caused memory problems. Then I had to leave the country for fear of being arrested once again. While in exile, I lost my mother.

Then came another round of ECT treatment, this time in Toronto, and two attempts at suicide. I stuttered when I spoke—I was in terror.

I was unable to leave my room. My memory deteriorated further. I avoided speaking about jail, avoided gatherings, avoided appearing in the media, because I would easily lose focus and feel lost, overcome by a desire for silence. This was all alongside a loss of hope in treatment, a loss of hope that I would heal.

This was the violence done to me by the state, with the blessing of an "intrinsically religious" society.

There is no difference between a bearded religious extremist who wants to kill you because he believes he ranks higher in the eyes of his god, and is therefore tasked with killing anyone who is different to him, and a non-bearded, well-dressed man with a new phone and a fancy car who believes he ranks higher in the eyes of his god, and so is tasked with torturing and imprisoning and inciting against anyone who is different.

Whoever differs, whoever is not a male Sunni Muslim heterosexual who supports the ruling regime is considered persecuted, untouchable, or dead.

Society clapped for the regime when it arrested me and Ahmed Alaa, the young man who lost everything for raising the rainbow flag.

The Muslim Brotherhood and the Salafists and the extremists finally found agreement with the ruling powers: they agreed on us. They agreed on violence, on hate, on prejudice and persecution. Perhaps they are two sides of the same coin.

We did not find a helping hand except from civil society, which did its job despite the state's oppressive restrictions on their work.

I will never forget the defense team: Mostafa Fouad, Hoda Nasrallah, Amro Mohamed, Ahmed Othman, Doaa Mostafa, Ramadan Mohamed, Hazem Salah Eldin, Mostafa Mahmoud, Hanafiy Mohamed and others.

The efforts of civil society, even after I was released, cannot be accounted for or appreciated with words on paper, but these are all I have. So I ask for the forgiveness of the lawyers and the rest of civil society for my inability to express my gratitude, except with words of thanks.

A year after the Mashrou' Leila concert, and after the musicians were banned from coming back to Egypt, after a year-long security campaign against homosexuals, a year after I announced my difference—"Yes, I am a homosexual"—I have not forgotten my enemies.

I have not forgotten the injustice which dug a black hole into the soul and left it bleeding—a hole which the doctors have not yet been able to heal.

Published in Mada Masr *in Arabic in September 2018 and in English in June 2020. Republished with permission of* Mada Masr.

A DEDICATION*

> Hello comrade,
> I am grateful to those
> who make no claim to perfection or excessive idealism!
> to those who [sacrificed]† to know the truth and are in constant
>   search of it, secretly or publicly
> to those who heroically persist
> to those who search for love on their own
> to those who live with the bitterness and the sweetness of the world
> to those who plant a rose inside their heart—and inside those of
>   others
> to those whose hearts were never orphaned
> to those whom depression cuddles like a loyal lover
> to those who feel terror when hatred ravages the world
> to those who care about rebellion, books, reading, and music

---

* The original poem is untitled; this title has been added by the translators.

† In the Arabic original, there is an ellipsis here; this interpretation has been added by the translators.

> to those who fell in love with Fairuz and Asmahan
> to those who were fondly in love with someone
> to those who find peace in solitude
> to those who search for love and beauty in ugliness
> to those who search for peace amid struggle and war
> to those who endured the struggle
> to those who collapsed in the face of the struggle
> to the person who loves and hates, and then reconciles with life and death

Written in Qanater Prison in 2017 and published as part of "Sarah Hegazy's Diaries in Qanater Prison 2017" on the "Pride for Sarah Hegazi" Facebook page, www.facebook.com/PrideForSarahHegazi/posts/150713143355081?_rdc=1&_rdr. Last accessed May 28, 2024.

FAREWELL

> To my brothers,
> I tried to survive but I failed. Forgive me.
> To my friends,
> The experience has been harsh and I am too weak to stand against it. Forgive me.
> To the world,
> You have been very cruel to me, but I forgive you.

June 14, 2020. Accessed on the Facebook page of Ahmed El-Hadi on June 15, 2020.

13

YARA SALLAM

YARA SALLAM IS A PROMINENT feminist activist and human rights defender. She was born in 1985 to a family that on her mother's side descends from migrant Jews who settled in Egypt in the nineteenth and twentieth centuries and converted to Islam in the 1950s. Her mother is the artist and translator Rawya Sadek and her maternal grandparents were the communist activist Dina Hanawi and the Marxist historian Ahmad Sadiq Saad, one of the founders of the Marxist magazine *al-Fajr al-Jadid* (1946) and a founding member of the Egyptian Worker's and Peasants' Communist Party (1942). Both Dina Hanawi and Ahmad Sadiq Saad were imprisoned during Nasser's crackdown against communists. Yara's father is the renowned poet and translator Rifaat Sallam.

A graduate of the francophone section of the law school at Cairo University, Yara specialized in International Human Rights Law in the US and her LL.M. degree led her to work at the African Commission on Human and Peoples' Rights (ACHPR) in Banjul, The Gambia. She worked in several capacities for ACHPR, for the Egyptian Initiative for Personal Rights, and for Nazra for Feminist Studies, among other organizations. She was arrested on June 21, 2014, two weeks after Sisi was elected president, along with at least twenty-two other activists, seven of them women, who were marching near Ittihadiyya Palace. They were accused of organizing a demonstration and violating the protest law. Condemned to three years in prison, which was later reduced to two, she was released by presidential pardon on September 23, 2015.

During her detention Yara was nominated for the Front-Line Defenders Award. The following are three blog entries that Yara wrote after her release.

"DID YOU SEE AYA IN QANATER PRISON?"

In May 2014, on a flight home from a business trip, I picked up a newspaper from a flight attendant and came across news of a group accused of exploiting children, among other allegations. It was obvious at the time that their case was fabricated. The paper did not mention the names of any of the accused, but when I arrived in Cairo, I discovered that the main suspect was Aya Hegazy, the co-founder of the Belady Foundation for the care of street children. A month later, fabricated accusations landed me in Qanater Women's Prison as well.

I got out five months ago, having spent fifteen months in prison on charges that included violating the protest law. A presidential pardon allowed our release after the court had initially sentenced us to three years in prison, later reduced to two years. For almost two years now, and ever since her arrest in May 2014, Aya has been in pre-trial detention at the prison in Qanater, attending court sessions that are adjourned time and time again. It is still unclear how long she will remain in prison.

I met Aya Hegazy in 2007, at a university-student activity that organizes artistic summer workshops for children in Palestinian refugee camps. Our group was fairly small, but despite having lived together for a month in the summer of that year, I had become friends with other people—perhaps because Aya was shy and talked very little. When I saw her again, in prison in the summer of 2014, she had not changed much.

This week, a stranger stopped me on the street and asked, "Did you see Aya in Qanater Prison?" I answered that I had.

He said, "I was a volunteer in their association. I just got lucky, because I was not there on the day they all got arrested. I could have been arrested too. You should leave Egypt," he said. "And don't come back until things have improved a bit. I know a lot of people who are unfairly imprisoned."

I was sick and in a hurry the day I met him. Upon my return home, I sat down and wondered what could possibly drive a person who is obviously staying in Egypt, with no plans to depart, to advise others to leave the country rather than have us all face this situation together.

Aya had returned from the United Studies hoping to bring about a positive change for children living on the streets. I had not seen her at all between the summers of 2007 and 2014, a period long enough for the birth and murder of hope.

The prison administration in Qanater forbade prisoners in our case from talking to other prisoners, forbidding me to speak with Aya even after I explained that I had known her long before the prison brought us together.

However, the few moments in which I was able to see Aya while I was imprisoned led me to feel that she had not changed at all. Although I am an optimistic person who has always been hopeful, I was always amazed by Aya's persistent hope. She was always touched to know that

Figure 7. From left to right: Activist Sanaa Seif, rights activist and lawyer Yara Sallam, and three other defendants appear in prison garb ahead of one of their trial hearings. Courtesy of the Free Sanaa Facebook page.

people outside still think of her. While in prison you always fear that you will be forgotten at some point.

We did not forget, Aya. We will continue to remind each other of those who have paid years of their lives for the hope we all dreamed of. When everyone is freed, life will hold a moment of silence to acknowledge the precious price that was paid by young people whose only intention was to make our country better.

Hope shall prevail.

Published in Mada Masr, *February 12, 2016. Republished with permission of Mada Masr.*

HOW WE GOT USED TO THE SCREAMS OF THOSE ON DEATH ROW

I had never really thought much about my position regarding the death penalty. After I watched the film *The Life of David Gale*, I started to ask myself how one might possibly work on an issue as difficult as this. I don't remember if I watched the movie before or after going to prison.

Some things are confused in my head. Nor do I remember when it was that I got used to the screams of the women in al-Makhsous (the death penalty ward, *makhsous* meaning *special*).

The Askari (military) ward, where I was held, was separated from the death penalty ward by the disciplinary room. Every time they took a woman to be hanged, we all heard them calling her name and wailing. It was the women in that ward who taught me that everything in this world passes, even if your cellmate, with whom you share your food every day, is taken to be hanged.

The next day they would put on the Qur'an, and after a while, when the rest of the prisoners had paid their condolences, everything would return to how it was before—jokes, laughter, and chatter.

They told us that al-Makhsous was full, and that nobody had been hanged since the beginning of the revolution. But they had taken a woman to be executed one or two days before I entered the prison, on June 23, 2014. I think by the time I was released fifteen months later, all the women in al-Makhsous had been hanged, and the ward had filled up again. The current president does not love life.

Published in Mada Masr, *October 10, 2017. Republished with permission of Mada Masr.*

I LOST TRACK OF TIME IN EVERY SENSE OF THE WORD: ON COPING WITH PRISON AND ITS AFTERMATH

How long has it been since our sudden release from prison? I have to concentrate to recall the date and calculate the difference. Four years. Do I not feel the passage of time, or am I still in the same place I was a year or two ago? To be able to write now, I read a text that I wrote more than two years ago. In March 2017, I wrote that I still had not recovered from my prison experience; now I feel a distance from the word *recovery* and no longer imagine a return to how I was before passing through that wooden gate. I no longer want to go back to who I was before. It's enough that I've come to know myself better in recent years and called up enough acceptance and maturity to understand and accept the changes in myself.

I am afraid of forgetting. I don't remember many things from before prison, and I've lost the names of some of those I loved while inside. Upon my release, I remember many people advising me to write, even if I published nothing, but simply in order to document and not forget. But I was busy getting my life back: going back to work five weeks after my release, therapy sessions, switching therapists more than once, remembering to eat even if I was alone, and recovering the skills I'd abandoned for fifteen months during my stay in Qanater. Perhaps I shouldn't use the word *stay,* which implies a kind of silent retreat punctuated by exercise, yoga, and abstaining from unhealthy food. That was the joke between my friends and me in our letters during my incarceration, and also the subject of arguments with my mother after my release.

This time, I will not write the text as it comes to me. I will write with intent, to remember.

Published in Mada Masr, *October 13, 2019. Republished with permission of Mada Masr.*

14

IBRAHIM EZZ AL-DIN

IBRAHIM EZZ AL-DIN is an architectural planning engineer and researcher at the Egyptian Commission for Rights and Freedoms, a Cairo-based human rights law firm. He works on forced evictions and housing rights, particularly for Egyptians living in the large number of informal or "slum" neighborhoods in Cairo (which in fact comprise the majority of housing in that city). He was twenty-six years old at the time of his abduction by security forces on the street near his home on June 11, 2019. He was forcibly disappeared for 167 days before appearing at the State Security Prosecution office, where he was linked by the State Public Prosecutor to case no. 488 of 2019.* He was accused of the usual trifecta of

---

* Case no. 488 was opened in February 2019 in response to small-scale spontaneous demonstrations and critical social media posts reflecting widespread anger over a train accident at Ramses Station that killed at least twenty-two people on February 27. Following the demonstrations of September 20, 2019, many people suddenly found themselves named as defendants in the case amid

charges: "spreading false news," "belonging to a terrorist group" and "misuse of social media." His pre-trial detention was repeatedly renewed, sometimes in his absence, until his release by order of the Supreme State Security Prosecution without probation requirements, on April 12, 2022, after 1,050 days of arbitrary pre-trial detention. It is not clear whether his release was part of a general pardon by President Sisi (after a previous release order, issued by the Criminal Court of Cairo on December 27, 2020, was never implemented), or whether charges against him, which were never dropped, could be reactivated. This was the first letter he wrote after six months of disappearance.

"BORED OF TORTURING YOU!"

Yes, it is me . . .

I had sworn before not to resume what I liked to do, I promised myself not to hold my pen and papers again; I have come to hate writing and with it I have come to hate everything that reminds me of the curse of ambition.

But on this confusing evening, those tiny tranquilizing pills, despite the increased dose, could not calm my thoughts nor my body, even for a few hours, as if they have sworn to make me break my promise to myself.

So here I am at dawn after my colleagues have fallen asleep. I pick up my cell companions—my cigarettes, which I do not smoke except in the hope that they might kill me. Everyday, I smoke a little more in the

---

a broad crackdown in which over 4,000 were arrested, many of whom are still detained. The defendants in case 488 are media, civil society, political, and legal professionals. Egyptian human rights organizations have long called for the closure of the case, which, at time of writing (May 2024), is still open. Source: www.cfjustice.org/egypt-close-case-488-and-immediately-release-all-defendants/.

hope that they succeed in what I have failed to achieve up until now. I take my pen and papers and now am trying to overcome this tremor which I have felt in my hands for months. I try to control nerves that have become independent of my body, so that I can write in the hope of attending to the wounds of the soul.

It is the 12th of June. We are approaching this hateful day; my heart shakes every time I remember its events; a day where I woke up in panic at 2:00 a.m. to the breaking of the door of my flat and in the dark, five masked men were pointing their guns to my head. And the same number of men raided the room of my friend. They blindfolded me, handcuffed me, and time stopped. I was not aware of the passage of time, but I am aware that the handcuff is still around my wrists until now and my eyes only see iron barriers. I remember everything no matter how much I try to forget. I see everything in front of my eyes when I am awake; even when I escape into sleep for a few hours, I see those horrible nightmares.

I see what happened to me within six months, I see the interrogation room in which the meaning of humanity is wasted, I see that sadistic interrogator—whenever he approached me, I felt his nerves tighten from the frequent practice of torture every day, he does not speak, does not discuss, does not understand, he only does his share of torture to get confessions, and perhaps also to please his sadism.

I see my return after the investigation to that grave, which they call a cell, led by that dreaded executioner who calls himself Abd al-Ma'mur (slave of his senior, who gives him orders), to complete the torture ordered by his master; I remember his words, "O my son, tell the Basha what he wants you to say, I am bored of torturing you." I laugh despite what I feel, and their cruelty gets worse.

I sit when I am allowed to sit for several minutes, my body weak, my soul lost; I hope that my eyes do not see the weakness of my soul, so I hide from it and secretly proclaim "O You, creator of the universe, for what am I being punished, who else do I have but You?"

I can still hear that damn sound, the screaming of the detainees whom the officer loves to torment with electricity until morning.

I still see that masked man they call a doctor, whose job is to treat the torture wounds so that the officer can begin another torture session.

Today I am writing to calm my mind and in the hope of finding a release from my loneliness, isolation, and fear.

I lost faith in people after being let down by so many around me.

I still wake up every day to a bitter reality, the reality of confinement and shackles, and my mind haunts me with its damned question, "What did you dream about and what did you do to find yourself here?"

And I answer that I did nothing but dream of hope and of social justice. I believed in the rights of the poor in their country and sought that. I hated the slums and demanded fair planning. I loved this country more than its thieves, and found myself in the ultimate scene in a dimly lit office . . . You are now in the Supreme State Security Prosecution . . .

You are accused of spreading false news and sharing the ideas of a terrorist group . . . The final scene . . . is not yet complete.

Written in Tora Investigation Prison, June 2, 2020. Courtesy of the Archives of El-Nadeem, Center against Violence and Torture.

15

MOSTAFA AL-AASAR

MOSTAFA AL-AASAR, A FREELANCER for regional newspapers including *UltraSawt* and *al-Araby*, was detained in February 2018, and his pre-trial detention renewed until Egypt's Supreme State Security Prosecution ordered his release on bail on May 7, 2020. He was not released until more than a year later, on July 18, 2021.

Police arrested al-Aasar in Giza on his way to work, along with his roommate and fellow journalist Hassan Al-Banna Mubarak. Cairo's national security prosecutor charged both men with belonging to a banned group and spreading false news, as part of a larger crackdown and a mass trial known as case no. 441. Mostafa's lawyer has stated that the charges were related to al-Aasar's work on a documentary film critical of President Sisi, with the investigation revealing that police recorded a call that al-Aasar made to a potential participant whom he wanted to interview for the documentary. In his public writing, especially for the online youth news platform Ultra Sawt (Ultra voice), al-Aasar criticized the lack of competition in Egyptian presidential elections, politically motivated convictions, torture in Egyptian prisons, and the authorities' blocking of news websites.

"WE ARE MUCH WEAKER THAN WE SEEM"

I have come to say I am guilty, take me to trial! But this open preventive detention is a curse . . . I don't know why I am here, especially with no reasons to keep me . . . I am not a danger to national security. There is no danger of messing with what they call evidence, for it is all in the possession of the prosecution. I am not a terrorist carrying weapons, committing crimes, and terrorizing people.

I have been in detention for 365 days; 365 days stolen from my life. Are they not enough to decide on my detention? . . . I have been deprived of my freedom for a whole year pending a case in which I am accused of spreading false news, and I do not know exactly what false news I published in order to be punished with unlimited detention.

I am only a young journalist who has ambition, dreams, and a future. I practiced my craft conscientiously, with professionalism and an objectivity derived from the journalistic code of honor. I rejected alienation and remained in my country with clean hands as well as a clean criminal record. Then suddenly my life stopped on the 4th of February 2018, and it has not moved since then.

The hearings ended a little less than a year ago. Since then I have been waiting for a just decision that does not come. Aren't those hundreds of days enough to look into my case? Imprisonment is not only devastating to the soul and spirit, it also negatively affects all forms of social, family, and professional life . . . One day is enough to destroy a person's life, so what about a whole year?

Prison is an ugly face out of the many faces of death . . . an ugly face of death, and unfortunately, we love life!

Courtesy of the Archives of El-Nadeem, Center against Violence and Torture.

"DESTINED FOR MISERY"

We are destined for misery like those before us.

Honesty often does not push things forward and does not improve our images to others or ourselves, but rather leads to the opposite, where things are complicated and where our voice and our confidence, in our own eyes and those of others, is shaken. Honesty makes things worse, but at at least this "worse" is real, clear, and not fake. What we need most in these circumstances is not to be fake to ourselves; it is a time of frankness, a time of shaming and shedding our defenses, a time for the real worst.

It is the phase of self-contempt, contempt for life with all its struggles, agonies, and lies, contempt for humans with jaws ready to smash everything, heads, souls, and hearts; contempt for the claws planted in the forehead of the earth to absorb its goodness and cast fire upon us. A phase of abhorrence and nothing but detestation.

Hope is the purest evil, it is the pain in every moment and the break when dreams collapse; it is the waiting for what does not come and the expectation of what will not happen, and talking to those who do not respond, and a call to one who does not hear.

Hope is weakness, it is a straw for the drowning and the dream of the lost.

We are the lost; we are sand grains in the wind, fluff in the middle of a storm, or pebbles wedged between the voids below a military boot.

I see myself as an ant suspended in a drop of water that falls from up high into a bottomless well.

It is the phase of decadence, which I clearly notice in every detail I experience. All this continuous degradation—of which I am an integral part—has made me an inanimate mass that does not feel but is capable of being broken by any knock or scratch on its delicate wall. The established lesson is that what prison implants in our chests is decadence. We are ashamed of many things when we think about them or they just pass through our minds.

We are ashamed to talk about them to ourselves and are afraid that others will know about them. Our moral failures, the ways we think in moments of weakness and collapse, our pursuance of the shame of others, of which they are ashamed, and which we share; all the things that rudely, brazenly, and calmly were thrown at us like saying hello to a stranger and then leaving. We present our hated self-image with a silly smile, like someone giving a free drink to an uninvited guest; we drink it like a glass of wine.

It is the phase of degradation that motivates us to act impulsively in order to feel that we are still human, even if we are degenerate. A decadent mortal is better than an inanimate object without a soul. Inanimate objects cannot become human, but a degraded human being may improve, change, and become a human being.

I triumphed over handcuffs, iron bars, and closed doors, and I was defeated by myself. I thought that, like a phoenix, I would rise stronger and younger from the ashes, but I found that the wings were completely burned and broken, revealing the wasted body and its weakness, impotence, despair, and fear, dangerous obstacles difficult to cross on the way back to myself.

I squeeze places of weakness without moaning to make them stronger; I flee from my helplessness as I would from a scorpion on the road; I swim in the sea of my fears towards a shore of safety and a little warmth from the suns of humanity. I jump over despair, I cross it, I walk along it, I crawl through its narrow solid paths, hurting myself on its spikes and rocks, bitten by its insects, reptiles, and rodents.

I continue crawling, bleeding in my feelings, and I dream, hoping for a spot of light at the end of the path of despair.

I seek the light.

A thousand motives may draw me towards writing, and I do not know which one is the real motive, but the thing I am sure of is that I am still writing because writing is my only means of resistance and my only means of life.

Written October 4, 2019, in Tora Prison, and published in Mada Masr, *October 16, 2019. Courtesy of* Mada Masr *and the author.*

RAMADAN NIGHTS IN PRISON

This is my second Ramadan without friends.

Friends: they are mine and I am theirs. Do I remember them? Forget them?

Remembering is painful and stabs me in my mind, diminishing its ability to keep pivotal moments of my memory intact, even though the moments aren't in a chronological and logical order—but the mind has its own methods, and it's impossible to just follow [whatever path] we want.

The blurry moments of memory exhaust me, as if a part of me is being separated from me and I cling to it so that it does not escape, and the clear moments destroy me like a punch with an iron fist in the face, but those in between kill me because they remind me of my condition, I am the one who is caught in the middle of two conditions, neither winning nor losing, neither happy nor sad, neither free nor constrained, neither alive nor dead, existing like a reserve player. I am the living embodiment of the irritating state of indecisiveness!

Prison kills us slowly. It empties us of our human content. Every night it sucks yet another drop of our blood, and in the morning it takes the breath from our lungs. It takes a step from our feet every time it prevents us from moving. It takes speech from our tongues in every situation in which we are impotent, unable and powerless to express, complain, or scream. It takes all of this and in return it gives us fear, insomnia, nightmares, rheumatism, osteoarthritis, muscle atrophy, emotional imbalance, slow reaction, calcification of the mind, and scars on the heart whose effects time cannot erase. It takes the rays of light from our eyes and from our vision. It strips us of everything except the dampness and cruelty of [our] prison cells. It strips our minds of memories, the past, ideas, and all previously stored images. The mind becomes an empty box, and the body becomes a corpse without a soul.

Sadness spreads in the mind like cancer, spreading in every cell until it completely forgets what happiness used to mean. Even the laughter that is forcibly stolen from our lips makes me wonder, why laughter in the midst of tragedy? Is laughter evidence of happiness and its logical synonym? Who is the stupid fool who came up with this ridiculous equation? We may laugh because—sorry—we are no longer good at crying.

The crisis in prison is not only that we strip naked in front of ourselves and in front of everyone with ease, and appear in that image that we do not hope for ourselves to the point that we hate ourselves, but rather that there is no way to present ourselves in an alternative image that we like, and that there is no way to escape from this disgusting reality. There is no way. It is effective for distracting the mind and diverting it from thinking. Whenever you try to move away and distract yourself by any trivial means available, your eyes collide with walls, bars, and closed doors, throwing you before your distorted reality, which is represented by weakness, helplessness, and lack of destiny.

There is no distraction in prison. This is a fact as certain as the reality of global warming. There is no distraction or escape. There is no way other than confrontation. Confrontation with an enemy we cannot stand and to whom we are not equal breaks us at every moment until we no longer have a healthy atom.

There are few experiences after which a person does not return to what he was: to experience death—for example—in one of his loved ones, or to experience death—in reserve—as a prisoner.

This new person who is born after the end of the ordeal may live eternally estranged from himself, his community, his acquaintances, and his friends. He may face contempt for the self that has been exposed. He may voluntarily choose death as an effective means of salvation from the knives that are tearing him apart, or he may immerse himself emotionally and intellectually in a radical way in every arriving experience without any thought, becoming like a newborn crawling towards life.

What is certain is that he suffers from dullness and hypersensitivity at the same time, becoming a strange, annoying, and difficult person who is not good at human interactions, and ordinary people do not know how to get along with him, so a new desire for isolation and exhausting distance is born in him, a new conflict that tears him apart . . . something like a strange virus. It affects the brain and prevents it from performing its cognitive functions with the required efficiency, something like a fatal error in human programming.

Harmful psychological experiences, like a thread of smoke from burnt cigarette tobacco, may disappear in seconds if the individual is able to blow them away, but their destructive effects nevertheless remain attached to him against his will, just as smoke clings to the lungs, blood, and bronchial tubes, and just as its flavor clings to the mouth to be clearly announced to every incoming stranger. About ulcers in the wall of the soul . . . and the longer the experience lasts, the more the destruction increases . . . so be gentle with us, for we are much weaker than we seem, and perhaps at the same time we are more solid than you think.

To friends I say, "Do you still mention me when you sit together? I don't want to lose the last seat, the last thing I can hold on to."

December 5, 2019. Previously published on the website Egypt Prison Atlas. Courtesy of the author.

16

SANAA SEIF

BORN IN 1993, Sanaa Seif is a revolutionary activist and film editor best known for her work on the Oscar-nominated film *al-Midan* (*The Square*). Like many of her generation, she first became politically active during the January 25 uprising. The youngest daughter of the late human rights lawyer Ahmed Seif al-Islam and March 9 Professors' Movement for the Independence of Universities co-founder and human rights defender Laila Soueif, and the sister of activists Alaa Abd El-Fattah (see chapter 2) and Mona Seif, Sanaa has been shaped by the experiences of detention—her own, that of her father and brother, and those of many friends—as much as by the street protests that defined the January 25 uprising and the revolutionary period that ended with the July 3, 2013, military coup. Sanaa was arrested for the first time in December 2011, during the "Cabinet clashes" that began in response to the appointment by SCAF of Kamal Al-Ganzouri as prime minister and in which twelve protesters were killed and upwards of a thousand were injured. Her next arrest occurred in June 2014, when she was detained along with some two dozen other women and men who were demanding the repeal of the law banning protests and the release of political prisoners, including her brother. After fifteen months in prison, during which time her father died of complications following cardiac surgery, Sanaa and a hundred other prisoners were released in September 2015 by a presidential pardon that was issued as a result of pressure by the US administration.

In 2017, when summoned for questioning on accusations of inciting protests, Sanaa refused to answer the investigating judge's questions, doubting the independence of the judiciary from the government. This resulted in her being charged with insulting a government employee while he was performing his duties, and Sanaa spent six months in prison.

Once she was liberated, Sanaa dedicated her life outside prison to supporting the struggle for democracy and justice in Egypt and fighting for the release of her brother Alaa and other political prisoners. On June 23, 2020, Sanaa joined her mother and sister's sit-in in front of Tora Prison, where Alaa was detained. They were brutally attacked by a group of female thugs, and when Sanaa went to file a complaint regarding that incident at the General Prosecutor's office, she was abducted in broad daylight in front of the building.

Sanaa was released from prison on December 23, 2021, after serving an eighteen-month sentence. She was one of the major speakers at the Civil Society Forum during the UN Climate Change conference, COP27, in Sharm el-Sheikh in October 2022.

Here, we include English translations of four of Sanaa's writings. The first is the Facebook post she wrote in 2016 before turning herself in to serve six months in prison for "insulting a public official." The second is a letter written in May 2020 in memory of Shady Habash, the artist who died in prison after two years of pre-trial detention for political reasons (see chapter 21). It expresses the grief of a generation. The next two statements were made by Sanaa in the wake of her arrest on May 23, 2020; the second of the two was leaked from prison in October 2020 and then published on Mona Seif's Facebook page.

The graffiti in the photo (figure 8) was painted in Berlin, a major site of the contemporary Egyptian diaspora (and especially of young people who were involved in the 2011 revolution); it celebrates Sanaa's braveness on January 25, 2015, when she challenged the ban on protests and walked alone to Tahrir Square in the footsteps of one of the largest 2011 marches wearing a sign on her back reading, "It's still the January revolution." The image is a tribute to her courage that speaks about the sense of community that her experience inspired among her peers.

WHEN THE LAW IS NOT THE LAW ANYMORE

I have just been sentenced to six months in prison for "insulting a public official." I had already decided not to attend my trial. And if there was a sentence against me I would not appeal it.

I am now on my way to Sayyeda Zeinab police station to hand myself in.

I'll try and explain how I arrived at this point.

In November 2011, in the events of Cabinet Street,* the army arrested me. I was held in the parliament building and beaten there. After I was released, I recognized—in a photograph—one of the officers who beat me, and I filed an official report with a copy of his photo. The police

---

* In November 2011, ahead of parliamentary elections, violent clashes exploded in downtown Cairo as security forces fired on protesters demanding the end of military rule. More than forty people were killed in four days, leading to the forced resignation of the entire cabinet, while the renewed occupation of Tahrir and strenuous fighting against the military galvanized the revolutionary coalition even as it made the dividing line with religious forces like the Muslim Brotherhood and Salafis ever clearer.

department sent me to a hospital, where I was examined and got a medical report. I went through their procedures for a year: My file was sent from one prosecutor's office to another's until it went before a judge. There were videos from security cameras that vanished after I'd watched them in an office in the Ministry of Justice. Then my medical report was lost, so we spent time looking for it in the archives. Ten months later, they asked me to go for another medical examination and get another report. The file became inactive—and I lost energy.

Three years later, in trials for these same events, it was the protestors who received life sentences.

In 2014 I helped organize a protest against the Protest Law and I was arrested. I admitted "organizing" to the prosecution because I believe that nonviolent expression of opinion is a constitutional right. In the end the charge of "organizing" was dropped and I and twenty-two others were sentenced to prison on false charges (possession of Molotov cocktails and destruction of property)—even though I had stated my actual role.

Throughout, I took the justice system seriously. Then I find a district prosecutor telling me, "I don't want to lock you up but it's not in my hands," and a judge asking, "What are you talking about, pre-trial detention?" while I'm standing in front of him, detained before my trial.

I've had the experience of dealing with the system as a plaintiff and as a defendant, and now I'm required to play, again, the role of the accused, and the lawyers are required to use up their energy defending me.

Well, this time, I will not play along. I just don't have the energy.

I am not making this decision lightly. Being in prison isn't easy and I know that. And going back in will be worse after I'd started seeing my brother again and after I'd started to get my career back on track. But since they insist on setting me up, it's clear there's going to be a price to be paid. So at least I'll pay it on my terms.

Figure 8. Graffiti celebrating Sanaa Seif in Berlin, 2016. Photo taken by Collective Antigone.

To the lawyers and my father's colleagues and his students and friends: I am sorry that this time I'm asking you not to do your work, work that I really respect. I was brought up in his house, the house of an activist lawyer, and I've seen how seriously devoted you all are. And because I respect you, and because I respect the law, I'll choose to spare you, and spare the law, these outrages.

Cairo, May 4, 2016. Translated by Ahdaf Soueif.

DEATH'S CHILD

When I learned that Alaa had gone on hunger strike my first thought was that this was a suicidal decision, and one without potential.

I was naïve. Shady taught me a lesson.

It's naïve to think that in Egypt today a prisoner will make a decision based on its usefulness. To think about "use" and "effectiveness" you need to believe in some kind of future. But if the horizon is empty, the formula becomes simple and cruel: there are no understandable givens, and you are the sole variable.

"In prison, your world shrinks and diminishes till you can measure it in handspans . . . only the space within you can accommodate you."

Ahmed Douma wrote this in Tora Investigation Prison five years ago. I don't know if his space is still able to accommodate him today. I hope so, but I doubt it.

I feel that the space within Alaa has almost run out, and that this is why he made the sanest decision open to him—to start his hunger strike. What's the use of the body's wellness when the horizon is blocked?

> Every defense I once built I have now discovered to be primitive and frail, all the energy I conserved ran out in the first hour, every bit of intelligence I developed was not enough to convince a guard, . . . every idea I invested in failed to get the attention of a guard, every image I had of myself I am now the first to mock, every feeling I had for my country was an invitation to be despised and belittled.
>
> All the meanings I'd worked so hard to arrive at could not hold up to the meanings I acquired here.
>
> This is the true meaning of fear and anxiety and depression and loneliness and weakness and want and deprivation and suspicion and exhaustion and boredom and oppression and despair and anguish and deformity and ugliness and estrangement . . . of pain and iron.
>
> HASSAN AL-BANNA MUBARAK
> Wadi Natrun Prison

This is how your space closes in on you. This is how Shady died.

Shady's family and friends met at Zeinhom morgue. They took his body and went to a cemetery in the desert of New Cairo to pray over him and bury him. I didn't hear anyone whisper, "How did he die? What did the coroner's report say?"

The reasons are many, but the end is one—prison kills, oppression kills.

And so I've come to believe in Alaa's strike: How can we guarantee the body's wellness when oppression kills?

They say you meet "Death's child" at the exit gate, and that everyone knows this, knows that the child was born to die. But no one tells him. What's the use? Why live the catastrophe before it, and its mercy, too, fall on you?

At the morgue, Shady's father said, "This is the first moment of peace I've had in two years. Shady is a child of death, he can't be with those people."

I used to get angry at the term; why do we use death to praise a person? But disasters have taught me to respect the myth. They say it was coined by Arab physiognomists—the people who study a person's character based on their appearance. They used it to describe people who had huge energy, who couldn't rest, as though they were on a mission that they had to complete in record time. I don't know who the Arab physiognomists were, and why they thought these youthful characteristics were closer to death than life, but it's hard to surprise me now.

If you talk to Shady's friends, they'll tell you he was going to be a great visual artist, not just because of his talent but because he was so full of energy, so prolific in his output, and a workaholic and obsessed with technology.

If you talk to Alaa's friends, they'll tell you he was going to be a great software developer, not just because of his intelligence but because he had a holistic vision and rare foresight.

I don't know if they were going to be great achievers in their fields, I don't care, what hurts is that they were robbed of the chance to try. I'm fed up with the oft-repeated story about someone who was so smart and promising but circumstances didn't permit it. This is the curse of our country and we've grown used to it.

Shady wrote last October:

> Prison doesn't kill, loneliness does. I need your support so as not to die.
>
> For the past two years, I've been trying on my own to resist everything that's been happening to me so I can come out the same person you've always known, but I can't go on. . . .
>
> I need your support. I need you to remind them that I'm still in prison and that they've forgotten me and that I'm dying a little every day because I know I'm up against everything alone. I know I have a lot of friends who love me and are afraid to write about me or think I'll get out without their support.
>
> I need you and I need your support now more than ever.
>
> SHADY HABASH
Tora Investigation Prison—until last Saturday

Shady is dead.

Shady is dead and this perhaps pushes me to accept the myth; all attempts to find logic, all attempts to deny or ignore, and all attempts to survive are useless.

But not for us the mercy of the myth, because they won't stop reminding us that we are children of death.

Freedom for them all . . . or for whoever's left of them.

May 5, 2020

ON THE VIGIL OF THE ARREST

The officers have now left, and all is quiet.

Six years ago, I was in a march near the Ettehadeyyah Palace [the office of the president] demanding the repeal of the Protest Law and the release of the prisoners. I had a personal reason to be in the march: a few days earlier Alaa had been sentenced to fifteen years (later reduced to five on appeal).

I was arrested, and released fifteen months later through a presidential pardon. After my release there was a series of negotiations. They wanted me to travel abroad, to study; they would even fund me, just go. My answer was: I don't want anything from you except give me back my brother.

Later I was offered work at DMC [the giant media company owned by an organ of the state] and I refused. My message was: even supposing I could turn a blind eye to all your crap, you have my brother. How and why would I work with you?

So the negotiation phase was over and we started the intimidation. They threatened me a bit, they pressured me at work, then they locked me up again. I came out after six months and I still had only one demand: freedom for Alaa.

Alaa came out after he'd served five years. He was out for a few months, half a day of freedom and half a day locked up in the Dokki Police Station under surveillance. And that wasn't enough for them, they locked him up again.

But this imprisonment is different. It started with physical insult and a beating and we've arrived at them cutting off our communication.

So please don't tell me to calm down, go home, your mom shouldn't be doing this. It's been seven years we've been stuck in this whirlpool. If they'd allowed us an exit maybe we would have calmed down. Personally, I'd have left the whole country and not looked back. But they're holding a hostage and we have no choice except to resist.

When anyone tells me to "calm down," what I hear is "forget your brother." And we're not letting go of Alaa.

Published on Facebook and translated by Ahdaf Soueif on June 22, 2020. Bracketed comments are by Ahdaf Soueif.

ABOUT PRISON, BOOKS, CHAOS OF THE MIND, AND THE STATE SECURITY OFFICER

I contemplated the book *Fantastic Beasts and Where to Find Them*, my one victory of the week; the only book I'd managed to get in. I'd seen Python. I could have stretched out my hand and snatched it. The State Security officer had flipped through it for a few seconds and made a quick decision: it couldn't come in, like the letter.

The book now sits—with a pile of others—on the desk of the Chief Inspector Detective a few meters from me. Every time I enter this office, I get the same idea: what if I grab the books and don't let go? What if I escape from the exercise hour, come into this office, and steal two books? Or maybe when I come back from one of the endless "investigative hearings." What would happen? They'll call me crazy? A book thief? Or would they launch another case against me? I like the idea. Maybe I really should steal my books from them; then we'd have a trivial case well suited to this whole situation I'm in.

I stop a moment and examine my thoughts. When did life become so foolish? My day revolves around silly details, details that should be simple, but here they're as far as can be from simplicity. I create for myself targets out of nothing, just to keep myself looking forward to the next day. When did I learn to adjust like this? Is this the best way to adjust to prison? Or am I adopting unhealthy practices that will slowly unhinge me? And why do I concern myself with what's healthy when I'm drowning in nothingness? And Alaa! Will he carry on inventing tricks to help himself adjust? I feel like my head will burst with thinking about nothingness, and I try to remember: what was my head working on before I came here?

We were absorbed in questions about the shape of the world after COVID-19; exciting, worrying questions. Do we look forward to a world in which technology plays a bigger role in communication and coproduction? Or do we dread a world where private spaces shrink and shrink as the justifications for government scrutiny and surveillance grow? And what about us—we who believe in the cultural commons and decentralizing networks and the accessibility of technology—what do these challenges do to us?

Do these questions still occupy you outside? Or have you dealt with them while I was busy negotiating the pen and paper I'm using now?

I go back to my book. It's only 293 pages. I won't read it today. We're still at the beginning of the week and maybe they won't let in another one from the next lot that will come to me. Maybe they won't. Maybe they will. I don't know.

The officer[†] said to me, "Think of yourself as forced to live in a building you don't want to be in, I'm your neighbor, so you're forced to deal with me. Your problem is you think the building has a foundation, but there is no foundation. This time I'll allow you a book, maybe next time I'll forbid books, maybe I'll allow a letter."

He carried on—with lots of different images and similes. He talked to me about the war in which you think you're moving forward while you're actually stuck in one place, and about the half-full cup that I can't see, and about a sign that he'll hang on the gate of the prison saying "State Security Can't Be Coerced," so that I won't forget, because I'm forgetful and stupid, and about the law that doesn't apply to me or to him, and about our meeting to which nobody was a witness except God.

For some reason he started his talk with "If the killer had had patience, his victim would have . . . " and waited for me to complete the proverb.

[†] The officer referred to in this article appeared on the first visit to Sanaa by her sister, but on a following visit by Sanaa's mother, a different officer attended.

The images crowded my head: a fragile building, an unwelcome neighbor, a helpless doorman, a cup that some see as empty and some see as half full, an impatient killer, internal matters and external affairs and a neighbor and a doorman who each have their distinct specializations.

I got lost trying to find a logic for the sequence of images. Then a terrifying thought hit me: lately, my thought processes too have become random. Is it the nature of this place? Is this the fate of everyone who lives in this building that falls outside the limits of logic and time and the pandemic?

At last I feel sleepy. I've exhausted my brain contemplating nothing, and time has passed. I shall fall asleep looking forward to a tomorrow in which I'll read my book. Tomorrow I'll throw out those stupid images he occupied my imagination with. Tomorrow I shall be saved for a few hours.

Sanaa
Qanater Prison 2020

Courtesy of Sanaa Seif.

17

PATRICK GEORGE ZAKI

PATRICK ZAKI IS A RESEARCHER at the NGO Egyptian Initiative for Personal Rights. At the time of his arrest in February 2020, he was enrolled in a master's program in gender studies at the University of Bologna in Italy. He was abducted from the Cairo airport in March 2020 as he was visiting his family, taken to a police station, tortured, and charged with generic accusations of terrorism. His lawyer has never been allowed to check the evidence of the accusations, and she suspects they are from a fake Facebook account under his name. Patrick's pre-trial incarceration was renewed multiple times. On April 6, 2021, his lawyer demanded the appointment of a new court for his case but the request was denied and his incarceration renewed. His case was closely followed by international diplomatic representatives, by the Italian section of Amnesty International, and by Italian civil society, particularly the university and the city of Bologna. Patrick was released on December 7, 2021, and his case

Figure 9. Portrait of Patrick Zaki used for the #FreePatrick campaign in Italy. Courtesy of the artist Gianluca Costantini.

remained pending until July 2023, when, in the space of several days, he was reimprisoned but then, after intense international pressure, was pardoned and released again.

LETTER NUMBER 1

I am fine, to the extent prison allows me to be. I want this to end. I want to return to my studies and until that happens, I want my books back and I want to be free to use the toilet.

March 2, 2020. Accessed on the Facebook page FreePatrick.

LETTER NUMBER 2

My dears—I hope you are all well and in good health. I send my love to my family and all my friends and dear ones. Yesterday I was in the hearing session, but nothing is new and it's the same repeated talk. Of course my time here has been too long and it gets heavier each day, but I'm trying. I lost the chance to take my exams for the second semester in a row . . . and honestly, this is one of the major issues that I'm constantly worried about. I want to send my love to my classmates in Bologna and to thank all my friends in Granada and Seville. I hope I'll be able to return to my university, classmates, and home at the soonest time possible. —Patrick (Tora Prison)

#FreePatrick

November 22, 2020 Accessed on the Facebook page FreePatrick.

LETTER NUMBER 3

I hope you are all well. I want to check on my family's health and all my friends in Egypt. Of course, the recent decisions are disappointing and as usual, without any understandable reason. I still have problems with my back and I need a strong painkiller and herbs to help me sleep better. My mental state is not very well since the last session. I keep thinking about the university and the year that I lost without anyone understanding the reason behind this. I want to send my love to all my classmates and friends in Bologna. I miss my home, the streets, and the university there very much. I was hoping to spend the holidays with my family but this will not happen for the second time because of my detention.

December 12, 2020. Accessed on the Facebook page FreePatrick.

18

MALAK AL-KASHEF

MALAK AL-KASHEF IS AN EGYPTIAN transgender woman and a gender diversity activist. She was arrested on March 6, 2019, by National Security Agency (NSA) officers at her family's residence in Giza. At the time of her arrest, she was nineteen years old. Malak's arrest was in response to her participation in protests calling for justice for two dozen people killed in a large fire in Cairo's main train station on February 27, 2019. Held incommunicado for twenty-four hours, her arrest became public when she appeared in front of a Supreme State Security Prosecutor, after which she was placed, without notification to her family, in solitary confinement at the detention facility next to the Al Haram police station in Giza. She was ultimately charged with "supporting a terrorist organization" and "using social media to incite crimes that violate the law." The Egyptian Commission for Rights and Freedoms documented that Malak was subjected to a forced anal examination and sexual violence in the hospital, a form of torture under international law.

On July 15, 2019, the State Security Prosecution ordered her release after more than 120 days in pre-trial detention. She continues to fight within Egypt for the rights of transgender and other LGBTQ+ people with the organization Transat, calling on the government and prison administration to respect the gender identities of trans people and ensure that their placement in prisons corresponds to their gender identity.

A HUNDRED DAYS

The fact that you are reading this message means that I broke the hundred-day mark and the conditions of my detention are known to everyone: solitary and every form of arbitrariness, because I protested about the train explosion in the country* and the negligence of the workers at the station, so I was accused of joining a terrorist group even though during past years I appeared on TV and in the press advocating against all forms of violence, discrimination, and racism, which I, as Malak, face, as do all transgender and transsexual people, leaving us in pain and fear.

Although we carry medical and Azhar reports that allow us to have sex correction operations, in the statistical evidence, the ratio of people transitioning from a male body to a female body is one for every 10,000 and from a female body to a male body five per 100,000. If we are a total of 120 million, it may seem that there are only a few of us, but we exist and we suffer abuse, beatings, harassment, racism; a suffering that deserved attention. I and a few others decided to use the media to do

---

* The massive metro crash on February 27, 2019, at Ramses Station in Cairo.

that, as well as social media, and although I was only nineteen when I started, for three years I did not shy away from fighting violence and discrimination and demanding for myself and all transgender people the right to live in peace. How could a person who suffers violence and discrimination and harm, and who demands to be allowed to live in peace, join a group that commits violence, discrimination, and harm? How would I fight using something that I am condemning? The evidence for my opposition to violence is present in TV shows and articles, recent ones. I have defended human rights and fought against violence, harm, harassment, and discrimination for years. The fact that I went public to defend the rights of an oppressed group did not grant me the peace I was longing for, because I appeared for the first time in the media when I was seventeen. I have experienced suffering and harm that left its marks on my body for demanding our rights and freedom.

I am calling upon you now to defend my right to my freedom, and the freedom of everyone who has not committed violence and who has expressed their views peacefully, without violence or harm. It is very obvious who expressed themselves peacefully and wanted to be constructive and who was aggressive, committed vandalism, and only wanted to destroy. We have the right to protest and to express our views in peace. The constitution grants us the right to freedom of expression. We carry IDs that grant us the rights of citizens, including freedom of opinion.

It is my right to continue my studies and to work and to walk my path, for which I have paid with many of my years and for which I have sacrificed a lot. It is not right that somebody be put in prison for expressing their views, no matter how much they differ from the mainstream, as long as they express them peacefully. In any case, we shall not stop expressing our views, because this is our right. We shall not stop hoping for a better and stronger society, one free of discrimination and violence, because we are the youth of this country and it is our right to see it get better. We are the youth who build and do not destroy.

May you always remain safe, defenders of your rights.

Published on the Facebook page of the Egyptian Commission for Rights and Freedoms, June 23, 2019.

19

KHALED LOTFI

KHALED LOTFI IS THE FOUNDER and director of the downtown Cairo bookstore and publishing house Tanmia (Development). In April 2018 the store was raided by security forces and Lotfi was arrested and charged with disclosing military secrets. The accusation was based on the fact that Tanmia published and distributed an Egyptian edition of the book *The Angel: The Egyptian Spy Who Saved Israel*, by Israeli author Uri Bar-Joseph. The book, which had already been translated into Arabic and published by the Arab Council of Social Sciences (Beirut), portrays Ashraf Marwan, the son-in-law of former Egyptian president Gamal Abdel Nasser, as a spy for the Jewish state. Lutfi was accused of "revealing military secrets and spreading rumours," tried in front of a military tribunal, and sentenced to five years' imprisonment. His appeal was rejected. The letter that follows was read by his brother on behalf of Khaled in a ceremony at the Seoul book fair, where he was awarded the Prix Voltaire in November

2019. In December 2019, the Egyptian Supreme Military Court of Appeals upheld his five-year sentence. He was released after five years of detention, on November 19, 2022.

WHY AM I HERE?

I am constantly looking for an answer, but I can't find it! I cannot find a justification for my suffering and for what I am living through.

And I wonder every moment: What did I do to deserve to be in a cell and between these four walls twenty-two hours a day?

What crime did I commit as a publisher to be punished with five years' imprisonment?

What offense did I commit in my work to reach this end?

My profession partners have always found me to be trustworthy. All I know is that we were doing our job to the fullest and with a lot of love.

Everyone would attest that we sought to support culture in Egypt and to support its ties with intellectuals in the Arab world. For five years, Tanmia was a destination for all of those looking for a useful book, as demonstrated by the praise expressed in articles and comments in official newspapers, praise that continues to be voiced by major writers and critics.

What I know first and foremost is that nobody had ever objected to what we have been providing over the past several years; it did not involve offense to anyone; our work respects the rules and laws and property rights and spreads positive values that help society progress and advance.

While I am writing to you from a dark "cell," I still look forward to the light, and I hope that everything I am suffering is just a dream and not reality; I hope it is a nightmare. I hope to wake from it and return to complete what my brother and I, who is now reading this to you, have started.

I want to go about my normal life and think differently about the future than I do now. I want to regain my right to have wishes that I strive to fulfill: I want to fulfill all my professional and family dreams, and to find an atmosphere that helps me do so.

For nearly two years, my life, the life of my family and of everyone near me and everyone who loved me has been suspended for no reason.

I want this to end. I want to see Tanmia and watch my little daughters grow up at the same time. I want to get out of here.

November 2019. Courtesy of the Archives of El-Nadeem, Center against Violence and Torture, and Khaled Lotfi.

20

SHADY ABU ZAID

SHADY ABU ZAID is a blogger and satirist. He studied mass media at October 6 University and worked as a correspondent for a satirical puppet comedy program, *Abla Fahita*. In January 2016, on the fifth anniversary of the 2011 revolution, he and friends videoed a prank in which they distributed condom-balloons to security forces in Tahrir Square. He was arrested in May 2018 at his home by guards in plain clothes and was accused of joining an illegal organization and conspiring to destabilize the Egyptian state. Although he was released from pre-trial detention in October 2020, he had to report to the police station twice a week for the next six months. "The ministry of interior never forgets" was the reply of a State Security officer to an inquiry by one Shady's lawyers regarding his crime.

FLOWER FOR A FRIEND

My dear friend Helmy,

I know it is not common to receive a flower, especially when this rose is sent by a "male" and especially if this male is "me," but...

Maybe there is no need.

I made this rose after twenty-one months of detention. In a few days I will turn twenty-two while being held in pre-trial detention. I remember the song that says "paint [it] black" and consider what I have gone through all this time and what I will go through again in the coming time . . . twenty-two months of blackness . . . Only blackness and nothing else, although I was trying to remain safe. I have not seen my father since my arrest. I remember his eyes on that day, when I was saying goodbye. He couldn't visit me even once. His health was deteriorating. He suffered a lot during my absence.

I saw him again for the first time at his burial. Everybody was wearing black except me. We wear white. I came from a grave to take him to a grave. I was devastated at the time. I saw life for moments, which I spent among my friends and family, and then I said goodbye, just as I had said to my father, to return to where there is no life.

I could not sleep on that day. Everybody was asleep while a voice was whispering in my ear, a real voice with no source, constantly whispering in my ear saying things I did not want to hear. Then the whisper turned into a loud voice screaming into my ear nonstop. I tried to respond in order to silence it or calm it down, but it only got worse. I suffered auditory hallucinations. I watched myself and listened to them in silence. It was very distressing.

I watch the blackness that has been controlling my life day after day . . . I lose hope and then renew it . . . I get released and am happy, then the decision is reversed and my detention is renewed. Not only that; I was denied visits at the same time for no reason. Then they were allowed again in the high-security prison, through a glass shield and

Figure 10. *Flower for a Friend,* a small wooden sculpture made by Shady Abu Zaid in prison in 2019. Courtesy of the Archives of El-Nadeem, Center against Violence and Torture.

over the phone, but only for a short time, about two months. Then the visits returned to my place of detention but in the company of an informer. All the while I do not understand why.

I observe everybody and I observe myself. I bear more than I can take. I pray, I scorn, and then I repent. Sometimes I cannot breathe. I contracted scabies, eating away my skin. I got it from the newcomers who could not obtain treatment before they settled in our cell.

Suddenly we wake up ... inspection ... they take everything we need. Sometimes they leave only three blankets for sleeping and to cover ourselves. Anything more they take away. Our ultimate dream becomes not freedom, but to replace what they took. In the beginning I used to think "It doesn't matter, this place is not ours nor are those things they took." But everybody is gone; people change and I remain. The inspections became more frequent until I began to care and to feel sad for what I had lost.

I am so sad, even sadness has become boring.

. . .

There is no longer a blackness like there was before . . . because there are no longer colors as you can see in that flower . . . and no smell either . . . it looks uncomfortable . . . the three leaves on one side of the stem, unusual, make it annoying . . . I am also upset . . . very upset . . . I do not know what is meant by the number of leaves: three . . . I saw this number a lot in my dreams and did not understand what it meant! It's so annoying!

A flower with a recycling symbol makes it unrealistic, but you know what? . . . This exaggerated imagination has become a real nightmare . . . Someone thinks that we are just things . . . things that are less than human, to be "recycled" from one case to another case under the heading of "pre-trial detention," and after nearly two years have passed, it is discovered that you are innocent . . . then you are recycled on another case with a new accusation and so on . . .

It is getting worse and is tragic for us and our families . . . simply because we are not "things" . . . we are human beings.

Tora Prison, March 3, 2019. Courtesy of the Archives of El-Nadeem, Center against Violence and Torture.

TEXT ENGRAVED IN BOAT

I saw in my dream that my molar had fallen out. I tried to retrieve it, but my father was gone.

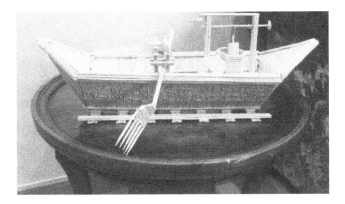

Figure 11. Small wooden sculpture of a boat made by Shady Abu Zaid, 2019. Courtesy of the Archives of El-Nadeem, Center against Violence and Torture.

Another day the waves were raging, but I was not afraid of drowning. I was afraid of things related to me, my mother and my sister, which seemed to relate to communicating with them. It was difficult to reach those things under the waves, but I managed.

Suddenly, without warning, the waves and all the water disappeared, the sunlight returned again, and my sister appeared to check on me.

You know there are always worse things, but I can still . . . breathe.

Tora Prison, March 2019. Courtesy from the Archives of El-Nadeem, Center against Violence and Torture.

21

SHADY HABASH

SHADY HABASH WAS A WELL-KNOWN young photographer and videographer/filmmaker who began his career in 2006. He was arrested along with seven other people and imprisoned without trial in March 2018 after he directed a video for the song "Balaha," by the exiled Egyptian revolutionary singer Ramy Essam, that ridiculed President Sisi as a "date." The song quickly racked up millions of views. Habash was charged with being a member of a terrorist group, spreading false news, abuse of social media networks, blasphemy, contempt of religion, and insulting the military. He remained in prison for almost 800 days, far longer than the mandated limit to pre-trial detention, and was thus being held—like too many prisoners—unconstitutionally, even given the broad latitude given to prosecutors and the Egyptian government to imprison people without trial. He died on May 1, 2020, in Cairo's infamous Tora Prison, at twenty-four years of age from undisclosed causes. The Arabic Network for

Human Rights Information declared his death a result of "negligence and lack of justice," while PEN America declared his death "a devastating blow to artistic freedom." The lyricist for "Balaha," Galal El-Behairy (see chapter 22), was sentenced to three years' imprisonment.

"PRISON DOESN'T KILL, LONELINESS DOES"

I need your support so as not to die. For the past two years, I've been trying on my own to resist everything that's happening to me so that I can come out the same person you've always known, but I can't go on. The meaning of resistance in prison is: you fight and protect yourself and your humanity from the negative impacts of what you see and experience every day, the most basic being that you might go crazy or die a slow death from being tossed in a room for two years and forgotten, and you don't know when or how you'll get out. The result is that I'm still in prison and every forty-five days I go before a judge and it's the same result: another forty-five days, and he doesn't even look at me or the case file, whereas everyone else involved was released six months ago. Anyway, my next hearing is Tuesday, November 19. I need your support. I need you to remind them that I'm still in prison and that they've forgotten me and that I'm dying a little every day because I know I'm up against everything alone. I know I have a lot of friends who love me and are afraid to write about me or think I'll get out without their support. I need you and I need your support now more than ever.

Published on Shady Habash's Facebook page on October 30, 2019.

22

GALAL EL-BEHAIRY

GALAL EL-BEHAIRY IS A POET, lyricist, and activist who is renowned equally for his poetry and the lyrics to many highly political songs composed and performed during the revolutionary era. El-Behairy is the author of several well-received books of poetry, including *Masna'a El Karasy* (Chair factory, 2015), *Sijn bil Alwan* (Colorful prison, 2017), and *Kheir niswan al-'ard* (The finest women on earth), which his publisher refused to release even after its printing because of the power of its social commentary. He has written lyrics for many songs by Ramy Essam, including for "Balaha," for which he was imprisoned for three years in 2018 along with Shady Habash (see chapter 21).

Not surprisingly, his poetry and lyrics have led to comparisons with Ahmed Fouad Negm, the most celebrated political poet-lyricist of post-1952 Egyptian history. Motivating El-Behairy's poetry is the belief that "each one of us loves their country and each one of us fears for their country.

However, each one of us has a personal vision that does not contradict the country's interest." The Egyptian government clearly does not agree, and El-Behairy was sentenced to three years' imprisonment in July 2021; he was then charged with four additional offenses, for which he reached the maximum legal limit of two years of pre-trial detention on September 5, 2023. On that date, with no end to his ordeal in sight, El-Behairy restarted a hunger strike he had begun in March 2023, and he attempted suicide four days later.

A LETTER FROM TORA PRISON

Opening:
You, something
in the heart, unspoken,
something
in the throat, the last wish
of a man on the gallows
when the hour of hanging comes,
the great need
for oblivion; you, prison
and death, free of charge;
you, the truest meaning of man,
the word "no"—
I kiss your hand
and, preparing for the trial,
put on a suit and pray
for your Eid to come.
I'm the one
who escaped from the Mamluks,
I'm the child

whose father's name is Zahran,*
and I swim in your name, addiction.
I'm the companion of outlawed poets.
O my oblivion, I'm the clay
that precedes the law of concrete.

In the heart of this night
I own nothing
but my smile.
I take my country in my arms
and talk to her
about all the prisoners' lives . . . out there
beyond the prison's borders,
beyond the jailer's grasp,
and about man's need . . . for his fellow man,
about a dream
that was licit
and possible,
about a burden
that could be borne
if everyone took part in it.

I laugh at a song
they call "criminal,"
which provoked them
to erect a hundred barricades.
On our account, they block out the sun
and the thoughts in the head.
They want to hide the past
behind locks and bolts,

---

* The Mamluks were the de facto rulers of Egypt and much of Syria from 1250 to 1517. Zahran is the name of a famous tribe on the Arabian Peninsula whose roots go back to the pre-Islamic era.

preventing him from whispering
about how things once were.
They want to hide him
by appointing guards—
weak-minded foreigners
estranged from the people.
But what wonder is this?
His fate is written
in all the prison cells.
His cell has neither bricks
nor steel,
and he was not defeated
within it.
Outside . . . a squadron of slaves.
Inside . . . a crucified messiah.
The thorns above his brow
are witnesses: You betrayed his revolution
with your own hands.
With shame in your eyes, you
are the Judases of the past,
whatever your religion, whatever
miniscule vision you have.
We've come back
and we see you.

You who imprisoned
the light, that naked groaning.
The light doesn't care
how tall the fence is;
it's not hemmed in
by steel bars
or officers' uniforms.

It cannot be forgotten.
You can take a public square away from us,
but there are thousands and thousands of others,
and I'll be there, waiting for you.
Our land will not betray us.
With each olive branch
we're weaving your shrouds.
And the young man you killed
has come back, awake now
and angry.
He's got a bone to pick
with his killer.
He's got a bone to pick
with the one who betrayed him,
the one who, on that night of hope,
acquiesced, fell silent, and slept.
His wound has healed; he's come back,
a knight
without a bridle;
he's setting up the trial
while an imam prays among us
and illumines the one who was blind;
he's rolling up his sleeves, preparing
for a fight;
he was killed—yes, it's true—and yet
he has his role in this epic;
he stands there now
and holds his ground.

We've returned
to call on God
and proclaim it: "We've come back,

come back
hand in hand."
Again we proclaim it: "We've come back,
and we vow
to spread the light,
the new dawn,
the keen-sighted conscience."
We've come back, and we can smell
the fear in your veins;
and our cheers tonight
are the sweetest of all:
"We are not afraid.
We are not afraid."

We saw a country
rise from sleep
to trample a pharaoh
and cleanse the age
of the cane and cudgel.
We saw a country sing:
those were no slave songs,
no harbingers of doom, rather
songs fitting
for a new kind of steel.
We saw it.
We saw a country
where no one is oppressed.

The English translation of this poem was published in May 2018 in the blog Artists at Risk.

23

WALID SHAWKY

WALID SHAWKY IS A DENTIST and a founding member of the April 6 Youth Movement. He was arrested at his clinic in the presence of his patients on October 14, 2018, and accused of joining a terrorist organization. He was released by the court on August 24, 2020, but his release was never carried out because State Security added him to a new case, case no. 880/2020, in a practice that human rights defenders describe as "recycling." He was also accused of participating in protests in 2020, even though he was in prison at that time. In February 2022, after four years in prison, he declared a hunger strike to protest his ongoing detention without trial. He was conditionally released—but not pardoned—two months later, in late April 2022, although charges have yet to be formally dropped and Sisi has not pardoned him. He is married and has a young daughter. The following article was published in *Mada Masr* while he was in prison.

SHADY HABASH: A TURNING POINT WHERE THE CIRCLE ENDS

"They say that the flapping of butterfly wings in India can, with time, turn into a powerful hurricane in Brazil." This is how I spoke with Shady about the butterfly wings theory, on one of our long days in prison when he brought "The Butterfly and the Tank" collection by Ernest Hemingway. After reading it, he—may God bless his soul—was impressed by the symbolism of Hemingway, which he used in the title of the collection, when he placed the butterfly in front of the tank. Shady commented, "This is my situation vis-à-vis the regime. I made a light song expressing my opinion of a work of art in the face of the tanks and cannons of the regime that do not understand art."

Shady was the first person I met in cell 2/2 in ward 4 in Tora Investigation Prison. His radiant and friendly spirit, his clear smile, and the sparkle in his eyes when he spoke about his artwork were always remarkable. He would talk to us about his ambitions, his dreams, his participation in the revolution, the tragedy of our whole generation. He talked about feeling broken when it was defeated, despite his young age. I lived next to him for more than sixteen months, we ate and drank together, we slept and dreamed, we resisted depression and oppression together, we succeeded sometimes and failed a lot. We agreed to treat his tooth (broken from a beating at the State Security headquarters), but unfortunately his teeth were in bad condition and the decay spread to his other teeth and molars, which caused him suffering. And I could not help him without my medical tools, all I could do was call the jailer and quarrel with him to get an injection of a painkiller. Shady used to wake me up a lot so we could talk . . . just talk. I remember his long sessions with our colleagues, studying books of photography and music.

The focus of our constant conversations was resistance, the idea of resisting prison and of being better, despite everything.

I remember well his being so touched by our conversation that he designed a necklace with the phrase "freedom fighter" and sent the design to his friends. My feelings towards him were more of friendship and a sense of parental responsibility, perhaps because of his young age and his impulsivity and sometimes his irritability; and perhaps for the sake of his virtuous mother, who always asked me to look after him when I met her during visits. I remember well his drawings and slogans on the cell wall: "Maybe if it were not for this wall, we would not have known the value of freedom's light." I remember the last thing he wrote, which is the title of a song, "No Time to Die." Unfortunately, my friend, in Egypt's prisons, there is always time available for death.

Circles in Life and Circles in Prison

I haven't absorbed the shock yet, and I admit that I am unable to think in a balanced manner, but I wonder how it all started? It is known that the beginning and the end are in straight lines, but here we are in extended and overlapping circles (from circles of suspicion to circles of terror). Everything is permanent, everything is circular, it returns to where it started, and interfering with each other, even the gears that drive the track of a military tank are circles that rotate and do not stop until they have hit all butterflies.

The doctrine of the National Security Apparatus, formerly State Security, after its re-establishment following the January revolution, relied on expanding the base of suspicion to include all Egyptians, as every Egyptian citizen is a potential threat to the regime. The circle expanded further to target all users of social media platforms, especially after they played an important role in bringing down Mubarak. The security apparatus was not satisfied with its success in stopping the traditional forms of opposition on the street and limiting its activity to social media, but extended its repressive machinery to pursue every opposition opinion holder in cyberspace (the tanks fight against the present age and do not accommodate development); most of the defendants of Supreme State Security Prosecution, subject to the Terrorism Law, have expressed an opposition opinion on social media platforms or liked, shared, posted, or uploaded a video in which they expressed their opinion. Any of that is enough to welcome you into the circle.

The accused is brought before the prosecution ten times, his detention is renewed for fifteen days each time, then he is presented to the counseling room (*ghurfa al-mashura*), which considers renewing his detention for forty-five days. Our cases are not referred to trial as they are intended just for storing us, like in refrigerators, to justify the continuation of preventive detention, the punishment. We are all potential terrorists in Egypt; in the face of oppression, we are as equal as the teeth of a comb. But what the regime and its apparatus do not see is that expanding the circles of suspicion and dealing with brute force with any opposing opinion may achieve a fragile, misleading superficial stability for a while, but it leaves tens of thousands of injustices that with time will explode in its face, one after the other. We are all collateral damage; our ages and our lives themselves are reason enough for the regime, which it deems necessary for its survival. What whoever arrested Shady twenty-six months ago did not count on is that his death in custody would have such an impact.

Your Soul Is a Turning Point

Shady left, taking with him a piece of our souls, our energy, and our ability to resist, and what matters to me—and what I am proposing now—is that Shady is the point at which the circle ends, that the regime must know and work to make Shady the end of the era of pretrial detention as a punishment, of medical neglect in prisons, and of political repression; and that Shady will be the last political prisoner in Egypt, and that his death will be the beginning of a much-delayed political change. We must all look at the matter from this angle, so that the tragedy of his death is the last of our sorrows and his noble spirit is the icon of freedom. Leave the beautiful butterflies free to breathe and flap their wings as they wish. . . . Know that the butterfly effect may not be seen, but it is never without an impact.

Endnote: "Prepare for me, O Lord, not to be a coward. I will not feel your grace except with your deliverance . . . but let me seize the grasp of your hand in my betrayal" (Tagore).

Published in Mada Masr, *May 7, 2020. Republished with permission of* Mada Masr *and the author.*

24

RAMY SHAATH

RAMY SHAATH IS A PALESTINIAN Egyptian and son of the former Palestinian minister of foreign affairs, Nabil Shaath. He is also the founder of the Egyptian branch of the BDS (Boycott, Divestment, Sanctions) campaign. On July 5, 2019, Shaath was apprehended at his apartment by heavily armed Egyptian State Security men, forcibly disappeared for thirty-six hours, and remanded in pre-trial detention in Egypt's notorious Tora Prison, where he would spend the entirety of his imprisonment. A dedicated political activist and human rights defender, he has been recognized as a prisoner of conscience by human rights organizations and his release has been called for by elected representatives and officials in the European Union, France, Palestine, the United Nations, and the United States. Shaath faced no formal charges, but despite the threat posed to prisoners by the COVID-19 pandemic, his detention was repeatedly renewed. When his wife Céline Lebrun-Shaath protested the confiscation of her private laptop on the day of his arrest, she was ordered to immediately leave the country. Notwithstanding the extent of the campaign for his release in France, in December 2020 President Macron conferred the Legion d'honneur on President Sisi.

Shaath was released on January 8, 2022, and since then he and his wife have relentlessly campaigned for the liberation of political prisoners both in Egypt and in Palestine. Their political biography and their politics are a testament to the coloniality of the carceral state in Egypt and Israel.

DEAR FAMILY AND LOVED ONES

I miss you very much . . . I hope everything is alright. I heard that visits are allowed again. Did you make a reservation? How is the visit going to be?

I love you very much. I am fine and look forward to seeing you soon.

A kiss to Mariam [daughter] and Randa [sister] and a warm greeting to my wife.

Please tell me how my father is doing. I heard his health is not good.

Ramy

DEAR LOVE

Céline only

Dear love,

It's the 4th of Feb. 2020, my 215th day in captivity, we got some good news of the released 135 prisoners through presidential pardon, and today some 25 guys in *ta7kik* [investigative unit] jail of mine got *ekhla sabeel* [release papers], they shall have to appear in 2 days for the appeal, but mood is there seem to be some plans for some releases.

I miss you a lot, and [it] got a bit hectic here, though finally Jan. is over. I was sick most of the month and I am trying to get back to some sport and some reading and maybe soon b[ac]k to French too.

I by the way sent Mimo a message and 5 chips [thumb drives] I had. I had to get them out of here for sec[urity] but I need one to be refilled with the 63 French lessons and one with all songs possible. And . . . the remaining 3 (after all being deleted and clean) [give] to Mohamed's wife so she can get me (the French + music) and of course your new voice messages that I wait for impatiently (I hope I am receiving one tomorrow). I miss your laugh, your smile, your dreamy tone, and your strong will. But surely I want everything too, even the bad moments that I hope never happen.

How is Mum, am very worried and I heard she has been moved to the hospital, plz *tamnini* [reassure me], and lots of kisses and hugs for her from me.

Also how [are] talks with dad? Any news?

I hear Mimo [is] coming to you in March, lovely, have fun both of you, maybe I join, lol *ya baktokom* [you lucky one], am also happy you told her she should ask me about the [word deleted by censorship] thing, I left her to decide but my advice she needs to decide on the relation before doing so and . . . [not] set herself to get hurt again.

Of course I am following up on the deal of the century [an aborted peace process do-over by Trump] and am giving so many lectures about it, but even more about the whole history of the Palestinian cause as I discovered so many don't know the basic details. But of course my sources of news is very limited . . . BBC radio and *Al-Ahram* newspaper so am not getting much news of what [is] happening and detailed int[ernational] responses also, what . . . [is] BDS planning to do in response?

Wa7ashani [I miss you] baby, it has been hard on both of us I know I am also confused, when will I be free and what will I do in life? Where? Work, money, politics, what the future looks like? Will our relation[ship]

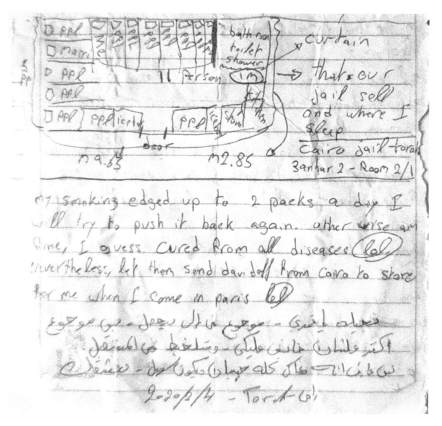

Figure 12. Fragment of a letter written by Ramy Shaath including a sketch of his prison cell, 2020. Courtesy of Ramy Shaath and Céline Lebrun-Shaath.

get affected by this? I know I still love you so much. And I know we need a vacation and some rehabilitation after this is over. I still feel by the way that from now till mid-March might hold some good news, but that's a feeling and some analysis.

By the way, do you know if anything happened during Abu Mazen's visit this week? Both on my account and on the deal of the century, details, also any news on elections?

Tell me *beta3mli aih* [what are you doing], are you having some fun?

Able to have a break and reenergising? Are you seeing friends? How is [our friend] Clem?

I miss our daily life. I miss holding you whenever I want, looking into your eyes and feeling the warmth of your hug, smelling your scent and hair 🖤 🖤 🖤

How is Harvard, doing well I hope? And any news about possible longer-term jobs?

My smoking edged up to 2 packs a day. I will try to push it back again. Otherwise, am fine, I guess cured from all diseases, lol. . . .

That's our jail cell and where I sleep. [See figure 12.]

[In Arabic:] I love you, my life. I feel pain because of what's going on, but I feel more pain because I'm worried about you and I'm confused about the future. But I know that with you everything will be clear and easy. I love and adore you.

Ramy

Tora

February 4, 2020. Courtesy of Ramy Shaath and Céline Lebrun-Shaath.

25

HAITHAM MOHAMADIN

HAITHAM MOHAMADIN IS A HUMAN rights and labor lawyer, and the son of famed labor leader Fawzi Mohamedin, whose career has focused on workers and independent unions. A member of the Political Bureau of the Revolutionary Socialists Movement, Mohamadin was among the activists who established the "Revolution Path Front" aimed at offering an alternative to the military/Brotherhood binary. Even after the front was forced to disband, Mohamadin continued working as a labor lawyer, and he criticized Egypt's ceding of the islands of Tiran and Sanafir to Saudi Arabia in 2016. This brought him the open hostility of the government, which seized his bank account and other assets and arrested him multiple times. In May 2018, he was arrested as part of the crackdown on demonstrations against the raising of metro ticket prices, even though he was not part of that effort, and six months after his release he was again arrested, in May 2019, on charges of supporting terrorism and broadcasting "false news aimed at destabilizing security and stability in the country and misusing social media."

He was released alongside forty-five fellow prisoners in September 2022.

"DO YOU LISTEN TO UMM KULTHUM?"

A cellmate asks me: "Do you listen to Umm Kulthum? Then write a letter to my fiancée for me."

I was taken aback by his question. I reply, "Why should I write it? Why don't you?" "Because I am illiterate." A young man who does not know how to read or write, from Kerdasa in Giza, made me smile when I felt very embarrassed. How can I write a love letter by proxy? What a situation. I felt bad denying his request when I can't find anything [else] to write.

Prison days delete earlier days and memories. In the beginning I thought I was a special case. Then talking with colleagues in prison I discovered they were complaining of the same thing, forgetting people and events. Here memories are being erased!

I searched for this state of forgetfulness so widespread among detainees. I thought it might be due to the suspension of time, or rather its boring repetition. Our eyes see but one repeated image, like in a cartoon, all the walls are the same depressing gray, the white a single color of all detainees, the same pale faces, the same rhythm of days and repetition of events, the narrowness of the place and its isolation from anything beyond its walls, the same stories being told and retold. Nothing is new. Nothing different. Maybe that is the reason. Forgetfulness is the confusion of memory.

I have been listening to Umm Kulthum since I was a high school student, I would be reviewing my lessons and her voice would be my companion. In my nights out with friends, I used to prefer the cafés and places that played her songs, so that the night was celebrated with her voice.

And because I love listening to Umm Kulthum's songs, and I also want to remember those nights that I spent with my friends, I had to get a radio and a hands-free speaker, which was the first obstacle. A cellmate lent me one. A bad radio made in China, as the prison administration requires it to be a single-wave radio in order to allow its entry.

Picking up the signal and adjusting the dial is a process that needs a lot of effort. Attaching a metal wire to the radio antenna, then moving from one place to another while keeping the hand that carries the radio steady are all things necessary to catch Umm Kulthum's voice.

I close my eyes and steady my hand and do not allow anyone to talk to me during the broadcast at eleven in the evening. A colleague asks me, "Why do you close your eyes?!" "So that I can see the inside rather than the outside!" I run away from the shapes and shades surrounding me, I remember evenings listening to her, I see the faces of my friends more clearly, their features are no longer blurry, as if the radio wave adjusts my memory with it.

I go back to my cellmate who wants me to write in his name a letter to his fiancée. It occurred to me that I would find a solution with Umm Kulthum. I wrote while listening to her, "All the love I loved in you . . . and all my life I lived for you." I signed it with his name and a drawing of a heart. He asks me to read it to him, and he says, "Sweet, when this song comes on again tell me so that I can listen with you and experience it."

There were many Umm Kulthum stories among the prison walls, between the Islamists who absolutely rejected the songs in their ward and others who joined me in listening, until eventually there were battles over the radio during the hours of Umm Kulthum's concerts.

Although I had listened to Umm Kulthum a long time ago, for the first time I listened to the presenter of the concert. The measures required to adjust the signal make me start listening early. The announcer knows that tonight's concert is from the Qasr El Nil cinema in Cairo, and last night's was from the Azbakeya Theater, and tomorrow's will be from the Great Conference Hall at Cairo University.

The presenter announces three songs: two of them have not been performed in recent years, and the third is a new one.* The presenter recites the lyrics of the song and names the lyricist and composer. Daily listening to Umm Kulthum has turned into a sacred act that I practice constantly. I interrupt any action or conversation and devote myself to tuning in the signal, listening, and enjoying Umm Kulthum.

Some people in the cell came to love Umm Kulthum because of me, and others hated her because of me, but in the end the moments of serenity, where I huddled with friends to listen to her, remain. "You joined me in the most beautiful story of my life!"

February 2, 2019. Courtesy of the Archives of El-Nadeem, Center against Violence and Torture.

---

* The singer and actress Umm Kulthum (1898–1975) is an Egyptian national icon. There is an Arabic radio station that still closes its nightly broadcast with one of her recordings. Her concerts at the Qasr El Nil theater on the first Thursday of the month were very special; at these, Umm Kulthum would sing a new song alongside the old ones.

26

ABDELRAHMAN ELGENDY

ABDELRAHMAN ELGENDY IS A WRITER and a human rights activist who was arrested with his father in October 2013 in Ramsis Square, Cairo. They were charged, along with over sixty others, with murder, attempted murder, vandalism, possession of weapons, and disturbing the public peace and were sentenced to fifteen years in prison, five years' probation, and a fine of 20,000 Egyptian pounds by the Cairo Criminal Court on September 30, 2014. In March 2016, their final appeal was rejected by the Court of Cassation. ElGendy had won a scholarship to study engineering at the German University in Cairo and was not yet eighteen years old when he was arrested. He lost his place at the university because of his imprisonment but never gave up writing and studying; during his detention he was enrolled at Ain Shams University and published multiple pieces in *Mada Masr*. After his release in January

2020, he moved to Pittsburgh, Pennsylvania, to pursue his career as a writer.

AMMAD

The first time I saw him, I was standing by the window outside my cell in our one-hour recess, watching the sky from behind bars. The painting of bars lining the blue canvas of the sky is a symbolic companion in prison; a distorted beauty that characterizes all the puny pleasures you fall upon—it's all the things you yearn for but can never taste.

Turning around, I found him sitting in that squatting position popular in prison, his back against the wall. He was thin to the point of frailty, short, with a thicket of frizzy hair. A bluish aura of loneliness emanated from him, with ripples of electric detachment; it was the aura of a choice, not an exclusion.

At first glance something about his face seemed different, and as I squinted, I realized what it was—he had Down's Syndrome. A normal reaction would be disbelief; his incarceration in an adult male detention facility, and not a special needs one, makes no sense, a disbelief that multiplies as one learns that his case is of a political background. But I wasn't surprised. I outgrew being flabbergasted by Egypt.

He was holding a cigarette and dragging on it as if it held the keys to his survival, not peril. I observed in wonder, the painstaking drags, given utmost care and attention; the several seconds of holding it in; the gratification of every moment in the gradual exhale of smoke, the way it swirled in the air around him, until the last whiff parted from his thin lips.

Approaching him, I observed his gaunt face, then squatted beside him and asked his name. He glared at me, an incredulous expression on his face at my interruption of his reverie. When I repeated my question, he looked away. I insisted. He eyed me in disdain; perhaps he'd been expecting the usual mockery and bullying that he'd no doubt grown accustomed to in this place, where sympathy and humanity, of both prison guards and prisoners, withered away with time. He then spat: "Ammad!"

Uncomprehending, I shook my head in inquiry, and he iterated: "Ammad!" Someone walking past us snickered, and told me his name was Mohamed, but due to a speech defect, he could only pronounce it in that manner. Later, I was to learn that the entire prison, prisoners and jailers, called him "Ammad."

I took a small piece of candy from my pocket and offered it to him. People here give those away all the time, and since I never eat them, my pockets are always filled. He eyed my hand dubiously, moved his gaze to my face, then slowly reached forward. His apprehension melted my heart.

He snatched the sweet after careful consideration and devoured it straight away. I watched in amusement, then held out my hand. "Abdelrahman," I said. He stared back, confounded, until I realized that the name was too long for him to catch. I tried again: "Gendy." I repeated it more than once; his face lit up at last with a great smile. The electric hum tuned down, and the aura softened into a baby blue. He spat the word that officially announced our friendship: "Shengy!"

I began to wave hello to him every few days. No one visited him and he owned nothing. He took to dropping by my cell for some tea and sugar, or a cigarette; as far as I could tell, that was all he survived on.

One day, passing in front of his open cell during recess, I saw him coming out of the bathroom after showering, dressed only in a long white undershirt that came down to his knees. One of his cellmates started to tease him and tried to lift it up. Ammad roared with laughter and ran away. Instantly, it became a game, with everyone in the cell chasing Ammad and trying to pull up his shirt while he bounded and circled around them, his guffaws echoing down the wing.

Mesmerized, I watched the alien scene, the palpable innocence; warmth caressed my soul.

A few days later, I awoke to a hand shaking me and a voice crying "Shengy! Shengy!" I struggled to open my eyes, "Yes, Ammad?"

"Ummaya," he said.

I asked if he wanted *mayya*—water.

He shook his head, frustrated by my stupidity, looked around, found a cup, and hurried to grab it: "Ummaya!"

"Ah, *kubbaya*?" Cup. He nodded in joy. He'd lost his cup. I handed him a spare plastic cup I had, only to have him shower me with a torrent of words I couldn't understand, but which radiated a gratitude that filled me with sorrow. How easy he was to please! All it took was a trivial plastic cup. I longed for the days when my happiness, too, lay within such close reach.

The last time I saw him he was coughing violently and yelling to be taken to the clinic. Everyone ignored him, as usual; he was an "imbecile," as they called him, so why shouldn't we expect him to rave? I watched him go up the stairs to his cell, still shouting in fury, repeating a phrase that only those privy to his personal lexicon could understand: "Wallahi lanmut hina!" I swear to God we'll die here.

Two days later, I found out Ammad went into a coma after a violent fit of coughing blood, and that he'd been taken to the hospital. Only a week after that, we knew what was wrong with him—he had tuberculosis.

I don't know if Ammad will die. I don't know if I'll ever hear that familiar "Shengy!" call again.

I've decided to write about him now before receiving the news of his death; I will no longer care to hold a pen when that luminous orb of innocence that has attached itself to my soul dissolves.

Repugnance bubbles inside me; I am in a world in which I don't know whether I ought to pray for him to live or die. I think I'll pray for him as I pray for myself: that he should have peace.

Abdelrahman ElGendy

Tora Maximum Security 2, May 9, 2018*

Published in Mada Masr, *July 14, 2018. This updated translation is courtesy of the author.*

LUMOS

I struggle back from the visitation hall to the cell block, my arms aching under the weight of the plastic bags I'm carrying, one in each hand. Sweat streams down my head, wetting my wild hair and trickling unto my back and chest like crawling insects. Despite that, I glow.

In the visit, my face lit up as my sister produced the magic wand from a long rectangular package, the kind you might find at Ollivander's. We chuckled as we pointed it at each other, my mum shaking her head and laughing at how giddy we acted because of this stick with round knots along its length. "The Elder Wand, mum," we said, by way of explanation.

The memory is bubblegum pink, buzzing with warmth.

I approach the guard blocking the entrance to the wing, ready for the second bag search and pat-down. I place the bags in front of him and he checks their contents one by one: food, clothes, sweets, soap. When he gets to the rectangular box, he peers at it, then opens it. He takes out the wand, turns it over several times in bemusement, then looks up at me.

"What's this?" he asks.

I hesitate, then blurt, "Ever heard of Harry Potter?"

---

* Ammad died the following month, on the first day of Eid, June 15, 2018.

He stares at me as if I'm speaking gibberish, then turns his attention to the wand and attempts to bend it. I decide I'd better tell him the truth before he breaks it.

"It's a magic wand," I say.

He looks up and stares me down. I reciprocate with utter seriousness.

"God protect us, whatever next?" he scoffs, slapping his hands together and shaking his head. He tosses the wand and its box into the bag and waves me through. As I pass, he mutters about prisoners these days. Little does he know—the wand he held just a few seconds ago was created by Death.

Later that night, after all my cellmates are asleep, I sit cross-legged in the far corner of the cell. It's one in the morning. The cell is cramped but intimate, with an orchestra of snores in the background. The ground is slightly damp, thanks to the leaking tap in the bathroom next to me, and only a dim bulb on the ground illuminates the bleak night with an amber glow. It reflects off the splattered water: translucent, soothing.

We call it the "kitchen" because it's festooned with Tupperware containing vegetables, onion, garlic, and spices.

Sipping coffee from my paper cup, I savor the strong taste, the sting it leaves in my throat, and the intoxicating fragrance filling my nostrils; I relish every second of the holy ritual.

I pick up the wand and contemplate it, running my fingers along its length, sensing the softness and the contrasting roughness of the infinitesimal dents on each knot. A bit of magic would come in handy in this stifling loneliness, to lift, for moments, the cloak of alienation that has shrouded me for years.

I raise the wand and point it at a wrinkled tomato.

"Wingardium leviosa!" I whisper-shout, moving my wrist. Swish and flick. A few failed attempts later, I abandon the tomato and turn the wand to my coffee.

"Incendio!"

Nothing; then I realize that had that spell succeeded, I'd have set the paper cup on fire rather than warmed up the coffee. Thank God for my magical disability; my memory is not as it used to be.

I enjoy marveling at the similarities between Harry and me. On the eve of my nineteenth birthday, I lay among the bodies suffocating me from all sides and traced out the words *happy birthday* on the cell's dirty floor, just like Harry did on the stone floor of the shack, when the door burst open and he learned he was a wizard. In my case, the door was flung open to reveal a gang of intelligence officers, yelling, kicking, and punching as they dragged us out for a vicious shakedown and ripped the cell apart.

I think, too, about how many people love Harry and consider him a hero, while others detest him and plot his destruction, all because of an unasked-for scar that he loathes. He only ever wanted to be normal.

Prison will scar me too, and I can already see the signs of infatuation from some and bitter hatred from others because of it. I have no more asked for it than Harry did his scar.

I glimpse a faint movement in an open tub of dates before me, and I squint in the dim light. A worm. A minuscule worm wriggling comically in half a date, slender segmented body barely visible in the faint light. I grab an empty jar from beside me, drop the date into it and shut the lid. The worm shuffles out of the date and extends itself along the bottom of the jar. It surprises me by embarking on rapid laps around the circumference—round and round it goes, not stopping once, like the thoughts in my head.

I point the wand at it. "Engorgio!" It continues its robust circuits nonchalantly.

A strange camaraderie fills me, watching the worm in the dark like this. Darkness is meant to be frightening, but these days I rarely feel at ease except in the dark.

I remember Dumbledore's words: "It is the unknown we fear when we look upon death and darkness, nothing more." Perhaps that's why I fear the future.

I decide to name the worm Hedwig, after Harry's owl. I give up trying to enlarge it with the wand; there doesn't seem to be any room for magic in this wretched place. I sing to Hedwig instead; I hum a lullaby, whisper the lyrics, my voice lost amid the snores.

I watch the scene from above; a young man with wild hair sits cross-legged on a wet floor, in darkness save for the dim glow nearby, clutching a magic wand for dear life. He sings while a worm shuffles in an Ouroboros before him, searching for meaning inside her jar, just as he too searches for meaning.

Another saying of Dumbledore's comes to mind: "Happiness can be found, even in the darkest of times, if one only remembers to turn on the light."

I turn to Hedwig.

"Lumos," I whisper.

And smile.

Published in Mada Masr, *September 16, 2018. This updated translation is courtesy of the author.*

27

ANONYMOUS

THE FOLLOWING TEXTS ARE ANONYMOUS testimonies collected by El-Nadeem and other organizations. They are drawn from prisoners' personal correspondence that was shared with El-Nadeem as well as social media posts collected by volunteers. This collection aims to shed light on conditions in the Egyptian prison system, both the abuses suffered and the attempts by inmates to retain some sense of agency and dignity in the face of routine mistreatment and harsh conditions. We have attempted to ensure gender as well as political, ideological, and class balance in the choice of letters, although as elsewhere, members of the Brotherhood, as well as Ultras and poorer Egyptians, remain underrepresented because of the difficulty in obtaining letters and the fact that there is generally less correspondence from these groups from which to choose.

A DAY IN THE LIFE . . . WE CREATED A DREAM
NO POWER CAN ERASE

Victory and defeat

Today is the 28th of January 2019. It has been close to a month and a half since I was detained. On the 28th of January 2011, I was held in a cell in the Alexandria security directorate in Labban. There were others with me. We shared the food, the cold, and the victory of the revolution.

Today, eight years later, here I am in another cell in Borg El Arab detention camp, and we also share food and the cold, but today we share defeat . . . defeat of the revolution. Eight years have passed since the dream . . . a dream of freedom and justice dissipated under the boots of the military, the business class, and opportunists, but we have another dream left that will grow and materialize, and no force will be able to dispel it.

Detainee at Borg El Arab prison, Alexandria, January 28, 2019. Courtesy of the Archives of El-Nadeem, Center against Violence and Torture.

"WE CANNOT HUG OUR CHILDREN": A DAY IN
THE LIFE OF A MUSLIM BROTHERHOOD DETAINEE

I am locked in a cell measuring about two meters by two meters, and I have two cellmates and every person has about four blankets that we lay on the floor, and everyone sleeps on an area of approximately fifty centimeters, and I put on the right and on the left a piece of cardboard to avoid diseases, especially as we all sleep touching each other, and our bodies are almost completely bound together. We hang our clothes at the top of the cell on something called *sahoora*, which is a hole in the wall of the cell, where we put everything from clothes to food, hygiene items, and medicine, and we try to arrange our belongings in it. We are three people of similar ages, and each of us has a special nature and specific characteristics, and we try to tolerate each other, support each other, and encourage each other, especially as we remain in the cell for twenty-three hours a day.

We go out for exercise only one hour a day in a place called the tube, which is a closed place, very narrow, about twenty meters long and about one meter and sixty centimeters wide. We breathe a sigh of relief when we go out for those minutes; it's as if you were giving oxygen to a person who nearly died to help him survive, but then quickly deprive him of this oxygen.

The prison administration releases detainees for the hour of exercise in stages and alternately, because it is impossible for all detainees to be released at the same time.

We wake up at around eight or nine in the morning, and we perform the Duha prayer [the non-obligatory prayer between the dawn and noon prayers], then go out for exercise, then we go back to the cell to have breakfast, and then we do the noon prayer . . . And after that, we read the Qur'an or enter a discussion about any topic or any personal or public issue until time for the 'Asr prayer, and we get together for a bit more, and after that we eat lunch and then wait until the sunset prayer comes . . . Every detainee has a daily ritual that he adheres to, and we may read the Qur'an together collectively, and then we perform the evening prayer and then return to reciting the Qur'an again, and there are those who memorize and others who recite, we teach and help each other . . . Then we wait a little until evening, after which we go to sleep, and we wake up a little before the dawn prayers, and then we go back to sleep.

If they allow us visits, we go out to our families while we are handcuffed with clasps (iron cuffs), and we sit with them for half an hour or an hour at most, and this visit is once a month or twice at most, and is an exception that is rarely repeated.

Of course, we cannot hug our children or our families during the few minutes of the visit—which passes faster than lightning—because of the restrictions and the shackles that we have on our hands, and it is no secret to anyone the amount of harassment and insults that we and our families are exposed to during the visit.

Women who come to visit detainees are often subjected to verbal and physical harassment by police officers, especially with regard to intense body searches, as well as the prohibition of many foods based on claims that the prison distributes the same foods to us every day—foods that are often bad and not edible . . .

With regard to medical treatment, patients, and the hospital, the prison doctor passes by every so often. If he finds that a detainee needs to go to the hospital, then this detainee goes to the prison hospital, but with great difficulty; of course he goes with his hands tied, and we are sometimes shocked to find that there are no doctors in the hospital.

When there is a prisoner in very poor health, all the detainees bang on the doors of the cells until the prison guards hear our screams and respond to our calls to transfer this detainee to the hospital, and sometimes the guards hear us knocking on the doors and screaming and do not respond, deliberately ignoring our calls . . .

If they respond to us, the police officers inform the prison officer and the prison administration of the detainee's condition, until the keys to the cell are brought in, and the nurse and the prison doctor are informed, and this may exceed two hours depending on the amount of screams and banging on the doors . . . Sometimes there is no response from the guards at all, and the sick detainee continues to suffer until the morning, no matter how severe the pain, and when we go out to exercise the next morning we try hard and in every possible way to make them take him to the hospital to speed up treatment.

. . .

There is a group of informants (police personnel) who manage everything inside the prison, and these are machines for carrying out orders only, without any human feelings or conscience.

There was a prison patient one time who asked one of the informants in the morning if he could get treatment and go to the hospital. The informant ignored his request and then came to him at the end of the day and told him that he was trying to provide treatment for him, so the patient was very happy and thanked him. Then the informant returned and told him the pharmacy was closed and it would have to wait until tomorrow. And when I told the informant that his condition was bad and was deteriorating, the informant replied sarcastically, "What should I do for you? Wait for tomorrow or even the day after tomorrow. You will not die; do not worry."

Everything inside prison is managed with the so-called bonuses that replace money and that we put in safe-keeping to buy things from the prison cafeteria. The prices we pay are always 30 or 40 percent higher than the prices outside prison. Anything available in the cafeteria is strictly forbidden to be brought in by our families, so that we have to buy it later.

Also, any repairs or other requirements in the cell are done at the expense of the detainees, for example, if there are any breakdowns in plumbing or electricity (including lamp repairs) or anything else, this is fixed at our personal expense. Nothing happens for free, even though these repairs are essential. The prison administration is supposed to bear the expenses.

The ugliest situation I experienced here was when the prison cell opened and the guards entered at dawn on a day when I was still sleeping and told me to accompany them. When I asked why, they said the moment of your execution has come, to relieve us of you and relieve you of your life in prison.

They took me forcefully out of the cell while I was trying to stand firm and read verses from the Qur'an and utter the two testimonies, but in reality it felt like a thunderbolt, and after I went out with them they took me to the exercise area (the tube), then they suddenly stopped and looked at each other and dissolved in a fit of laughter and sarcasm, saying, "You will not die today. We will leave you until tomorrow or maybe the day after tomorrow. But be sure that this day will inevitably come. Today, we were just laughing at you and testing your nerves."

Muslim Brotherhood detainee, July 2019. Courtesy of the Archives of El-Nadeem, Center against Violence and Torture.

I AM AFRAID TO DIE IN PRISON

I do not demand more than my rights as an Egyptian citizen, I am a thirty-year-old young woman who has not yet married; I am an orphan, many stations have passed in my life that I cannot understand, I have found myself classified as a terrorist; I had dreams and hopes that were never realized, not even started; and I never would have imagined that my field of work, which I adore, would be the reason for my unhappiness and the theft of my freedom. I have been unjustly accused of publishing the video of the Helwan brigades and I swear that I have no relation to any group or organizations. What happened came out of the blue and it turned my life upside down and I found myself behind bars in 2014, accused of joining a group and publishing the video.

My imprisonment has lasted about three and a half years, I am currently living under very difficult psychological pressures and struggles, which has led to my suffering from many diseases, including a uterine tumour, acute anaemia, asthma attacks, an anal fistula, and others that I cannot mention. I had many surgeries, but unfortunately my condition is going from bad to worse and when I finish one operation I enter into another because of the poor medical care in addition to the lack of availability of any of my family members. I badly need psychological support and it is difficult to obtain because I am deprived of my freedom and every night panic attacks take my breath away. I fear that I will die inside prison . . .

I submitted all my medical reports, in vain. I demand my release, especially given that I have been released before and proved my good intent by attending all court sessions. I need to follow up on my health condition under the care of my family.

In gratitude

Female detainee, name withheld, August 2019. Courtesy of the Archives of El-Nadeem, Center against Violence and Torture.

AS IF PRISONS WERE DESIGNED TO KILL US

When I was in State Security and after a serious torture session that lasted for hours while I was blindfolded and handcuffed behind my back I was taken to a place . . . like a hole in the wall . . . like the one they use for a CT scan, or at least that is what I thought.

After I was stripped of my clothes, a security man used a device (not a Taser, because I know that well) and pressed this device on my left leg. I felt very severe pain, but the truth is it only lasted for a short period and ended after a few moments. Then I heard the officer tell those present, "Turn on the fan to end this smell." A shower of cold air poured on my head. The truth is, I did not smell any smell! Also, I did not pay attention to the matter at the time . . . I was counting the moments for this humiliating torture to end.

But for a while now I have had a problem with my left leg where they used that device. I cannot extend my leg properly and have pains every now and then.

A while ago I fell ill. I thought it was a common cold, but then I went into a coma for three days, interrupted by two incidents of awakening, once for an hour, the second for two hours. I had a severe cough. I feel these prisons were designed to kill us with health problems or chronic illnesses.

I wish that doctors would tell me if there is something like that . . . does it cause bone disease . . . or is it the prison years . . .

Anonymous, December 2019. Courtesy of the Archives of El-Nadeem, Center against Violence and Torture.

28

ISLAM KHALIL

ISLAM KHALIL IS A YOUNG man from the Nile Delta city of Tanta, where the governorate is notorious for its cruel State Security department. In May 2015, agents from the National Security Agency came to his home searching for his brother, a refugee rights activist. The arresting officers mistreated Islam's father, pushing him around, which led Islam to push one of the officers back, the beginning of a long journey of forced disappearance, arrest, torture, release, and further arrests. Islam initially remained forcibly disappeared for 122 days. He was then questioned by prosecutors without a lawyer present based on a forced confession, and was placed in pre-trial detention on charges of belonging to the Muslim Brotherhood, inciting violence, and attacking security forces, charges which could have led to the death penalty. He was released in February 2019.

FIVE BIRTHDAY CELEBRATIONS

My first birthday in prison, that was my twenty-second birthday. I spent it inside Ahmed Jalal Military Station prison, crawling on the hot sand on our stomachs as punishment for the whole prison . . . to this day, I don't know why . . . and then standing in the sun all day long. Anybody who hesitates or appears to object is forced to continue crawling on the sand. The day ends with us in a dark, suffocating cell with the smell of urine, stools from the bucket, and bottles for relieving our needs. My twenty-second birthday was one of the bleak, sad, and miserable days I spent in prison.

My twenty-third birthday was celebrated inside Benha Public Prison, forcibly stripped of all my clothes except for my boxers, on rocky ground inside a dungeon measuring one meter long and two meters high . . . inside it you feel like you are in a mousetrap, or you are a cockroach jammed inside a matchbox turned upside down. This was the disciplinary dungeon. My food was one loaf of bread a day, a small piece of cheese—if I wanted to be precise, it was just a stick of cheese on a loaf, one bottle of water, and a bucket to relieve myself. The terrible smells in that place, its tightness, and the lack of any ventilation make it a real grave. I spent the day singing loudly, smiling, hoping against hope that this was the worst I would face.

My twenty-sixth birthday might have been the worst, but I could celebrate it my own way. At that time, I was "forcibly disappeared"; I was secretly held inside the headquarters of the National Security department in Lazoughly, I was blindfolded with a piece of thick black cloth and handcuffed with an iron handcuff and I sat on the floor forbidden to speak or move. There are no names in that place. There you had to forget your name because it may indicate that you exist or are alive. You are only a number that you must memorize well; you will be subjected to the most severe punishment if you forget your number.

I had spent three months in this situation during which I could not shower. The effects of torture were still visible on my body and on the body of all detainees. Everyone's clothes were full of bloodstains. We lived in this situation, with the stench of sweat and wound sores that accumulated for months on our bodies. Everyone waiting for his turn in torture, which could come at any moment, everyone lived in fear, anticipation, and despair, everyone was waiting for death, which might be a relief from all this suffering. On that day I defied him. I asked him a provocative question. The bystanders laughed and he got even angrier. He started a long list of abuses and then dragged me and suspended me from my hands for two or three hours. I am not sure. Time is strange in that place. The suspension was very painful, but all the same I felt I had achieved something by making his juniors laugh at him. Despite the pain I felt, despite everything, I was still strong.

My twenty-seventh birthday I was in the Borg El Arab prison. On that day, after protesting a violation of a prior agreement with the prison administration following a prison-wide hunger strike, I was dragged and after a long series of kickings, beatings, and miserable resistance from me, I was dragged to the disciplinary cell, which was a meter and a half wide and about four meters long, containing fourteen prisoners, all naked except for boxers, with a bucket behind the door of the cell. I laughed and told my cellmates that it was my birthday and asked them each to sing me a song. The sound of the songs mixed with the stench of urine and stools in the bucket and the smell of stinking sweat and the stickiness of naked bodies in that narrow space, I felt I had gone back in time to the Middle Ages. I kept telling myself, "You have been through worse than this; this too will pass; be strong."

On my twenty-ninth birthday . . . I was inside the Cairo Prison for preventive detention in the Tora investigation complex. I spent that day on a hunger strike, a strike that I had started five days earlier to protest the intransigence of the prison administration with me and my mistreatment in addition to being confined to the disciplinary cell for no reason except to satisfy the prison administration's passion for cruelty.

These are brief scenes, five birthdays inside prison. That is not the worst that I went through, but there is always worse. Perhaps the best condition in prison is to have two and a half hands of space to sleep in, in a relatively clean dungeon, which makes you feel the homeland is shrinking to this miserable space; but despite all the distress that causes pain, the homeland remains and will remain great in our dreams.

January 4, 2019. Courtesy of the Archives of El-Nadeem, Center against Violence and Torture.

29

JOURNALISTS IN PRISON

SINCE 2011, EGYPT HAS CONSISTENTLY ranked among the worst countries in terms of journalists harassed, imprisoned, and forced into exile. In the words of the Committee to Protect Journalists, reporters "have faced unprecedented threats" since the 2013 coup, while *Mada Masr* and Reporters without Borders have affirmed that "in the ten years President Sisi has been in power Egypt has become one of the biggest jailers of journalists," ranking as high as third in the number jailed. The following entries reflect detained journalists' specific experiences of prison life and the harm it inflicts on them as writers, and through that, on the health of the Egyptian body politic.

SOLAFA MAGDY

Solafa Magdy is a journalist and a human rights defender whose work focuses particularly on women's and minority and asylum seekers' rights. She is a co-founder of Everyday Footage, which provides training programs in mobile journalism. Along with her husband Hossam al-Sayyad, she was arrested and imprisoned from 2019 through 2021. Her then seven-year-old son Khaled was not told about his parents' imprisonment. Both Solafa and Hossam were accused of joining a terrorist organization and spreading false news, and she was subsequently added to another State Security case, this time accused of joining a terrorist organization from inside prison, "misusing social media," and "spreading false news." After refusing to become an informant, she was subjected to severe maltreatment, including both physical and sexual assault, by State Security intelligence as well as prison personnel. The couple was prevented from seeing each other during their pre-trial detention, which only ended on April 13, 2021, Soon after her release she left Egypt for Paris, where she presently lives and researches and campaigns for political prisoners.

Message on Her Birthday from Qanater Prison

Today, I turn thirty-two while in prison, far from my only son, far from my husband and companion Hossam, separated from him by high walls, prison, guards, and iron . . . But the love and dream remain.

I hope that we will soon return to our seven-year-old son, because he does not deserve to live apart from his parents, and he does not even know that we are political prisoners!

From my cell, I appeal to every colleague to fight for the sake of the profession, to be proud that you are journalists, and to complete what we are unable to implement while we are prisoners against our will . . . Journalism is an honor and a covenant, so rise to the responsibility and uphold the covenant . . .

In the end, I hope that the price that we and others are paying for our freedom will be a sacrifice for everyone who deserves to live in freedom . . . I am not guilty because I am a journalist doing my work and defending freedom of the press and opinion; I am proud to be a journalist . . . and proud to be a prisoner of conscience. Prison is not luxurious but it will never break us.

We will still love this country despite the prison and the jailer.

Qanater Women's Prison, January 31, 2020. Courtesy of Solafa Magdy.

On Mother's Day, a Letter to Her Son

Forgive me my little one. I will come back and hug you all the time. My detention has now gone beyond 120 days, away from my detained husband, photojournalist Hossam al-Sayyad and my little son.

One hundred and twenty days and to this day I do not know the reason for my arrest. I only know that I am an Egyptian journalist who loved my country and tried hard through my work to shed light on everything that needs reform to advance our society and provide a better life for us and our children.

First and foremost, I am a mother. I spent a hundred and twenty days in prison and my heart broke at every moment for my little son, who is six years old, my son who has not tired of waiting for the date of my "return from travel" and who has not stopped asking those around him, and asking me in his letters, "Tell me exactly what day will you come back."

My love, every time I receive a letter from you, my heart is writhing in pain, and I cry for my absence from you and your father. My heart breaks every time you write to me "I miss you." Your simple words never leave me. In all my court sessions I look for answers to your questions and I repeat those questions to everyone I meet. But to no avail!

Isn't it time to decide upon my situation? And that of every mother and prisoner who did not commit a crime that deserves imprisonment and punishment?

Today is Mother's Day, I should have been with my son, cuddling and caring for him. My dear son, I miss you so very much, and as I told you in the past, I will come back to you my love, I don't know when, but I hope it will be soon, I will come back and hug you all the time.

Forgive me my little one.

March 21, 2020. Courtesy of Solafa Magdy.

ESRAA ABDEL FATTAH

A blogger and the creator of the Facebook page to support the April 6 strike, Esraa Abdel Fattah was at the forefront of the January 2011 uprising and considered one of the "most iconic leaders" of the uprising era. She was known as "Facebook Girl" because of her role as one of the first activists in the country to organize protests through social media, and after the January 25 uprising was nominated for the Nobel Peace Prize and named a "Woman of the Year" by *Glamour* magazine.

Subjected to a travel ban in 2015 (which lasted until 2021) after being accused of receiving foreign funding, Abdel Fattah was arrested in her car in October 2019 by plainclothes policemen, likely for her support of an initiative launched to release political prisoners. Her arrest was part of the same sweep that saw Alaa Abd El-Fattah and over 3,000 other people arrested as a result of protests launched in response to large-scale corruption accusations leveled against the Sisi regime by exiled former construction contractor Mohammed Ali.

Abdel Fattah was systematically beaten and tortured during her arrest and interrogations after refusing to unlock her phone. Despite informing the court of of this, she was returned to the same prison, generally a guarantee of further mistreatment. After going public about her mistreatment, she went on a hunger strike, prompting former prisoners and colleagues like Solafa Magdy to publicize her case and ask supporters to stand by her and talk about her situation. In July 2021, Abdel Fattah received a Democracy Courage Tribute from the

World Movement for Democracy. She was released from prison on July 17 of that year and her travel ban was lifted. The excerpt below is from a message that Abdel Fattah asked her sister to publish on social media on the anniversary of the fall of Mubarak, while she was in prison.

Hope from Pain

Hope is born from the womb of pain. Recall the moments of hope and be always proud.

Justice and rights and freedoms will inevitably come.

February 11, 2020. Courtesy of Esraa Abdel Fattah.

SHEREEN BEKHEIT

Born in 1982, journalist Shereen Bekheit was arrested on October 19, 2016, from her home in Shabin El Kom, Menufeyya governorate. The police that came to the house were searching for her husband; when they did not find him, they arrested her instead. She was taken to State Security intelligence, where she was held in a narrow, dark, dirty cell and was subjected to threats of rape if she did not confess to crimes she did not commit. She was also subjected to beatings by inmates who were being held on criminal charges. Accused of joining a banned organization, disseminating false news, and inciting illegal demonstrations, she remained in prison until 2017.

From Prison: Journalism Is Not a Crime

There are days that I shall never forget. I have not forgotten what happened in them, from the moment they stormed my house and broke the door of my apartment and terrorized my children and prevented me even from talking to them; my house was [suddenly] a military barracks, my heart almost stopped after that, they forced me to leave with them without changing my clothes, I was putting on my niqab by the door. I went out and felt that I was dreaming and was taken away in a white Toyota.

The voice of the interrogators, the accusations, the threats, the handcuffs, forcing me to make a video of my "confessions."

I spent six hours in State Security headquarters in Cairo. Then once again a return to State Security in Chebin El Kom (in the Nile Delta). New threats . . . new confessions until dawn.

The first call for the dawn prayers . . . then a solitary cell . . . the insects . . . the darkness . . . without food . . . without water . . . the sound of the opening of the cell . . . the terrible sound of the guard calling me, until I came to hate my name . . .

I did not wake up from this nightmare until four days after the fifteen-day renewal, when I moved to live in the midst of criminal prisoners, and despite the difficulty of life with them, it was easier than in State Security . . .

I am still deprived of my freedom, no lawyer is allowed to attend my questioning or renewals . . . I am not even allowed to defend myself.

((Oh God, I count that with you))

My message to you:

Bring our girls out of the cells

I miss my children, my family, my brothers, and everyone I loved

I do not know my destiny, do not forget to pray for me

I love you in God

November 23, 2016. Courtesy of the Archives of El-Nadeem, Center against Violence and Torture.

KARAM SABER

Karam Saber is the founder of the Land Center for Human Rights, which focuses on promoting and defending human rights in Egypt, including the rights of children and the economic and cultural rights of farmers, and putting an end to corruption. He is also a writer and poet. He was arrested for publishing a novel that was considered insulting to religion and sentenced in absentia in 2013 with contempt of religion, atheism, and inciting sedition and bloodshed under Article 98 of the Egyptian Penal Code, also known as the Blasphemy Law.

Existence Is Resistance

I know that the public and private climate is despondent and does not provide defenders of the oppressed any opportunity to protest or express anger, but your resistance and your insistence on revealing the truth make it difficult for those who surrender and trade in people's dreams to defeat or break us. Your presence is resistance, my friend, and despite the darkness of the cell, I am not worried about my children.

January 2019. Courtesy of the Archives of El-Nadeem, Center gainst Violence and Torture.

HISHAM FUAD

Hisham Fuad is a journalist, socialist, and political and trade union activist.

Please, Wait

Please wait for me at the café where we used to meet, so that we can complete the path of the martyrs of the January revolution, which is paved with trees of equality and hope.

July 2019. Courtesy of the Archives of El-Nadeem, Center against Violence and Torture.

AHMED TAREK (ARNOUB)

They Gave Me a Number and Told Me "You Have No Name"

Hundreds of days ago, for reasons I could not comprehend, they stripped me of everything, took me to the top of a mountain and then pushed me from the ledge and left me to fall. For a whole year I have been falling—neither have I hit the ground nor have I been saved. That is what pre-trial detention is like. You remain suspended in the air, waiting, falling, unable to add or change anything. Fear surrounds me from all sides, turns me on all faces, defeats me cruelly and empties my soul without allowing me to move. A whole year in prison, where I slept on the ground and in the permanence of darkness. I knew complete loneliness and brutal alienation, I was exiled inside the country, rotten boredom, and madness.

How can I be accused of publishing if nothing has been published? Where shall I find strength when I weaken? Who will console me when there is no consolation? Who can decide my case? Or is able to put an end to this misery? I don't belong in this place.

Maybe others can, but I am unable to describe prison. Words are too weak to explain and accurately describe a world full of sadness, failures, patience, tears, torture, time passing slowly, death surrounding us, and where a person is humiliated and is forced to be other than what he wants for himself. There is no normal laughter. Only hysterical laughter when you are asked to smile and be optimistic. Only cynicism that ends in more despair.

Tora Prison, February 2019. Courtesy of the Archives of El-Nadeem, Center against Violence and Torture.

ANONYMOUS FEMALE JOURNALIST
Writing Is Resistance

Hope is pure evil, it is the pain in every moment and the break when dreams collapse . . .

A thousand motives may draw me towards writing, and I do not know which one is the real motive, but the thing I am sure of is that I am still writing because writing is my only means of resistance and my only means of living.

October 2019. Courtesy of the Archives of El-Nadeem, Center against Violence and Torture.

REEM QOTB GABARA

Reem Qotb Gabara is a journalist with *Al Jazeera* who was arrested at the airport upon her return from Turkey in the beginning of January 2017. She was accused of joining the international Muslim Brotherhood and was added to State Security case no. 1173/2016. Her detention was renewed until her release with precautionary measures in March 2018, after she had spent a year and four months in Qanater Women's Prison.

"I thank God for the death of my mother"

For the first time in my life, I thank God for the death of my mother, who would not have endured my imprisonment and my affliction over the people of my country . . . Months passed by, with all that was in them, with their traumas, their pain, and their sweet moments too.

My dream has become a sin, my sincerity has become sin, and my honor has been taken maliciously. Because I do not live like others and my path is not drawn by my predecessors, I am guilty until proven otherwise; what a joke.

I do not want help from you, just as I do not need your encouragement; your differences and interests do not concern me, so leave me to address the humane people; I only ask to refine the humanity in us.

I heard about injustice and sometimes thought that I was treated with injustice, but it is only a fleeting moment; I found it to be my close friend and confidante, I recognized it as an embodiment, I am not Joseph, but I am still waiting.

I still wonder every day . . . does my country intend to break people and dreams?

Hope still survives inside me, my feathers are on the alert.

It is my father, a spirit that runs with me, he always taught me to stand in pride, courage, and also love, how wonderful he is, my father. Sorry, darling, I hurt you and tired you out worrying about me, so forgive me . . . you who said, "I live for you."

Written in Qanater Women's Prison. Courtesy of the Archives of El-Nadeem, Center against Violence and Torture.

HASSAN AL-BANNA MUBARAK
Meanings

This is above all a slow, but effective, process of physical and psychological liquidation, I can attest to that . . .

Every defense I once built I have now discovered to be primitive and frail, all the energy I conserved ran out in the first hour, every bit of intelligence I developed was not enough to convince a guard. Every vanity I developed did not raise me above his military boots, every idea I invested in failed to get the attention of a guard, every image I had of myself I am now the first to mock, every feeling I had for my country was an invitation to be despised and belittled.

All the meanings I'd worked so hard to arrive at could not hold up to the meanings I acquired here.

This is the true meaning of fear and anxiety and depression and loneliness and weakness and want and deprivation and suspicion and exhaustion and boredom and oppression and despair and anguish and deformity and ugliness and estrangement . . . of pain and iron.

Letter written December 27, 2018, in Wadi Natrun Prison. Courtesy of the Archives of El-Nadeem, Center against Violence and Torture.

30

MAHIENOUR EL-MASSRY

MAHIENOUR EL-MASSRY IS A HUMAN rights lawyer. Born in Alexandria in 1986, her political activism was inspired by the writings and memory of her aunt Sana' al-Masri—a prominent Marxist and feminist intellectual who had been part of the student movement in the 1970s—and by the wave of student political activism that spread around Egypt in the wake of the Gulf wars and the Second Palestinian Intifada. In the early 2000s she joined the Youth Coalition for Change (the youth branch of the well-known Kefaya movement) and later the Revolutionary Socialists. During this period she developed a broader understanding of workers' issues, especially by taking part in the sit-ins and the protests organized by the labor movement between 2006 and 2011.

Mahienour was arrested multiple times for her political activism. Her first arrest was in July 2008, but her case was never prosecuted. When she was arrested again on March 29, 2013, during a sit-in to protest police violence against a fellow lawyer in Alexandria, she was referred to the prosecutor's office. She was released the following day. In 2014 she was sentenced in absentia for breaking the protest law, for which she was imprisoned from May until September 2014. Her celebrity crossed Egyptian borders in October 2014, when she flew to Florence, Italy, to receive the Ludovic Trarieux International Human Rights Prize, an award given annually to a lawyer for contributions to the defense of human rights. The award was established in memory of the founder of the Ligue des droits de l'homme and the first recipient was Nelson Mandela, in 1985. However, not even this prestigious award protected her from being convicted again. In May 2015, prosecutors reopened the 2013 case against her and she spent one year and three months in prison. She was jailed yet again from November 2017 to January 2018 for participating in protests against the Egyptian government's decision to cede Tiran and Sanafir Islands to the Kingdom of Saudi Arabia.

On September 22, 2019, Mahienour was arrested once again, this time on pending charges, in the wake of the protests that erupted in Cairo and across Egypt on Friday, September 20, 2019. Plainclothes police took her away while she was attending the hearing of a fellow lawyer at the State Security Prosecution in Cairo. She was provisionally released on August 3, 2021, after twenty-two months of pre-trial detention, with an investigation still pending on charges of "publishing false news" and "involvement in terrorism-related offenses."

What characterizes her writing is her attention to social justice with a specific focus on the need to address class inequalities.

PRISON IS A MICROCOSM OF SOCIETY

I don't know a great deal about what is happening on the outside since I was sentenced to prison. However, I can imagine it is pretty much as we used to do when somebody we knew was imprisoned. The online world is flooded with slogans like "Free this or that person" or "We are all so and so."

However, ever since I set foot in Damanhour Women's Prison and was placed with my inmates in "Block One"—the cluster of cells assigned to those accused or convicted of embezzlement—only one thing has been on my mind and I repeat it like a daily mantra: "Down with this classist system."

Most of my inmates have been imprisoned for defaulting on the payment of installments or small loans. They are loans taken out by a mother buying some direly needed items for her bride-to-be daughter, or by a wife who needed money to afford treatment for her sick husband, or a woman failing to pay back a loan of 2,000 Egyptian pounds on time, only to find herself slammed with a fine of 3 million pounds in return.

Prison is a microcosm of society. Those who are slightly more privileged than others find ways to get all they need inside, while the underprivileged are forced to work to meet their basic needs.

Prison is a microcosm of society. Prisoners discuss what is happening in the country. You can find the whole political spectrum here. Some of them support Sisi in the hope that on becoming president he will issue pardons to all those who have been imprisoned for defaulting on payments. Others want him to become president believing that he will take a strong stance against "terrorist protests" and rule with an iron fist, even though they sympathize with me and feel that I am probably innocent. Others are pro-Sabbahi, as they see him as one of them. "He promised to release prisoners," they say, only to be bellowed at by other inmates who say he only promised to release prisoners of conscience. And there are those who see the elections as a farce, which they would have boycotted if they had been free.

Prison is a microcosm of society. I feel I am amongst family. They are all giving me advice about focussing more on my career and my future once I'm out of here. In response, I say Egyptian people deserve much better, that justice hasn't been served yet, and we will keep on trying to build a better future. At this point, news reaches us of Hosni Mubarak's three-year sentence for charges of widespread corruption, embezzlement of funds, and financial fraud in the "Presidential Palaces Case." Cracking up, I ask them, "What kind of future do you expect me to have in an unjust society, in which the regime thinks that Umm Ahmed, who has been incarcerated for the past eight years and still has six more to go for signing a bad check worth no more than LE50,000, is more of a dangerous criminal than Mubarak?"—the same Mubarak who supports Sisi, whom they see as their savior.

Here they speak of this classist society and dream of social justice without complex theories. We should never lose sight of our main objective in the midst of this battle, in which we have lost friends and comrades every other day. We should not turn into people demanding the freedom of this or that person, while forgetting the wider needs and anxieties of the Egyptian people, who merely want to survive hand to mouth.

While chanting against the Protest Law, we should be working on abolishing this classist system; on organizing ourselves and interacting with the underprivileged, on speaking out for their rights and building a vision for how to solve their problems. We should be chanting, "Freedom for the poor," so that people don't feel we are isolated from them and their problems.

And finally, if we have to hold up the slogan, "Free this or that person," then let the slogan be, "Free Sayeda," "Free Heba," and "Free Fatima"—the three girls I met at the Security Directorate accused of being members of the Muslim Brotherhood and of committing murder, among other things. They were randomly arrested and have been incarcerated since January without trial.

Freedom for Umm Ahmed, who hasn't seen her children for eight years. Freedom for Umm Dina, who is the sole provider of her family. Freedom for Niamah, who agreed to go to prison instead of someone else in return for money to feed her children. Freedom for Farhah, Wafaa, Kawthar, Sanaa, Dawlat, Samia, Iman, Amal and Mervat.

Our pains compared to theirs are nothing, as we know that there are those who will remember us, say our names from time to time, proudly mentioning how they know us. Instead, these women, who deserve to be proudly remembered, will only be mentioned at most in family gatherings.

Down with this classist society, something we will never accomplish if we forget those who have truly suffered injustice.

Block 1, Cell 8, Damanhour Women's Prison. Translated by Radwa al-Barouni and published in Mada Masr, *June 7, 2014. Republished with permission of* Mada Masr *and Mahienour El-Massry.*

WE SHALL CONTINUE

Khaled Saeed's anniversary has passed without reviving his memory, while at the same time one of Mubarak's men has been inaugurated to rule the state, a man who says he'll deliver the martyrs' rights. Nonetheless, he's imprisoned thousands of oppressed individuals, and until we are delivered the rights of the martyrs, the revolution will continue.

As I said in my first letter, even if the court upheld my sentence, and even if I'm granted a new jail sentence in the Raml police station case (the court session will take place on June 16), still . . . we shall continue. And by the way, our sacrifices are trivial compared to the suffering and anguish of the impoverished. I repeat again that the ward where I'm imprisoned—a ward related to public funds fraud—isn't what we think it is. It isn't for criminals and corrupt moguls but specifically for the poor who can't provide for themselves and are imprisoned for defaulting on the payment of installments or small loans. That's why a frail regime like this one won't stand for long.

Figure 13. "We don't like prisons but we're not afraid of them." Graffiti on a wall in Alexandria depicting Mahienour El-Massry, by Rania Youssef.

I refuse any form of amnesty, because the regime is the one that's supposed to ask for amnesty from the people. I will not leave my prison until the Protest Law is abolished completely.

Down with all traitors . . . military junta, *feloul* [regime remnants], Muslim Brotherhood . . .

Block 1, cell 8, Damanhour Women's Prison, June 10, 2014. Published on the Facebook page FreeMahienour. Courtesy of Mahienour El-Massry.

ABOUT GAZA DURING THE 2014 ATTACK

Via attorney Mohamed Radwan today [July 7, 2014], Mahienour El-Massry's fourth letter from prison regarding recent events in the Gaza Strip.

The liberation of Palestine starts with the liberation of Cairo. The Palestinian cause has always been a card among many in the hand of various regimes, be it Morsi's that used it in an emotional context without providing any real support for the cause, or the current regime that closely abides by the Camp David Accords and thus, as expected, considers the resisting oppressed a criminal, while presenting the oppressor as the victim, all the while sacrificing the Palestinian cause in exchange for excuses to justify its incompetence.

The current regime that imprisons thousands of wronged citizens (be it under political or criminal charges) will surely view Palestinians as traitors, just as it views any human demanding their just rights as an agent and saboteur.

Praised be every one of our brothers and heroes of Palestine and all the soldiers of the resistance, and shame upon all traitors and sell-outs.

Block 1, Cell 8, Damanhour Women's Prison, July 7, 2014. Courtesy of Mahienour El-Massry.

ON THE ANNIVERSARY OF THE ASSASSINATION OF SHAIMA AL-SABBAGH[*]

Imprisonment is what always confirms to me that we were not mistaken when we dreamed of a better world and our revolution . . . We may have made mistakes on some paths of the revolution, but we were not mistaken in our participation in it . . . and there are a thousand reasons that confirm our lack of confidence and belief in a regime that is against the poor. If there was a good place to celebrate International Women's Day, surely it would be prison . . . among the toilers, the poor, and those struggling for a better life for their families . . . Freedom for the deprived.

This is the fifth anniversary of the revolution. I almost cannot believe that it has been five years since the chants "The people want to bring down the regime" and "Bread. Freedom. Social justice. Human dignity." Maybe because even in my cell I am full of dreams of freedom and hope.

[*] Shaima al-Sabbagh was a young poet, the mother of a toddler, and an activist in the Socialist Popular Alliance Party in Alexandria. She was shot dead by the police while bringing flowers to Tahrir Square during the vigil on the fourth anniversary of the January 25 revolution. Her image became iconic of the violence of the police state.

Some believe that since years have passed, the revolution has been defeated; others believe that nothing better could have been achieved. And the regime thinks that it has won. But are these answers correct and decisive? Are we defeated and is the revolution over? Were we only victims the whole time? Has authoritarianism fixed its feet by using force and tyranny most of the time and being soft-spoken at another time?

There are lessons for everyone . . . lessons we learned through pure blood that was poured out for us.

The first of those lessons: There is no individual salvation, despair and trying to escape to the outside or inside will not help us make our day better. When we only looked at ourselves and demanded freedom only for those we knew and did not move for the freedom of the people as a whole (for example, there are not only thousands of oppressed political prisoners, there are also thousands of citizens whose charges were fabricated or who became aggrieved due to the state's economic system and many other issues), that is how we gave the regime an opportunity to separate us from the street and our goals and to achieve victory in the final rounds.

Second: We were eaten the day the white bull was eaten. Revolution is humane in nature; it should not allow us to accept any injustice that occurs even to those who disagree with us in opinion, and even to those who want to erase us. Accepting injustice for one will extend injustice to all.

Third: It is not enough to have had the honor of trying. We must not continue to walk in the same circle. We must translate the objectives of the revolution into activities and initiatives and start organizing ourselves. If they are united by the interests of counter-revolution, we who believe in freedom and who stand against all forms of authoritarianism and reaction must be united by the drive for survival.

Fourth: A terrified regime is the one that arrests thousands and cancels elections (student union elections, for example) and shudders on the anniversary of a certain day despite the passage of time. A terrified regime is the one that treats equally those who demand life and those who demand death. Oppression never mattered, but rather deepened the sense of injustice and strengthened resistance. The people who took to the streets for two days on January 18 and 19, 1977, and did not touch the head of the regime absorbed the lesson and attempted to topple the head of the regime in 2011, but the attempt has not been completed yet . . .

Fifth: The revolution is the perpetual life and the dream and does not depend on individuals, and sooner or later, in our lifetime or that of those who come after us, the revolution will be completed because human beings deserve better, and ugliness, no matter how it tries to beautify itself, will reveal its face.

Oh Shaima . . . on the first anniversary of your death, carry our regards to our martyred angels . . . and tell them that we are still full of hope and that imprisonment and oppression have only increased our adherence to our dream and our revolution . . .

Qanater Prison, January 24, 2016. Courtesy of Mahienour El-Massry.

31

MOHAMED RAMADAN

MOHAMED RAMADAN IS A HUMAN rights lawyer who previously worked for the Arabic Network for Human Rights Information. His work includes protecting human rights defenders and political prisoners. Ramadan was part of Mahienour El-Massry's defense team (see chapter 30) before he was arrested in a case in which she and others were convicted of violating the Protest Law, assaulting security forces, and disrupting traffic. On February 9, 2015, El Raml Misdemeanor Court in Alexandria sentenced them and Ramadan to two years' imprisonment.

In April 2017, Ramadan was falsely accused under the counterterrorism law and the Alexandria Criminal Court sentenced him in absentia to ten years in prison, followed by five years under house arrest and a five-year ban on using the internet. He was released in August 2017 and rearrested in December 2018 by plainclothes security officers. He was nominated, with four other imprisoned Egyptian human rights lawyers, by the Law Society of England and Wales for the CCBE Human Rights Award 2020. Ramadan was pardoned by President Sisi and released on July 25, 2022, and is currently practicing law in Alexandria.

KNOWING YOUR TORTURER

There is no prisoner in Borg El Arab detention center who is not familiar with Ezbet Abu Lebas. It is one of three forms of torture used if a detainee commits any breach or violation. The three are disciplining, *falaka*, and Ezbet Abu Lebas.

Disciplining: This is the official punishment for any detainee who may commit a violation, whether criminal or political. The prisoner is deposited in a cell measuring one meter by three meters for a whole month; there are six other prisoners and only one blanket, and a bucket in which to urinate and a liter-and-a-half bottle of water daily for the seven to use. As for food, it is a loaf of bread for every prisoner each day, with a small pack of halva and a tablespoon of white cheese.

Falaka: This is an unofficial torture method for criminal prisoners only. It is a long thick stick with a thick rope on both ends, and the legs of the detainee are placed between the rope and the stick. Then the detective wraps it around several times until the man is crammed between the stick and the rope and cannot move his legs, and another detective holds in his hand a heavy power cable, with which he beats the detainee on his feet until his feet are swollen.

Ezbet Abu Lebas: This is an unofficial torture method for criminal prisoners, and it is a swamp of sewage on the outskirts of the prison in which the detainee is forced to swim back and forth several times until he is covered with shit and rotten water all over his body. Then he is forced to dip his head in several times, and of course the reason for calling this swamp "Ezbet Abu Lebas" is because the detainee is swimming stripped of all clothes other than his boxers (*lebas*).

Ward 2, cell 12, Borg El Arab detention center. Courtesy of the Archives of El-Nadeem, Center against Violence and Torture.

32

MOHAMED EL-BAQER

MOHAMED EL-BAQER IS A LAWYER, human rights defender, and the founder of the ADALAH Center for Rights and Freedoms. His practice focuses on cases related to the protection of human rights defenders, political activists, minorities, and refugees, as well as student rights and academic freedom. With the outbreak of the 2011 uprising, he volunteered to defend civilians before military courts, joining the No Military Trials for Civilians group as well as working with the Front for the Defense of Egyptian Demonstrators and the Front for the Road of Revolution.

El-Baqer was arrested on September 30, 2019, from the premises of the State Security Prosecution office where he was performing his duties as a lawyer for Alaa Abd El-Fattah (see chapter 2). His first interrogation took place in the absence of a lawyer. He was then taken to Tora Prison, where he was beaten and mistreated in what is known as the "reception party" in Egyptian prisons. He slept on an iron platform without a

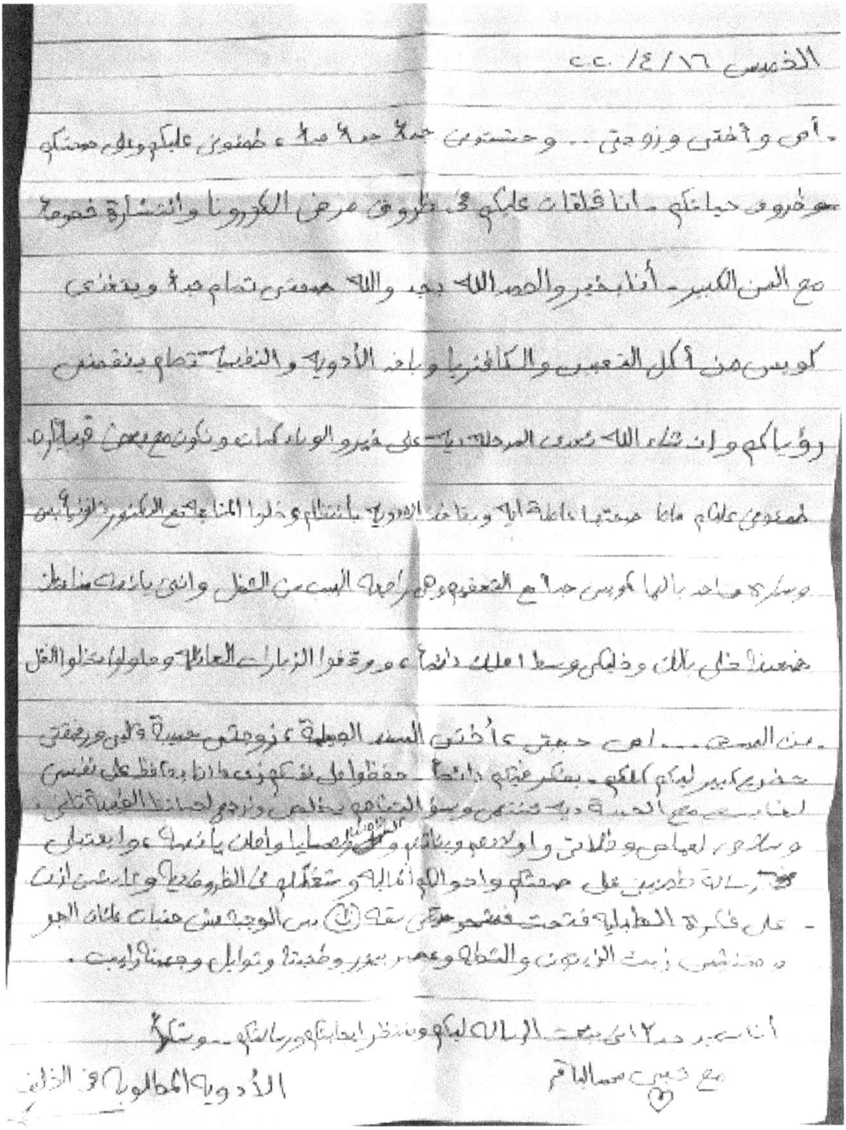

Figure 14. A letter written by Mohamed El-Baqer. Courtesy of the Archives of El-Nadeem, Center against Violence and Torture.

mattress or pillow and only two blankets, and without access to books, radio, or any other privileges, all in contravention of prison regulations.

While still in detention El-Baqer was added to several newer State Security cases; he ultimately underwent a trial devoid of due process, access to case files, or legal representation and was sentenced by an exceptional civil court under military jurisdiction and without the right to appeal. El-Baqer spent three years in the maximum-security Scorpion Prison wing of Tora Prison, under inhumane conditions, before being transferred in October 2022 to Badr Prison for another year. In April 2023, his wife, Neamatallah Hesham, was arrested in their home after she publicly denounced the torture, ill treatment, and poor conditions of her husband's and other prisoners' detention. This led to eleven Egyptian organizations publicly appealing her arrest. El-Baqer's work for human rights has been acknowledged by international organizations, including Amnesty International and the Council of Bars and Law Societies in Europe (CCBE), which honored him and six other Egyptian human rights lawyers (Haytham Mohammadein, Hoda Abdelmoniem, Ibrahim Metwally Hegazy, Mahienour El-Massry, Mohamed Ramadan, and Zyad El-Eleimy) for their courage, determination, and commitment to defending human rights in Egypt.

Without warning, El-Baqer was pardoned and released along with detained student activist Patrick Zaki (see chapter 17) in July 2023. Six months after his release, he was still subject to security restrictions, including a travel ban, that limited his professional activity.

THE PANDEMIC IN PRISON

To my mother, sister, and wife,

I miss you very, very much. Please tell me how you are doing, your health and your life in general. I am very worried about you, considering the corona pandemic and its spread especially among the elderly. I am fine, thank God, really. My health is fine and I eat well from the prison food and the cafeteria, and I take my medicine and I am psychologically fine. I only miss seeing you, and God willing we shall pass through this and will soon be together again.

Please tell me about yourselves. How is mom's health? I hope she is taking her medicines regularly and can follow up with her doctor by phone. And Sara please take care of yourself and always use disinfectants on your way to and back from work. And you Neama, your immune system is weak. Please take care and always remain with your family. Please reduce family visits and try as much as possible to work from home.

My beloved mom, my beautiful sister, and my wife, the love of my heart and my companion, a big hug to all of you. I think about you all the time. Take care of yourselves, like I am taking care of myself until this detention ends and the misunderstanding is cleared and we can return to our normal lives.

My regards to my uncles and aunts and their sons and daughters and all friends and my father-in-law, don't forget, Neama. Write to me about your lives and the financial situation and your work under these circumstances.

By the way, they have allowed food to be brought by families, so spoil me ☺

But note that the meal cannot sit out overnight or it will go bad in this weather. Don't forget the olive oil, juice, tahina, spices, and powdered milk.

I am very happy to be writing to you and await your news and letter. . . . Thank you.

With all my love ♥

Mohamed El-Baqer

The needed medicines are on the back of this letter

April 16, 2020. Courtesy of the Archives of El-Nadeem, Center against Violence and Torture and Mohamed El-Baqer.

33

COLLECTIVE LETTERS

THE FOLLOWING LETTERS WERE COLLECTIVELY written by various groups of prisoners between 2019 and 2022 to express their joint outrage to authorities or their own leadership about their treatment, conditions in prison, and lack of justice in society.

TO THE LEADERS OF THE MUSLIM BROTHERHOOD, FROM THE YOUTH OF THE MUSLIM BROTHERHOOD

The situation inside prisons has become very worrying. The prison population is exhausted and fed up by the least provocation. Despair has become their partner, hopelessness their colleague. They are defeated, helpless. The hardship has become too heavy and lasted for too long. Men have been broken. The elderly have been insulted. Humiliations, financial burdens, bodies drained by uselessness and filled with illnesses. Spirits are destroyed and disfigured.

Fleeting ideas, conflicting opinions, dreams were killed, the future is bleak and unknown. Children have been deprived of their parents, wives of their husbands, and families consider it a holiday when they can see you. In the not so distant past we thought this would not last long. But days followed days, years have elapsed, and the crisis continues and magnifies. Despair is engulfing the hearts of everyone, young and elderly, and it is no longer useful to talk about steadfastness inside those terrible cells with all the broken spirits. Now everybody is talking as if they will probably spend their full sentences in prison. What a disaster.

Hundreds received life sentences, and many others received sentences of five, ten, and fiteen years, and there are those whose sentences exceeded all barriers and reached more than fifty years. Our weaknesses are exposed. Young people are imprisoned with older prisoners. A brother has seen the weakness of his brother. Small problems have become major ones. Intellectual differences have appeared between the elderly and the young, to the extent that the youth no longer see the elderly and the leaders as anything other than another prison inside prison. We have seen strange things from leaders in prisons: attitudes that we cannot believe belong to the senior members in the biggest [Muslim] organization, illogical ideas, and concerns that are—to say the least—insignificant, a striving for power even in prison, and disagreements on the slightest things, while proclaiming to the young false slogans and fake steadfastness; claims that have nothing to do with the truth; pretentious endurance and patience, while they are the most tired and exhausted, having been consumed by despair as we are. But they insist on their arrogance and every day they lose more of their popularity, their youth, their followers. The prisons the group described as faith camps have become a great loss for the group, draining its members, feeding on their youth, and eroding their confidence and trust.

We the youth confess that prison has become the strongest influence on our ideas and tendencies, and you cannot miss the indicators. Some of the youth entered prison without any ideology or orientation and developed them inside prison; some lost them and acquired new ones; but the most numerous are those who entered prison with the ideas of the Brotherhood, of which they were deprived by prison, forcefully stripped away, leaving the Brotherhood to be the most affected and harmed by the prison crisis and its duration.

The question is: What role is leadership playing inside and outside prison to put an end to this crisis? Or more accurately: Is the group trying to reach a solution? Or are you really waiting for the people to revolt again in Egypt, as claimed by leading member Dr. Mahmoud Hussein? What logic or mind would believe that? Have you not learned the lesson summarized by this saying: "A rebel for an ignorant people is a person who sets himself on fire to light the way for the blind"?!

By describing to you only a portion of the situation in prisons, we have thus reached the goal of our mission . . . We, the youth among the detainees, from within the Brotherhood and others, call on all the leaders of the Muslim Brotherhood inside and outside prison and the borders of Egypt to act with all their strength towards a solution to their crisis with the military and the regime in Egypt, and not to hesitate to take a step backward to preserve what remains of the group's membership and to protect the few of their youth who remain, and to preserve our youth, our future, our present, and what remains of our dignity and humanity.

We reject all that is conveyed to you by the young leadership in prisons about our steadfastness and high spirits. These claims are furthest from the truth. Most of what these leaders hear are sentences such as "Solve it, will you not put an end to this farce," and they know very well that the situation is different from what they say. Indeed, many of those leaders curse the prison and oppression that we are in, and they utter words of steadfastness and strength that are contrary to what they believe, and they await the amnesty lists and search for their names on them . . . !

In the end, spare your efforts to decide the final scene in a movie that we are tired of watching. We conclude with a few words to the regime in Egypt: If you really want to end this crisis and save Egypt from this calamity, then bring the top leaders among the detainees in prisons, bring M. Khairat Al-Shater, Dr. Mohamed Badie, and the rest of the leaders and put them among the youth until it becomes clear to them how things have turned out. Then renegotiate; that is, if a rejection really comes from them. But if your desire is for the scene to continue and the crisis to drag on, or if you have other desires or agendas that are fulfilled by the Brotherhood's stay in prisons, then you know best the damage of this crisis and the severity of its consequences. In each of our lives there comes a stage where the slogan is "It no longer makes a difference. I shall not lose more than I have already lost," and that is when the individual becomes a time bomb waiting to explode, and you above all know the outcomes of that!!

Wait for us. Our intent is guided by God and He is the One who shows the way. Please spare yourself the effort of replying to us or trying to denounce our message or prove its opposite and accuse us of betrayal.

Signed,

The Youth of the Muslim Brotherhood, August 2019

Courtesy of the Archives of El-Nadeem, Center against Violence and Torture.

FROM WOMEN PRISONERS

In view of the fact that we, women prisoners in Egyptian prisons, who are subjected to the pain, suffering, and deprivation of our parents and children . . . including mothers who are deprived of a normal life, and

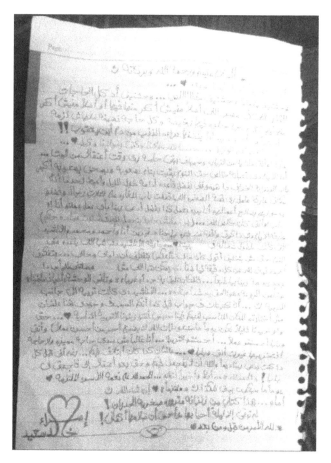

Figure 15. Collective letter handwritten by women prisoners. Courtesy of the Archives of El-Nadeem, Center against Violence and Torture.

young girls who have been deprived of completing their education and exercising their natural right to life, and elderly women who are close to their sixties and suffering of many diseases, while ignored by all parties concerned . . . we decided to send this message as an appeal to whoever is of a rational mind . . . and everyone who is in charge of this crisis . . . to look upon us with humanity and to not involve us in the political struggle into which we have been forced for more than six years.

We are trying to find a solution in which we can return to our normal lives, and we are trying to express our solidarity with the reconciliation proposed by our young male counterparts in Egyptian prisons.

August 2019. Published on the Facebook page Aswat Khalf al-Judran.

CRY FOR HELP FROM QANATER WOMEN'S PRISON

May God's peace, mercy, and blessings be upon you; a cry for help from the women's prison in Qanater to the compassionate hearts, and to humanity if it still exists in this time in which we live, to the whole world, to everyone who hears us and bears witness . . .

Last week Hajjah Safia died and returned to her creator thanks to medical neglect and lack of patient care in the prison hospital, or what they call a hospital. It has the name "hospital," but it is not a hospital. It kills patients instead of curing them.

Hajjah Safia kept vomiting blood until she died, and there was not in the hospital nor in the whole prison a single ampul of Zofran to save her life. When her medical report came out, it appeared that her death was due to low blood sugar.

Now the same is happening with Rabab Abdel Mohsen, who suffers from hepatitis C, a malignant tumor in the liver, gallbladder dysfunction, reflux, esophageal varices, and a hearing condition.

She is now vomiting black blood, indicating that she is in the terminal stage of this fatal disease, due to the negligence of the hospital administration and the prison administration and their failure to treat her for a period of three years since her illegal pre-trial detention began. Unfortunately, the authorities do not want to recognize her deadly diseases and they dismiss any reports proving her condition. They have been so cruel as to remove her from the hospital with the cannula still in her hand before the IV drip was even finished—and that by order of the prison administration, despite knowing that she had very thin veins and that she hardly receives any hydration or IV treatment. The reason was to avoid her being seen by anyone in the human rights delegation that was visiting the prison. That was on Monday August 26, 2019.

After that, her condition deteriorated further but was still met with neglect on the part of the prison administration, even though they knew very well that she needed treatment in an outside hospital, and they pretended that they were waiting for medical reports to allow her to be transfered. She now lingers between life and death, and has no one but God Almighty. Save us before we lose her . . . save the mother of orphans. . . . Save a soul . . . Or is human life in our society no longer worth anything . . . Are we in a time of no mercy . . . no humanity . . . no conscience . . .

Documented by WeRecord.org, September 2019.

LETTER OF DISTRESS FROM DETAINEES AT SCORPION PRISON

We live in very difficult and tragic circumstances and what is happening to us is a crime of genocide against humanity for nearly a thousand people. We have been starving for six months, and we shiver from the cold. The cold is eating away at our bones, and hunger is eating into our bodies and intestines. The quantity of food we receive is very, very little . . .

We are deprived of clothes and blankets, everyone has one blanket and some have two blankets but they are not enough to warm us from the cold . . . The blankets are thin and worn out, and the clothes, each of us has only one set, we die from the cold dozens of times a day.

The cold enters from everywhere inside this concrete box, as if it were jets of air coming out of the refrigerator, the constant pain is terrible, we cannot lean back against the concrete walls. Although there are many among us who are still young, we wake up in pain, our backs are bent from all the pain, anyone who sees us would think we are in our seventies or eighties. Can you imagine what this cold does to the elderly among us, such as Muhammad Suwaidan, Dr. Issam Hashish, Dr. Mahmoud Ghazlan, Dr. Issam Al-Aryan, and many others.

We have lost a lot of weight. Some of us have lost ten kilos because of the poor quality and quantity of food, a deliberate attempt to starve and break us. Many of us are suffering from malnutrition and other ailments such as indigestion, hemorrhoids, and anal fistulae and bleeding. And nobody cares or helps. Allah is sufficient for us, and Allah is the best trustee.

Collective letter of distress from detainees at Scorpion Prison

December 2019. Courtesy of the Archives of El-Nadeem, Center against Violence and Torture.

34

BASMA REFAAT

BASMA REFAAT, A PHYSICIAN, was convicted of "killing a public prosecutor" in 2016 and sentenced to fifteen years' imprisonment. Her husband was sentenced to life imprisonment. During her imprisonment she was one of several women who were severely beaten, isolated, and otherwise punished by prison authorities for attempting to protect a fellow inmate in the midst of a beating. Her health also deteriorated as a result of a botched procedure by prison medical staff. As of late 2023, Refaat remains in 10th of Ramadan Prison in Sharkeya governorate.

QANATER WOMEN'S PRISON

My baby boy does not know me anymore, he is not aware that I am his mother, and every time he looks at me his eyes punish me (where did you go and why did you leave me?!).

My five-year-old daughter entered school and I am not with her. There is no one to take care of them except my father and my mother, who are more than seventy-two years old. My husband is also imprisoned in the same case, and he is in the death prison (Scorpion Prison).

May God curse the oppressors. . . .

Courtesy of the Archives of El-Nadeem, Center against Violence and Torture.

35

MONA MAHMOUD MOHAMED

MONA MAHMOUD MOHAMED ENTERED the prison labyrinth after participating in a 2018 interview with the BBC during which she claimed that her daughter, Zubaida, had been abducted, raped, and tortured by police and then, after being released, was recaptured again and detained for a year before her mother spoke out about it. Mona was arrested immediately after the video was broadcast. The human rights lawyer who first brought Zubaida's plight to the public's attention also disappeared. After an initial imprisonment of fifteen days, she was rearrested and charged with spreading false news and attempting to harm the national interest. After the initial burst of attention, Zubaida appeared in pro-government media saying she was free but was not in touch with her mother, before disappearing again. The Egyptian government saw the BBC broadcast as a serious threat and called for a boycott of the BBC as well as a further crackdown on journalists. Mona was eventually released in 2020.

WHY AM I IN PRISON?

Is there not a rational man in this nation who would answer my questions?!

Hasn't God created all His creatures with a mother's instinct?

Why am I being punished for looking for my daughter?

And why are my release papers being torn after they have been endorsed?

Doctors, tell me, can you excise the mother's instinct from inside me, so that they can let me out of prison, so that they are assured that I won't look for my daughter again?

My heart is heavy with the pain of loss and the pain of prison, and my soul is tired of all the hope that never rises in the darkness of detention. I know that only he who has been handcuffed can feel the torture of the pain of handcuffs; the bitterness can only be felt by those who have tasted it.

August 2019. Courtesy of the Archives of El-Nadeem, Center against Violence and Torture.

36

ISRAA KHALED SAID

I'M HERE BECAUSE YOU DID WELL, MOM

Peace be upon you, Beloved Mother
Many greetings,

I miss you Mom, I miss you very much. I miss you as much as all the ugliness in Egypt, which is so much, which is the only thing existing in Egypt, where everything beautiful is cheap and everything clean is useless; a country that disowns anyone who tries to redeem or clean it.

Allah is my suffice, and the best deputy.

You know, after the visit ends and you leave me, I feel exactly as I felt at the time of my arrest from home. I am very tired these days, even sleep has become difficult, and I wake up with greater difficulty. This horrendous cell door is killing me. I spend the night in front of it, gazing at it and crying until I fall sleep, exhausted, on the spot. It is like the story of the stone that closed the cave over three men and they kept praying to God, reminding Him of the good they did. I do the same. I keep praying to God in the name of everything good I have done (but nothing happens; God has His reasons and wisdom).

You know, these days my memory goes back to the time when we were young, I, Ahmed, and Mohamed, and the religious songs that were on all the time at home . . . You know it is those songs that protect me from regret; they prevent me from saying "why did I get involved," they remind me to renew my pledge for goodness every minute I am here . . . Maybe it is those songs that prevent me from despair, that help me count on the mercy of God . . . This place is really for strangers, where you reconcile with loneliness and the ghosts of the past and feel safe in fear, believing in the Truthful One who mobilizes its soldiers. Those songs were an additional education. I wrote to you in an earlier letter that you are the ones responsible for my being here, not because you chose this place for me, but because you raised us in the proper way . . . Even if our lives are short, one day we shall return, because God will not waste the good that people do . . . and you and Dad did good, you brought us up well. I don't have anything to be proud of except you and Dad . . . That is why I am being tested, although I always used to pray to God that I would never have to feel sorrow for something that happened to you, even after my arrest and the sorrowful fate of Dad! Thank God . . . First and foremost, our pledge is to God, and I thank God for a committed family. One day my family will be like this. Committed. If God wants.

Mom, this is a letter from a disgusting cell with stone walls. I have one night to live and feel its darkness is my shroud.

God's will shall be in any case

Courtesy of the Archives of El-Nadeem, Center against Violence and Torture.

37

GHADA ABDEL AZIZ

"FROM THE WORST PLACE"

My name is Ghada Abdel Aziz. I am a university student. I was in my final year in the faculty of commerce at Ain Shams University. I am twenty-two years old. I was engaged for a year. I was kidnapped on the 11th of May from my father's house and taken to State Security headquarters. There I was physically and psychologically tortured. There I learned that the person I was engaged to was wanted by security, so they charged me with the same offenses. I do not have any ideological or political affiliation. Since then, I have been in detention.

Mom . . .

I miss you very much. Forgive me, I try to show that I am well in front of you so as not to worry you, but the situation here is worse than anyone can imagine. Try to get me out of here any way you can, because I cannot stand spending another hour here. I am so very tired.

I am sorry I am not able to write you letters. I am unable to hold a pen. For most of the day I am silent, unable to speak with anyone. It has been a year and two months. I remember every moment since the day I was taken. I shall never forget the night I opened my eyes to find someone waking me up, shouting at me, and the house full of people. I was scared by the way they looked. I didn't know who they were or what the matter was. They had each one of you sitting on a chair, prevented from moving. I shall never forget when he pulled me and blindfolded me and took me out of our building. All I wanted to know at the time was what happened!

One day, after a month had passed, they took me to a place they called the prosecution, and a few days later they took me to a worse place . . . the prison.

I don't know what my charges are for all this to happen!

Mom, pray for me and ask everyone to pray for me . . . I want to get out of this place. I want to go home. I am very tired and I know that you, more than anyone, can feel me.

Mom, honestly, every time I want to tell you not to make any more food. I am unable to eat the food you bring, although I would very much like to. But when I look at it I remember us gathering around the dining table. When we eat, I cry and am unable to eat.

Bye Mom, I so wish you could hug me to sleep.

Ghada

From the worst place

Qanater Prison

Courtesy of the Archives of El-Nadeem, Center against Violence and Torture.

38

MARWA ARAFA

MARWA ARAFA IS A PROFESSIONAL translator who was abducted by security forces from her home in Cairo on April 20, 2020. At time of arrest, Marwa's Facebook feed was mostly populated with photos of her twenty-one-month-old daughter. Marwa disappeared for two weeks and then reappeared in front of the prosecutor, accused of terrorism. Since then, her detention has been automatically renewed, despite the fact that her family asserts that she is not a political activist and the prosecutor has not provided evidence to prove her alleged crimes. The day after her arrest, another young woman translator, Khouloud Said Amer, the head of the Translation Unit in the Publication Department at the Bibliotheca Alexandrina, was also arrested by security forces and disappeared. Like Marwa, Khouloud also appeared a week later before the prosecutor, accused of being part of a terrorist organization, and her detention was renewed multiple times until December 13, 2020, when the Cairo Criminal

Court ordered her release. However, Khouloud was never released; instead, she disappeared again, then reappeared in court with a new case having been filed against her.

Prosecutors use the practice of "recycling" cases to start a new two-year pre-trial detention period. By bringing the same charges in a new case, they circumvent the law that limits pre-trial detention to two years even for maximum offenses. Marwa remains in pre-trial detention in the 10th of Ramadan Prison in the Sharkeya governorate.

DEAR BIG WAFAA[*]

I am now sleeping on the new red bedsheet, covered with the new red blanket and turning on the lightbulb I bought from the electrician for three packs of cigarettes (to help you picture the situation, it is a lousy normal lightbulb connected by a wire to the socket in the wall). I am reading "Principles of the Egyptian Penal Code." The light of the bulb is reflecting on the ceiling of the tin bed, against which I bump my head every now and then. The blacksmith should have come a month and a half ago to lift it a little. The old base of the bed was broken in the middle and I asked for a new one. They brought me one for the ground-level beds, which is too wide. I rent it for ten packs a month. I am still waiting for the blacksmith to lift the bed and its roof from above my head! We keep everything under the bed, so it is a disaster when the bed is low! The storage, the clothes, the bed covers, there's not room for everything. I have tied a plastic bag to the foot of the bed to put my toothpaste and brush in, to keep them away from cockroaches. Also,

---

[*] Wafaa is also the name of Marwa's two-year-old baby daughter, who is named after her grandmother.

the bristles of the new hairbrush broke in my hair. I am so unfortunate with hairbrushes in prison.

Since I am in Alcatraz Egypt and it is very cold, I need two black blankets like the red one to wrap around the bed. Also because I like to hide from the light and from people, so that I don't literally lose my mind. I cannot believe I have not been home since the 20th of April and that I might not go home for another two or three years.

Prison is very bad, Mom. But worse than prison are the people inside it. They are liars, tricky, harmful, and rude. Real criminals. The real punishment is having to live with them.

Wafaa should not stop going to the nursery, or else the nursery too will become something that is not constant in her life. That is very wrong. I told you she was in shock and needs a psychiatrist other than the one in the nursery. Go to Dr. Marwa, the child psychiatrist in the wellness hub in Heliopolis, and tell her that I am in prison and she will tell you what to do. There is a puzzle application on my iPad. Get it out for Wafaa and let her play with it.

I want a big box of tahina sweets every month, because I make sandwiches of it every day for the girls who help us.

This month I woke up in the nick of time to spit out a big cockroach that flew into my mouth while I was sleeping. Also, the cutest mouse ever jumped out at me while I was on the toilet at 3:00 a.m. and I didn't even scream. So I win the first prize for emotional stability. Wow me. F**k my life.

The girl who used to cook for us left and now I have to cook. So, who has to stand over the heater that gives electric shocks and makes explosive noises? I do.

I want to go home.

Courtesy of Marwa Arafa's family, via the Archives of El-Nadeem, Center against Violence and Torture.

39

ESSAM MOHAMED ATTA

ESSAM MOHAMED ATTA was a university business student and the owner of an advertising and design office in Ismailia. Charged with the murder of the assistant to an investigation officer in Ismailia, he was detained from November 21, 2013, until the day of his execution, July 27, 2020, when he was executed alongside six other detainees.

Atta's trial lacked all the standards of a fair trial. In his testimony to the court, he said that he was tortured until he confessed to acts he did not commit.

LETTER

I now stand at the edge of death and wait to meet my destiny. Who of you will demand my right, which I was denied coercively but also willingly. Yes, willingly because I surrendered to their threats.

Whoever said "confession is the master of evidence" did not clarify which confession. Confession by coercion, under torture, or under threats?

I will not talk about all the possible means of torture: electricity, crucifixion with iron cuffs, cigarette burns, heavy beatings with hands, sticks, and other things, all of which is documented in the forensic report describing my injuries.

All that is easy compared with threats that violate my dignity and pride! For whom?

What made me surrender to them were those filthy threats to assault my mother and sister in front of me. That was after they had arrested my uncle and tortured him in front of me. What happened was a full, systematic crime to change the path of the case. The script—the report—was written and the roles were distributed over us, and we accepted them because we had no other choice. The prosecution had come to the police station, to the room they call the "fridge," in the presence of the torturers who flogged our backs in front of the room. The torture series continued without a censor to delete scenes that showed human rights violations.

Was the end written despite you and despite the law? To whoever has tasted injustice and psychological collapse, I cannot defend myself because I do not have the documents. I hope to capture your conscience.

Will our fate be determined by law or by what they want? Are we the fuel for maintaining national security? Are we the victims of chaos in our Egypt? What if the murder victim had been a laborer and not a person of authority and status? Is it acceptable for the torturer to be the judge as well? Is it justice for the claimant to also be the witness? These are all questions awaiting answers from decision makers in Egypt!

From the graves of the living

Essam Atta

November 26, 2016. Courtesy of the Archives of El-Nadeem, Center against Violence and Torture.

40

ANONYMOUS

LIFE ON DEATH ROW
The Prison Authority

The Prison Authority, based in El Qollaly in Cairo, is the general administrator of prisons that according to the law, periodically inspects prisons and the conditions of prisoners and receives prisoner complaints, etc. I was therefore glad to hear that in Borg El Arab, we were about to have an inspection by the administrator; I thought it was a golden opportunity to present complaints and the violations we have suffered. But I discovered I was too naïve. In reality, a visit by the administrator means one of three things:

1. A death sentence will be executed,
2. *Tagreeda,*
3. *Taghreeba.*

1. The Execution

It is only natural that the execution take place in the presence of the administrator, in accordance with certain proceedings and rituals. But what happens is that on the day of the execution, time outside the cell is canceled, so we are denied the hours we spend in the open air, walk around, and wash our clothes or blankets. As long as the administrator is in the prison, we have no access to the sun, even if the visit lasts a few days.

2. *Tagreeda*

This means a raid of the cell by informers and officers of the administrator, with the help of prison informers and officers, where they confiscate the belongings of all of the prisoners except the uniforms they are wearing, their slippers, three blankets each, and the Qur'an. Otherwise everything is taken: the rest of the clothes, bags and plastic bags, cleaning supplies, books, medicines, plates, spoons, plastic cups, pencils, papers, kettles, sheets, towels, and anything else apart from the items I mentioned. The strange thing is that 90 percent of the items they confiscate are sold in the prison canteen. Of course the detainees have to buy them all over again once the administrator has left—quite an income for the prison.

3. *Taghreeba*

A prison employee enters a cell and calls a number of prisoners and takes them out of the cell without any of their belongings except what they are wearing but without their slippers. Then the cell is closed again and those detainees never return. After a day or more their cellmates learn that their colleagues have been transferred to another prison, barefoot, without anything other than their uniform. The new prison is usually in a governorate farther away from their families. *Taghreeba* is a punishment.

Undated. Courtesy of the Archives of El-Nadeem, Center against Violence and Torture.

41

IBRAHIM AZAB

IBRAHIM YAHIA AZAB was one of six men convicted in 2015 of terrorism-related charges in connection with the killing of a police officer the year before. All six were sentenced to death in 2017, a verdict upheld by Egypt's highest criminal court, the Court of Cassation, despite claiming that their confessions (three of which were made on national television) were coerced and they recanted them, and despite the inconsistent testimony of major witnesses against them.

KISS MY COMBAT BOOT

We were sitting in the transfer van, our eyes blindfolded, our hands tied behind our backs. They had left only my underwear on me. I don't know what the others were wearing because we could not see each other.

The van stopped and they started getting us out. They released police dogs on us in the van . . . we were running and falling on top of each other inside the van and trying to find the door to get out. The lucky ones jumped and found themselves outside the van. Some fell on the steps of the van . . . what I felt was that we were falling on top of each other. We had barely stood up when the beating began . . . whips, wooden sticks, and an iron electrified rod . . . they kept beating us and abusing us with the most terrible obscenities while ordering us to stand straight. Every time we tried to stand we would fall again from the beating . . . we remained like this—we trying to stand, they beating us, we falling again—for about four hours. Then the beating stopped . . . we tried to stand . . . I had two, maybe three people on top of me and I felt my bones were cracking because of the weight. I was breathing with difficulty . . . I was pleading to God . . . every time I mentioned God, I felt a cold breath on my face.

Eventually I managed to stand, and still I could not see anything and did not know whether the rest had stood up or not . . . somebody pulled me by my hair and pushed me aside . . . later I realized they were making us stand in queues. They removed the blindfold . . . they would beat each of us on the back of the legs . . . we would drop on our knees, and they would push our heads down with their hands.

Then somebody came . . . they said the prison warden has arrived.

He began to speak. "This is the Scorpion Prison, you sons of b——. . . . Whoever enters here comes out with a burial permit . . . that is if he shows good conduct . . . if he tries to make trouble there will be no burial permit because he will be left to the dogs to tear his flesh." He said, "Lift your heads each one of you so that you see what I mean by good conduct." He took one of us, tied a rope around his neck and pulled him while he was not allowed to stand up, just crawling on his knees until he reached the warden . . . the warden pressed his boot on the prisoner's head, forcing his face into the dust, then he said, "See this boot that stepped on your head? Kiss it." The young man did what the warden ordered him to do. Then the warden kicked him and said, "This is what I mean by good conduct here. Take them in!"

They brought ropes and tied them around our necks and dragged us by the ropes while we crawled on our knees. Whoever fell was beaten with the electric rod.

We were taken to a cell that was originally a toilet. We spent some time in there and then they divided us over the wards.

I was put in solitary in the basement.

February 7, 2019. Courtesy of the Archives of El-Nadeem, Center against Violence and Torture.

42

ANONYMOUS

SOUNDS OF THE EXECUTION CHAMBER FROM THE ROOM NEXT DOOR

In the Cairo appeal prison, I was held during the period of examination in a room next to the execution room.

The appeal prison is the dirtiest, darkest spot in Egypt, where executions of prisoners from several prisons around Cairo take place. I am separated from the gallows by a wall. People taken to their deaths pass by my cell door every Sunday and Tuesday at sunrise . . . wearing their red uniform . . . the black hood on their heads . . . their hands tied behind their backs.

The night before, there would be a different activity on the floor. The floor is washed with soap and water; there is incense burning, a sheikh from Al Azhar, and there is swearing and screaming from the second floor, the one with the death row cells. Some recite the Quran in panic. Some lose their minds and groan, shaking the ground from the death they experience every minute waiting for their turn on the floor just below.

The gallows have to be checked and operated several times the night before the execution . . . it has its rituals . . . when they open the room for testing, the door makes this screeching sound, then comes a terrible sound of something heavy hitting something heavy . . . it is a scary sound . . . your soul is filled with fear, your heart shatters, your eyes see horror.

This sound foretells a black day for the death row cells and for me too.

Those taken to their death are terrified by the time they get to the door of the gallows room, and they rush to the closest door—the door of my room—asking to escape from death. Through the hole in the door, I have seen terror that I cannot describe. Some of those taken to their death have thrown themselves against my door screaming "I don't want to die!"

I feel I am dying before they do. They are dragged, pulled, pushed, beaten towards that door, the Quran is recited, the final submission to God dictated . . . then the room opens and the heart jumps from the sound, squeaking and collision, O my God. One morning they executed eight prisoners. They enter on their feet and leave as corpses that are cast aside, that I can see if I look through the opening in my door. Then the second and the third, the gallows and the squeaking, the collision, the screaming, the terror . . . the building shakes, screams from the death row cells, Quran recitation, and corpses lined up one next to the other. I rush to prayer, kneel, and lift my head to glimpse a pair of eyes staring at me . . . I scream . . . one of them was not hooded . . . he stares at me . . . my God . . . I fail to pray and tremble while looking at him . . . What should I tell him? How can I speak when his look has frozen me? Until they dragged him away from in front of my cell . . . for a few moments there is silence. . . . Then the collision.

September 4, 2019. Courtesy of the Archives of El-Nadeem, Center against Violence and Torture.

43

ANONYMOUS

I AM NOT A FAMOUS DETAINEE

I write to you after 425 days behind bars in my prison in Cairo, the Tora Investigation Prison, wearing white prison clothes, lying on the floor in an area not exceeding two handwidths on blankets lined one next to the other, gazing at the roof of my cell, after I lost my most basic rights in life, waiting to hear the ruling tomorrow in a case I know nothing about.

I am in prison for no reason, in a state of non-state, calling on my Lord to be kind to me and remove me from this scourge and save me from the oppression of the oppressors. I have been left on my own. I am not one of the famous detainees, so I don't have media support, and the Press Syndicate is busy with elections, and neither local nor international human rights organizations declare their solidarity with campaigns to demand my freedom, and the famous lawyers who claim to be a shield for the oppressed, and some of whom I thought were my friends, do not line up to defend me.

Even the entity I belonged to ten years ago did not go to the trouble of issuing a statement protesting what happened to me during my arrest and disappearance until I was imprisoned in a governorate other than my own. All the glory goes to the celebrities, while the insignificant are lost and forgotten.

In the end, I thank everyone and inform you that despite everything that has happened I still raise my head high, I remain steadfast, I do not regret any word I uttered in defense of the detainees who came here before me; I didn't care about prison or prison guards during my work as a journalist or as a party activist.

I do not want to prolong my speech to you; I ask you to remember me in prayers for my freedom and return to my family and my loved ones, and if my Lord wishes otherwise, I am satisfied with His wish and judgment. I am always grateful to Him; our only consolation is that we loved our country. ((The evildoers will know what they will return to.))

Undated. Courtesy of the Archives of El-Nadeem, Center against Violence and Torture.

44

YASSIN

YASSIN AND HIS PRISON PAINTINGS AND NOTES

One of the most absurd consequences of the dramatic events of 2013 and the military domination is the detention of very young people for years, and mostly without trials. When Mahmoud Mohamed Abd el Aziz, known as Yassin, was arrested in November 2013, tortured, jailed nine days later, arrested again in January 2014, and sentenced to more than fifteen years in prison, he was not yet twenty years old. Ultimately, he spent five years of his life in six different Egyptian prisons and was released at the end of 2018. As documented in his unpublished prison diary,* he had led an extremely dramatic life since his late childhood: conflicts with his family, especially with his father, dropping out of school and

---

* I'm grateful to Yassin for our conversations and for making these unpublished manuscripts available to me.

leaving home twice at an early age, joining the 2011 revolution and taking part in the protests until the beginning of 2014, in addition to many violent confrontations with the police and the security apparatus. His name, Yassin, might be one of very few things in his life in which he had a choice. In his writings, he recalls having met a person after leaving his family home. The person asks for his name, but he does not answer, and then the person suggests "Yassin!" He likes it more than his real name, and ever since, he has only been called Yassin. Because he left home and dropped out of school, he had to do menial work, but he always loved to paint.

With paintings and with words written in his secret notebooks, he documented, during the years of his imprisonment, much of his life inside and outside of prison. He managed to smuggle two small notebooks and his small-format paintings out of jail. Unfortunately, he lost a large number of his paintings in a house fire in 2019. In the fragments he wrote, he remembers his life since childhood, his family, his early experiences with people and streets far from home, his struggle for an independent life and freedom at an early age, his engagement in the revolutionary events, and the brutal encounters with the security state before his imprisonment. Yassin's prison notes are not chronological; we find him frequently going back to his cell, reflecting on prisoners and on prison life, and as he goes back to his memories of the outside world, he tries to make out why he is in this ugly place. In his writings, he is not only documenting facts and events, he is willing to create an alternative fictional world. He does that not only with words, but also in painting, in which he changes reality. Yassin was inventive in creating beauty within the ugly space of prison, planting plants in small pots made from plastic water bottles, or building a swing.

The world of prison represented in his paintings is less a documentation of prison life than an attempt to capture exceptional moments of different human and aesthetic experiences within this depressed reality. Therefore, the paintings cannot be judged by the normative criteria

Figure 16. *Green Portrait* of a young woman by Yassin. The original is saturated greens to blue-black, and the lighter areas are yellows to yellow-green. Courtesy of the artist. This was painted with his fingers in Tora Prison, cell 14, December 2017.

Figure 17. *Stick Figures* by Yassin, March 10, 2018. Courtesy of the artist.

of art, but gain their value and meaning through the true moment of the creative experience in such an exceptional situation. The story and the conditions of production depict an essential part of such works of art. Each painting has its own significant story. For example, the colorful portrait of a woman is painted using only three colors, blue, yellow, and green.

The reason is very simple—he only owned two tubes of color. Even more impressive is the fact that he did not have any brushes or painting tools, so he used his finger to paint the portrait, which was inspired by a photo of the woman in an old newspaper in the cell. We often feel this material limitation in his paintings: small formats, poverty of color, use of pencils. The results can be simple and sometimes innocent, but genuine, unique, and powerful. An interesting black-and-white sketch painted in March 2018 in Tora Prison, is divided into twenty squares and represents his life over the past five years.

The first story begins in the top right square (like Arabic script, the images should be read from right to left) and represents the event of Maglis ash-Shurah, on November, 26, 2013, when Yassin was arrested, interrogated, and jailed, as depicted. The second row represents his participation, on January 18, 2014, in a protest against the abuse and torture of women by the Egyptian police and depicts his arrest, torture, and imprisonment by State Security. The third line tells the story of his participation in protests against the agreement with Saudi Arabia regarding the islands of Tiran and Sanafir, and again, arrest, interrogation, and imprisonment. The fourth line is the story of his escape, disappearance, and surrender to the police, and finally, in the fifth row, jail, jail, and jail.

One of the most touching paintings by Yassin depicts an old man from behind, wearing the white uniform of administrative detention, and on his back the word *interrogation* is written.

This is "am Hisham," or uncle Hisham, who spent three years in administrative detention after being accused of belonging to a terrorist

Figure 18. *Seated Figure in Corridor* by Yassin, March 22, 2018. In the original, the corridor is beige, brown, and black, opening out into white beyond the prison door, and the ceiling is a rich blue with hanging green plants. The white-uniformed figure is seated on a red stool. Courtesy of the artist.

Figure 19. *Rainbow Swing* by Yassin, October 3, 2018. In the original, the rays beaming through the bars are a vibrant rainbow. Courtesy of the artist.

organization. He was eventually acquitted by the court. In the painting, we see him waiting for his release, as he did every single day. Am Hisham, however, did not live to see that day; Yassin reported to me that he passed away while waiting to hear his name being called for release. In April 2018 Yassin also painted the swing he built in prison.

His joy and pride in this simple achievement beam through in the painting. He expressed his feelings on this small act of hope in verse on the cover page of his second notebook:

> In prison I built a swing
> To caress those years of pain
> And shine through the darkness of formal restrictions
> I felt, though only a little, the rare spirit of childhood
> In a world full of adults' struggle
> For their own existence.

Text by Atef Botros and images by Yassin.

45

MAHMOUD ABU ZEID (SHAWKAN)

SINCE 2011, IMAGES OF WOMEN and men in white uniforms behind bars have widely circulated in the Egyptian public sphere. For the first time in history, Egyptians saw their rulers and state leaders as prisoners: in 2011, it was Mubarak, his two sons, and the most powerful men of his regime; in 2013, it was Morsi and the leading figures of the Muslim Brotherhood. Later, it was many members of the Muslim Brotherhood, as well as young revolutionary activists from leftist movements who played a prominent public role in the years after the revolution. This highly dramatic staging, which changed rapidly, one prisoner after the other, was quite new in the Egyptian media. In many cases, the emerging and circulating images of prisoners in white gained an iconic quality.

One of the iconic figures belonging to the left-wing resistance of this period is the young photojournalist Mahmoud Abu Zeid (born 1987), also known as Shawkan. He was

Figure 20. Shawkan in prison, March 2016. Courtesy of Moustapha El-Shemy and Heba el-Khouly.

arrested for covering the Rabaa massacre on August 14, 2013, and remained in pre-trial detention until March 2016, when these pictures were taken in the courtroom (see figure 20).

In September 2018, he was sentenced to a five-year prison term. Already suffering from deteriorating health, he was infected with hepatitis C during his imprisonment. Shawkan was released on March 4, 2019.

Shawkan's story speaks for many other journalists, activists, and lawyers who were arrested on a massive scale after June 2013. Due in part to these photos, he became one of the most famous icons of that decade. Two years into his imprisonment, he wrote a long letter to the chairman of the journalists' union that was published in July 2015 in the Egyptian opposition press and went viral on social media. It declared in part, "My emaciated body, besieged by diseases, can no longer help me to endure the difficult circumstances of my detention within four walls. It has been two years without any charges or accusations. I just carried my camera and recorded the events neutrally and professionally. Still, I am not afraid of death. I am waiting for it because it is certainly better than this life."

In several letters from prison, Shawkan wrote about his illness and about the circumstances of his imprisonment and asserted that he was not politicized, that he had only been doing his job as a photojournalist. Numerous actions and petitions for his release were organized in vain by his colleagues. An annual award in photojournalism was named after him. After about a thousand days in pre-trial detention, he wrote a letter titled "Excerpts from a Thousand and One Days," which was published by Amnesty International.

What do the four 2016 courtroom photos say? The photos were grouped together in a frame and have circulated expansively on social media. Together, they build a square. The same person appears in all the photos, a young prisoner in the usual white uniform of Egyptian pre-trial detention. He stands right next to the grille and looks directly at the observer or the person taking the photos, who stands, of course, on the other side of the grille. His facial expressions, gestures, and hand movements produce figurations in the space of his cage, seemingly to convey a certain content or message to the outside world. In the upper right picture, the prisoner appears as if he were taking a closer look at the outside world through binoculars. He closes one eye and looks at us (the observer/photographer) in a concentrated and constant manner. In the other pictures, the white uniformed man appears as if he were holding a camera and using it to search for, record, and capture precise objects outside his cage. Is he trying to document specific moments of the reality beyond the grid, to freeze, fathom, question, reveal, or chant conditions or grievances? Who is observing whom? Who photographs and documents whom?

Prisoners, by definition, are banished behind walls, especially political prisoners, who are to be kept invisible and silent. Yet this type of photograph of prisoners behind bars makes them visible and present again. The grid highlighted in the photos makes the boundary between the two worlds quite visible to us, but at the same time allows us a clear insight into the world of the prisoners, who appear as if they were in an aquarium. All of this information and these impressions flow immediately in a moment of sensual visual perception of the image. The prisoner here is a performer in an interactive presentation, and his cage is the stage of a play. The spectator is the outside world, society, the collective, or the public, which is watching the images online or in the media everywhere. The powerful and complex irony of these photos is mainly due to their visual mimicry. The complexity of this irony unfolds when we realize that the character in the cage is the photojournalist Shawkan, who was arrested due to his photodocumentation activities.

The photo composition expresses the complex relationship between politics, ethics, and aesthetics. Does his visual mimicry remind us of the cause of his loss of freedom? As a photojournalist, he merely wanted to document the bloody events of the Rabaa al-Adawiya massacre with photos. Does he want to denounce the silence of society, or is he pointing at the double barbarism of the regime: the massacre itself, as well as the arrest of thousands afterwards? There will be no clear answers and interpretations, including of the question as to what constitutes the aesthetic through the visualization of the political and ethical.

The political, ethical, and aesthetic complexity of the images also includes the dialectic of power that emerges from them. A young photographer stands against a violent military regime. He is behind bars, powerless, at the mercy of brute force, without a weapon, without even a camera, and yet he can set an example with his artful, artistic pantomime of simple movements. His signs were visually fixed, recorded, composed, and circulated again through photography, perfectly and at the right moment. These photos were extremely widespread on Egyptian social networks, often as profile pictures. Another dialectic level is the tension between the inside and the outside, the activist and his community. The strong visual rhetoric of the photo composition is no less effective than Shawkan's powerful words in his letters.

INFORMANTS IN THE MORNING

At 7:45 a.m., a tall, hard-hearted and thick-minded informant with barely recognizable facial expressions shows up; his accent betrays his countryside origins. His mission and assignment inside the prison, like those of his other "team" members of informants, are to stand near your head and shout the following: "Stand up buddies, all of you; it is inspection time."

These informants are alike in terms of traits, characteristics, and expressions—perhaps they only differ in height from each other. They all have small faces, untidy moustaches, bald heads, sunken eye sockets, and flat palms and long arms that match their stature. This was the third time we were being searched this month, the twenty-sixth time by the Prison Authority within the last 900 days, and the ninety-fifth time by the Prison Intelligence service. The lion's share of such incidents were carried out by Mr. Selim, chief of intelligence, who conducted the search in person this time.

I lazily and gradually opened my sleep-heavy eyes; it sank in slowly—I realized it was another inspection. Leaving all my belongings inside the cell, I went outside with my cellmates for the physical tap-search of every one of us. We lined up next to each other like slackers for the inspection to take place under the supervision of the chief prison informant. An hour passed, with all the denigrating looks and verbal insults one can think of.

The cell was ransacked, all of our belongings scattered around, the clothes torn and insulted like their owners. Another hour passed; it seemed that it was quite serious this time, as all the prison informants and their boss were conducting the inspection. Can you imagine what it is like to have ten people searching a 2- by 1.8-meter cell?!

I stood wondering to myself, "What is this? Am I the [Muslim Brotherhood] Supreme Guide? Or am I [Al-Qaeda leader Ayman al-] Zawahiri? But Zawahiri left prison years ago? So what is this? Why does this happen to me? So, could I be [leader of the armed group calling itself the Islamic State] Abu Bakr Al-Baghdadi? This whole commotion just for inspection!"

By the way, each time there is an inspection, the informants steal our belongings. On top of that, my colleague's eyeglasses were crushed in the cell; this poor guy, Iskander, is nearly blind. The remains of the poor glasses were ground up like corn kernels in a mill under the guy's foot. Nothing was left. Regardless of the justifications they might resort to, nothing really justifies a human being treated with this cruelty, harshness, and insult.

I have no answers other than that this is a matter of persecution by the chief informant. But what have I done to deserve his oppression? The two of us have nothing personal going on between us, inside or outside prison, that would justify me being insulted and searched for the third consecutive time this month. He spared all the criminal prisoners, the Brotherhood, and the ISIS inmates, only to oppress a journalist who was betrayed during the performance of his duty and thrown in prison for a nearly a thousand days without being able to see the judge.

Is he doing this on his own or has he been instructed by his superiors to persecute me? If so, the state, represented by the government, has decided to leave its Brotherhood and ISIS enemies alone and teach a journalist a harsh lesson—a journalist who has no affiliation but to his profession; a journalist who answered the call of the government itself to cover the dispersal of the [Rabaa al-Adawiya] sit-in.

Can any sane person tell me what is going on? Why am I being unfairly placed in solitary confinement?

Has it not been enough to have spent almost a thousand days in detention, unfairly and on false grounds? A thousand and one nights?

Why are my two elderly parents being prevented from seeing their son after being dragged for eight hours and a full day to bring me things I need?

Why on earth do ten men search a matchbox-like cell for two hours?

Although the inspection failed to find any violation, "the informant block" threatens to come and search again. What do the chief informant and his men want from me?

Why all this oppression and persecution? Has there not already been enough?

March 9, 2016. Letter to Amnesty International. Initial English translation at www.amnesty.org/en/latest/campaigns/2016/03/cruelty-insult-photojournalist-letter-egyptian-jail.

This entry was originally published in German in Atef Botros, "Von der Straße zum Gefängnis. Die Verschiebung des öffentlichen Widerstandsraums im heutigen Ägypten," in Elisabeth Büttner and Viktoria Metschl, eds., Figurationen von Solidarität *(Berlin: Vorwerk 8, 2018), 226–40.*

46

SONG OF SUBMISSION

> CHANCE FOR LIFE (FURSA AL-HAYAT)
> He is able to be a new person
> Who has the right for a chance at life
> We will help him start over again
> With all the love
> We will always be beside him
> We will assist him to learn
> To benefit from and survive in life.

These lyrics are from a song, "Fursa al-Hayat" [Chance for life], that accompanied a promotional video for the new prison complex in Wadi Natrun.* Produced by YN Studio in Dubai and Cairo-based Fortissimo Audio Production, and featuring images of a gleaming white complex of structures

---

* Egyptian Interior Ministry, "Ughnia bi-'anwan 'fursa al-haya', Markaz islah wa-ta'hil wadi al-natroun, al-jadid," 2021, www.youtube.com/watch?v=h1B06B0cS9w.

Figure 21. Screen capture from a promotional video for Wadi Natrun Prison, located in the desert 100 kilometers outside Cairo.

of panopticonic proportions, the video shows three new tourist buses approaching what looks at first like a mall, until the camera zooms out to show what is clearly a massive prison complex (one of the largest in the world, according to *al-Araby* newspaper). Prisoners exit the buses in slow motion, surrounded by security; they could easily be rock stars on the way to a stage were it not for the handcuffs joining each pair together. As we are taken through a tour of the prison, whose clean cells, ample ventilation and light, and workshops and classrooms for learning all sorts of skills are the ontological and phenomenological opposite of the reality of Egyptian prisons today, we see the "American-style" carceral vision of the Sisi regime, whose ostensible goal for whoever is lucky enough to be transferred there is "rehabilitation" rather than pure punishment.[†]

[†] See Mandour, "Egypt: Mega Prisons Deepen Sisi's Dystopian System of Repression," *Middle East Eye*, November 9, 2021, www.middleeasteye.net/opinion/egypt-repression-deepens-sisis-dystopian-vision.

Of course, there will be no rehabilitation for the vast majority of political prisoners, who constitute an ever larger share of the total prison population. The most compliant prisoners may indeed be transferred to Wadi—one recently freed female prisoner told us that the video was actually shown to prisoners in Cairo, who were told that if they behaved exceptionally well they might be transferred there to finish their sentences. For most political prisoners, entering prison will continue to mean a "welcome party" and other forms of brutality and humiliation that remain the core and the point of the prison experience.

The fact that the Egyptian government would build such a complex, never mind use it as an incentive for good behavior, speaks to the carceral future of Egyptian politics, where violence and imprisonment are used to prohibit any possible challenge to the regime while disciplining those who run afoul of it so that they leave prison as compliant citizens of the new Egypt. For those who don't comply, Scorpion—the most feared high-security wing of Tora Prison, where the most important political prisoners are remanded—will ensure they leave broken and brutalized, if they survive.

Despite the violence and the propaganda, the courage of Egypt's political prisoners remains an inspiration to a world where such treatment will by necessity become increasingly common as governments resort to violence to stifle protests against conditions and policies they are unwilling or unable to change. Still, not all hope is lost. Angela Davis once remarked that she was freed by the people, not the US government. Constant public pressure and recognition left the government no choice but to let her go. In the same way, enabling prisoners' words and writings to travel far and wide is akin to breaking them out of prison, not metaphorically but literally, because as long as their words are free, they can never be silenced. This book is a testament to the humanity, yearning for freedom, and power of Egypt's stolen generation, and of the importance of listening and learning from it as we continue to struggle to build a world free of authoritarianism, violence, and mass imprisonment.

NGŨGĨ WA THIONG'O IN CONVERSATION
WITH COLLECTIVE ANTIGONE

AFTERWORD
A Message to Egyptian Political Prisoners

> COLLECTIVE ANTIGONE (CA): It is a great honor to have you here, knowing that you have read this collection of prison writings, and to discuss them with you.
>
> NGŨGĨ WA THIONG'O (N): It's a pleasure for me as well.
>
> CA: Reading your prison memoir *Wrestling with the Devil* [recounting his imprisonment in Kenya, 1977–78], we can't help but be struck by how relevant it is to the situation of Egyptian prisoners today. We'd like to begin with something that was said by Egyptian human rights lawyer Mahienour El-Massry, several of whose letters are included in this book: "We don't like prisons, but we are not afraid of them." It seems you had a very similar sentiment of defiance fifty years ago when it was your time "behind the sun," as Egyptians describe being imprisoned.

N: Her words remind me of the lyrics from a famous Mau Mau song, which go: "You can take us to prison and to concentration camps. But we shall never give up the fight for our lands and freedom. Kenya is a Black people's country." Settlers used to think of Kenya as a white man's country, what they called the "White Highlands." This song was a resistance response to their claim that Kenya was a white man's country, where the native people were often killed, taken to prison, concentration camps, just to break their collective spirit in the struggle for their land and freedom.

CA: One supposes this feeling is not unique to activists.

N: It's not just about being politically active. If you are politically active, which is important, but armed with an ideology and coherent belief system, it's very difficult for the oppressive measures to break you. Call it resistance backed by a belief that comes from the heart.

CA: This resonates with the words of Alaa Abd El-Fattah in his book *You Have Not Yet Been Defeated*. Being positively defiant seems to be central to the act of survival in prison.

N: Belief in the cause is a very important part of resistance and survival. And resistance in prison is not a matter of fighting your warders or guards, but finding a way to stick to your beliefs, to know who you are. The foundational act of resistance in prison is understanding why you are there.

CA: There's that scene in *Wrestling with the Devil* where you're standing up to the warden and you don't know whether you should resist the order to hold out your hands to be handcuffed so you can go to the doctor. You're arguing with yourself: Should you just do what he wants or speak up? And ultimately, the voice that says you have to speak up prevails.

N: Yes, there are two voices wrestling within you. One voice tells you to resist and the other tells you, "Submit." And it's good when the voice of resistance wins. You know that what you stand for is right, and what the other side stands for is wrong. If you stand against oppression armed with belief, you can't suddenly bow down to it. So, resistance is essential to the survival of a political prisoner, and by political prisoner I mean someone who is politically and ideologically clear, be it an ideology rooted in political or even religious beliefs.

CA: What also struck us in thinking about our volume as we read through *Wrestling with the Devil* was how tied together being a political prisoner and a writer are in prison. Yet at the same time, the idea that thirty to forty years after your experience in Kenya there are young people who still go through this—across Africa, including Egypt of course, but globally as well—is quite telling. The dehumanization of imprisonment, of children, women, activists, anyone challenging the dominant set of beliefs, remains great.

N: Well, it is still a problem. Survival was not inevitable. Many young people of my generation died in dictator Moi's prisons. But they died for the collective survival of a community, which is the whole point of resistance. It is an act for a survival greater than one's own physical survival. And by resistance I don't mean fighting with prison wardens who are armed and outnumber you. I mean standing for your beliefs. As Martin Luther famously declared, "Here I stand; I can do no other." These words were echoed in the title of Paul Robeson's book, *Here I Stand*.

CA: Several of our friends who've been in prison have said the same thing. You have to find something and if you don't stand up for yourself, you are doomed. Whatever you think you're saving yourself for, you're not.

N: Yes, if you give up your belief you'll be broken forever. When political prisoners stand up for their beliefs, they tend to survive. At Kamĩtĩ Maximum Security Prison, I met Wasonga Sijeyo, who had been in that prison for ten years, but he was strong because he knew what he stood for. To know what you believe, and therefore what you stand for, is absolutely necessary for survival. Look at Mandela: twenty-seven years as a political prisoner, eighteen of them on Robben Island. He came out strong and ready to continue the fight against apartheid.

CA: We can see this when we look at the strength and courage of most of the prisoners whose letters are collected in this volume.

N: I can relate, for example, to Alaa Abd El-Fattah because he and I were both in prison for what we'd written, at least in part, and we both turned forty in prison. The idea of standing up and being defiant no matter what is exemplified by him and the writings of other contributors to this volume, such as Ahmed Douma and Ahmed Naji. You have to choose the minimum you have to stand for. Some prisoners fight everything they're asked to do and fight all the guards. I didn't fight every normal order or pick fights with the guards. I told myself, they are not the ones imprisoning me. They are the employees of the system. My enemy is the system. But there were minimums for which I stood my ground. For example, I would not raise my hands to have them handcuffed. I could not cooperate with my own imprisonment, but I told them that since they had the power of the gun, they could reach for my hands and put them in cuffs. But I wouldn't participate in my own handcuffing.

CA: You write about the urgency of writing, the urge to write that enabled you to defy daily the intended imprisonment of your mind: "Writing this novel has been a daily, almost hourly, assertion of my will to remain human and free despite the state's program of animal degradation of political prisoners." This notion of the urge to write is very powerful and helps elucidate the central premise of this book.

N: Well, Ahmed Naji writes in the foreword to this book that "I realized the trap. I couldn't publish anything while in prison, yet during my release anything I had written while here would be scrutinized, and I would likely be forced to burn it." As I describe it in *Wrestling with the Devil*, it was a constant "game of write-and-hide, with inquisitive guards prying and prowling constantly." But that trap can as well become a trapdoor to a kind of freedom, as I was to discover when I was taken to Kamĩtĩ Maximum Security Prison. The reason I was taken there, as I write in the book, is that I'd worked with ordinary men and women of Kamĩrĩthũ, Limuru, to produce a play, *Ngaahika Ndeenda* [I will marry when I want], written by Ngũgĩ wa Mĩriĩ and me, in Gĩkũyũ, the language spoken by my community. It was wonderful for me to see the transformation of a community when it sees its struggles communicated in its own language. So, when I was arrested, I could never apologize for that; nothing could make me apologize for that, ever.

In prison, we were supposed to write a confession. And you're not told what to confess. It's a confession of your sins of revolting against the government, but I knew there was no way I would say I was wrong. I'd seen the transformation in the people, and I knew the regime was wrong, so there was no way I was going to bow down to their lies. Writing helped me a great deal. For me, writing became an act of resistance. I didn't have regular paper, so I used toilet paper. I got the pen from the prison guards. I told them I was going to write a confession. There was no confession, of course; I wrote the novel *Caitaani Mũtharabainĩ* (*Devil on the Cross*) instead—perhaps the novel was actually a long confession of my beliefs. As important was that I wrote it in my mother tongue. The biggest transformation for me was the discovery of the power of my mother tongue.

CA: In your memoir, one of your prison-mates says, half-jokingly, that "it may sound a strange thing to say to you, but in a sense I am glad they brought you here. The other day—in fact, a week or so before you came—we were saying that it would be a good thing for Kenya if more intellectuals were imprisoned." But then when you're in prison, they started jailing a lot of intellectuals. The assumption, we presume, is that once you remove the intellectuals it's much harder for the people to organize, because the intellectuals play a key role in organization. Egyptian prisoners have similarly joked about wanting to have friends and comrades imprisoned with them in order to have company.

N: Yes, that's natural. But more seriously, imprisoning so many intellectuals can have the opposite of the intended effect. They may want to silence the ordinary people by removing the avant-garde, but sometimes doing so awakens the people instead. A good example: The women and men of my village were just enjoying doing a play in their own language for once; they didn't realize it had any larger significance. But after I was arrested, oh my God, they saw the larger significance. That's why imprisoning writers and intellectuals, and even torturing them, often does not have the intended result of silencing others. It might even encourage them to resist.

CA: You write that imprisoning intellectuals and activists shows that they have been seen by the authorities, and that people have seen through the government's official lies and use of morality and tradition to justify what they are doing. It's a recognition that the people have started to organize to oppose the plunder of the nation and its wealth and heritage.

N: With the participants in the play, the actors weren't saying, "We've performed something anti-government or revolutionary." They were just enjoying the play and the performance. My imprisonment made them look at the play again. That's why in history, oppression has never been able to silence voices of dissent, ever, as the persecution of the early Christians reminds us. The early followers of Jesus were workers and fishermen, and even prostitutes; when they were persecuted, they found other ways of living, even in catacombs. They found new ways of sharing communally, and so Christianity spread rather than disappearing over time. They formed communist communities, where sharing whatever they had was the moral norm. All that changed when Christianity became the religion of the empire.

CA: You talk a lot about the relationship between what you call "the colonial affair and neocolonial affair." Specifically, can you elaborate on how Kenyan jailers, and through them the postcolonial government, were treating prisoners exactly how they'd been treated by the British (this includes President Jomo Kenyatta, who was himself imprisoned by the British).

N: That's what neocolonialism does. Think about it. Kenyatta was in prison, imprisoned by the colonial regime. I had written about him very positively in my second novel, *Weep Not, Child*; he's a very heroic figure. He was like a semi-God to us growing up. He inspired us, even those who went on to fight in the mountains. So I've always respected him for that; yet we have to be able to criticize him for the neocolonial part of our history.

But the "affair" can be more complicated still. In the struggle, you can find situations where people in the same family, and who love each other, are on opposite sides. In my own family, one brother was fighting against the British and the other was a member of the Home Guard, working for the British auxiliary force, paid very poorly to do the dirty work of the colonial government. Two brothers who loved each other—my full brother was a guerrilla, but the half-brother was working for the

British, and they were friends. One day they met at the house of a third brother, one leaving and one coming to visit, and they ran away in opposite directions, because they each thought the other was there to get him. Yet years later, when I was myself arrested again by the police, the two brothers came to see me together. They'd realized that in the struggle they were serving two different systems, so they didn't hold the grudge against each other forever.

CA: You wrote the following in your memoir about composing a letter to Kenyatta when you were in prison.

"I am writing to Jomo Kenyatta in his capacity as an ex–political prisoner."

"His case was different," the guard argues.

"How?"

"His was a colonial affair."

"And this, a neocolonial affair? What's the difference?"

"A colonial affair . . . now we are independent—that's the difference," he says.

"A colonial affair in an independent country, eh? The British jailed an innocent Kenyatta. Thus Kenyatta learned to jail innocent Kenyans. Is that the difference?"

N: The word *affair* came from a memoir I was commissioned to write, what would have been my third book. I had just gotten an agent and he succeeded in obtaining a very big advance for the book. The book was supposed to be about the lifestyle of the British settlers, who were always drunk, committing adultery with each other's partners. He told me the title should be *A Colonial Affair*, so I was playing around with that. Now, I never wrote the book, and the advance was paid back from future royalties from other books. But the title remained with me.

CA: You did write about this. Part of *Wrestling with the Devil* is about the issue of adultery, how louche and loose the settlers were.

N: Yes, because of the area called the Happy Valley, which was a very colonial and louche place. The settlers were known for that kind of lifestyle. That's why they called it "the Happy Valley," ironically. Because they didn't do any work. They were always there drinking, chasing each other's wives and girlfriends and husbands, et cetera. But I was also playing around with the idea of colonialism and neocolonialism as "affairs."

CA: You also argue that colonialism didn't produce anything artistically of value, but rather "was the culture of hedonism without morality, a culture of legalized brutality . . . desperately trying to impose total silence on a restive oppressed majority. This culture was sanctified by the very structure and practice of the colonial administration." In this regard, you emphasized the central role prison plays in such a carceralized society.

N: The performance of authority was central to the colonial culture of silence and fear. In the colonial period a white person was not supposed to be seen by a native picking up luggage. You make a Black man take the luggage for you. A white man couldn't be seen being polite to a native. You just order him. If you're Black and a white person talks to you, you're supposed to say "Effendim!" I don't know what it means.

CA: *Effendi* is an Ottoman term meaning "my lord" adopted by the British in their African colonies.

N: Yes, we had to use that word for any white person who stopped you and if you didn't, you'd be slapped or whipped. The culture of silence and fear, we used to call it. But see the irony. The settlers couldn't do without the Black workers. You think your performance of power shields you from being seen for who you are, but you're being seen. Your cooks, your house cleaners, all who make your bed, all the colonized see everything you do; you're not hiding anything from them. Because of that, the settlers had to perform authority all the time in order to reinforce it, at least for themselves, but the colonized could see right through the performance of power.

CA: You talk about how important theater was in this regard, to the point where the British tried to create their own theater in Kenya and elsewhere.

N: Theater for the oppressed was very important because you could perform the opposite of the current colonial reality. Not just any theater, but theater rooted in the people. If you produce a play in your language, the mother tongue of the community, it can fundamentally change it. Every oppressive system has economic, political, cultural, and even religious aspects. In such a system, culture is used to control the minds. But theater, as culture, can also be used as a tool of resistance, resisting the oppression of the mind. That's how writers survive in prison, because when they write, the resistance helps keep the spirit alive.

CA: You talk about writers several times, and obviously you're a writer, as are many of the prisoners whose letters are featured in this volume. But the majority of the people arrested in Egypt today are picked up merely because they are in the wrong place at the wrong time. Such random imprisonment is, we believe, a way to scare the population at large. Even if you're innocent you can be guilty, so you better really watch yourself. You better do nothing, because even if you do the littlest bit, they'll grab you. But for a writer prison is very particular. But you must have encountered other prisoners who weren't writers or artists. You have your writing, but what do they have to sustain themselves?

N: Even if you're not a writer at first, you start to write in prison in order to survive. For me, as a writer in prison, writing was even more important. They could handcuff me, but they could not handcuff my mind or my imagination.

CA: Yet they somehow allowed you to write.

N: Well, they wanted me to confess, in writing. I pretended to be writing a confession, but instead I wrote a novel, *Caitaani Mūtharabainī* (*Devil on the Cross*); I made notes on the walls during the day, or even in the margins of the Bible—similar to the story of the anonymous Coptic prisoner in this volume who wrote his letters in its margins. Then I'd rewrite and expand the notes on toilet paper at night—the paper of so many imprisoned writers.

CA: Yet, as you've written, while they are in prison most people begin to feel that the people have betrayed them. And that's a big issue.

N: Yes, it is; part of the way they try to break you is to make you feel that "the people" have abandoned you. That's why you have to know what you stand for in order not to feel abandoned; that's the biggest weapon of resistance. For me this was epitomized by the language question. Yes, I had been imprisoned for writing a play in Gīkūyū, my mother tongue. Now, in prison, I started thinking more about the language question, and it became a revelation—the role of language in the system of oppression. Look at Ireland, Scotland, Wales, Native Americans, Native Australians, the Maori in New Zealand, et cetera, and the pattern is the same—the colonized being made to feel ashamed of their language, their mother tongue. Their language was full of gory; the language of the oppressor was full of glory.

Humiliation for your mother tongue and glorification if you master the language of the colonizer. Under colonialism it's not just a question of knowing your master's language; the master's language must negate your mother tongue. But this now continues into the postcolonial era, with English, in our case, continuing to be what constituted proper language, knowledge, and education. I call it normalized abnormality. Perhaps there's a similar dynamic with Coptic and Nubian Egyptians.

CA: What about the significance of gender relationships in resistance movements, and especially the erasure from the record of history of women's role in them. What does this tell us about resistance?

N: This is an equal problem, erasure of women from our histories, a product of both colonial and neocolonial patriarchy. Women have to tell their own story. Nawal al-Saadawi told her story. Many more women are telling their stories.

CA: You talk about the disappearance and silencing in prison and refusing the psychological terror of being silenced. This is the same in Egypt, where people disappear for months, and no one knows where they are until the family gets a phone call from the police station, the office of a prosecutor, or even the morgue.

N: This is part of psychological torture. Let's go back to the picture of me refusing to extend my hands, my refusal to participate in being handcuffed. What am I doing psychologically? I didn't want to be part of the deception, so I refused to participate in my own oppression. I wasn't abusive to the warders or anything like that, but I stood my ground when necessary for me to do so. Of course, the situation in prisons today is perhaps even more violent. In my time, I was blindfolded and driven around for hours on the way to prison so I wouldn't know where I was, but I was not physically tortured. Today the violence is more ubiquitous and direct. But the performance of terror, anything to make you submissive, is what is constant then and now, here and there.

CA: One prisoner in the notorious Scorpion Prison in Cairo wrote in a letter included in this collection, "I am the one buried alive! I am the one who was put in a solitary dark cell, with no air like a grave. The only difference is that I am breathing, my heart is beating, my limbs are moving, my eyes see all this blackness. Otherwise, I would have thought I was dead!"

N: Can you imagine the experience of being buried alive in a cell for years—no books, newspaper, or radio? Imagine me as an intellectual being without books, newspapers, radio, television. It's not literally being buried alive but it's not that far off. Just getting hold of a pen becomes a victory, one sheet of paper a conquest. What is clear is that in prison your writing takes on greater precision, a kind of razor sharpness. You are recording history, being a scribe of your own experience. For me, to write a novel, in my own language—the first ever in Gĩkũyũ—in a prison cell, hiding it in plain sight, was my resistance, and more. I was imagining another world, out there, of flight to freedom, like a bird you see from the window. Time, which stops in prison, begins to move again, at least on the page.

This volume reminds of my friend Nawal al-Saadawi. She was imprisoned for a year and her husband for twenty years. I remember her at our meeting in Eritrea, at the conference that came up with the famous Asmara Declaration on African languages. She said "Let us get Egypt back to Africa." I think she may have been thinking of all the centuries of attempts to show that the great Egyptian civilization that produced the pyramids, discovered ink and writing paper, and was a pioneer in every field of human endeavor including medicine was somehow not Africa. Egypt is an integral part of the African continent and African civilization. I salute all my writer and intellectual brothers and sisters in Egyptian prisons. Ra will rise again and again.

Selected Bibliography

'Abd al-Hakim, Tahir. *al-Aqdam al-ariyya* [Bare feet]. Beirut: N.p., 1978.

Abd El-Fattah, Alaa. *You Have Not Yet Been Defeated: Selected Writings, 2011–2019*. London: Fitzcarraldo Editions, 2021.

Abdelrahman, Maha. *Egypt's Long Revolution: Protest Movements and Uprisings*. London: Routledge, 2015.

Aflatun, Inji. *Mudhakkirat Inji Aflatun. Min al-tufula ila al-Sijn* [Inji Aflatun's memories: From childhood to prison]. Cairo: Dar al-Thaqāfa al-Jadīda, 2014.

Agamben, Giorgio. *Homo Sacer: Sovereign Power and Bare Life*. Stanford, CA: Stanford University Press, 1998.

———. *The State of Exception*. Chicago: University of Chicago Press, 2003.

al-'Aqqad, Mahmud Abbas. *'Alam al-Sudud wa al-Qiyud* [The world of bars and shackles]. al-Mashreq Bookstore, 2015. First ed. 1937.

Al-Arian, Abdullah. *Answering the Call: Popular Islamic Activism in Sadat's Egypt*. New York: Oxford University Press, 2014.

Al Jazeera. "Qawwat al-'amn al-masriyya" [Egyptian security forces]. February 2, 2011. https://aljazeera.net/news/arabic/2011/2/2/الأ-قوات-المصرية.

Alsharif, Asma, and Yasmine Saleh. "Special Report: The Real Force behind Egypt's 'Revolution of the State.'" Reuters, October 10, 2013. www.reuters.com/article/us-egypt-interior-specialreport/special-report-the-real-force-behind-egypts-revolution-of-the-state-idUSBRE99908D20131010.

Améry, Jean. *At the Mind's Limits: Contemplations by a Survivor of Auschwitz and Its Realities.* Trans. Sidney Rosenfeld and Stella P. Rosenfeld. Bloomington: Indiana University Press, 1980.

Amnesty International. "Egypt: Rampant Torture, Arbitrary Arrests and Detentions Signal Catastrophic Decline in Human Rights One Year after Ousting of Morsi." July 3, 2014. www.amnesty.org/en/latest/news/2014/07/egypt-anniversary-morsi-ousting.

———. "Time for Justice: Egypt's Corrosive System of Detention." 2011. www.amnesty.org/en/wp-content/uploads/2021/06/mde120292011en.pdf.

Arabic Post. "'Wasilatan linaza' al-'itirafat minhum' . . . Taqrir huquqiun: Mu'ataqalun fi misr yuajihun 'unfaan jnsiyyan maminhajan" ["A means of extracting confessions from them." A human rights report: Detainees in Egypt face systematic sexual violence]. September 4, 2022. https://arabicpost.net/أخبار-مصر-في-عنفاً-يواجهون-مم-جنس/2022/04/09/معتقلون/.

Armbrust, Walter. "Trickster Defeats the Revolution: Egypt as the Vanguard of the New Authoritarianism." *Middle East Critique* 26, no. 3 (2017): 221–39.

Awad, Hani. "Egypt's New Authoritarianism from an Institutionalist Perspective: Formal-Informal Interactions before and after the Egyptian Revolution." *British Journal of Middle Eastern Studies*, 2022. https://doi.org/10.1080/13530194.2022.2113503.

Beinin, Joel. "Egyptian Workers and January 25th: A Social Movement in Historical Context." *Social Research* 79, no. 2 (2012): 323–48.

———. "Labor, Capital, and the State in Nasserist Egypt, 1952–1961." *International Journal of Middle East Studies* 21, no. 1 (1989): 71–90.

Benigni, Elisabetta. *Il carcere come spazio letterario. Ricognizioni sul genere dell'adab al-sujun tra Nasser e Sadat.* Rome: La Sapienza Orientale—Ricerche, 2009.

Bianchi, Robert. "The Corporatization of the Egyptian Labor Movement." *Middle East Journal* 40, no. 3 (1986): 429–44.

Blackmon, Douglas. *Slavery by Another Name: The Re-enslavement of Black Americans from the Civil War to World War II.* New York: Doubleday, 2008.

Booth, Marilyn. "Women's Prison Memoirs in Egypt and Elsewhere: Prison, Gender, Praxis." *Middle East Report*, no. 149 (1987): 35–41.

Cairo Institute for Human Rights Studies. "Egypt: National Strategy for Human Rights a Ruse to Show International Community and Donor States that Political Reform Is Underway." November 15, 2021. https://cihrs.org/egypt-national-strategy-for-human-rights-a-ruse-to-show-international-community-and-donor-states-that-political-reform-is-underway/?lang=en#_ftnref15.

———. "Egypt: Systematic Torture Is State Policy." 2019. https://cihrs.org/egypt-systematic-torture-is-a-state-policy/?lang=en.

Cattaui, Rene. *Le regne de Mohamed Aly d'après les archives russes en Égypte.* Cairo: L'Institut français d'archéologie orientale du Caire, pour la Société royale de géographie d'Égypte, 1931.

Cole, Juan. *Colonialism and Revolution in the Middle East: Social and Cultural Origins of Egypt's 'Urabi Movement.* Princeton, NJ: Princeton University Press, 1993.

Daly, M. W., ed. *The Cambridge History of Egypt.* Vol. 2, *Modern Egypt, from 1517 to the End of the Twentieth Century.* Cambridge: Cambridge University Press, 1998.

Dikötter, Frank, and Ian Brown. *Cultures of Confinement: A History of the Prison in Africa, Asia and Latin America.* Ithaca, NY: Cornell University Press, 2007.

Echebiri, Chiamaka. "The Carceral State and White Supremacy, One and the Same—A Tale of State Sanctioned Violence." *Georgetown Journal of Law & Modern Critical Race Perspectives*, November 4, 2019. www.law.georgetown.edu/mcrp-journal/blog/a-tale-of-state-sanctioned-violence.

Egyptian Interior Ministry. "Ughnia bi-'anwan 'fursa al-haya', Markaz islah wa-ta'hil wadi al-natroun, al-jadid" [Song with the title "Opportunity of a Lifetime," from the New Wadi Natrun Correction and Rehabilitation Center]. 2021. www.youtube.com/watch?v=h1B06B0cS9w.

El Amrani, Issandr. "The Murder of Khaled Said." *The Arabist*, June 14, 2010. https://arabist.net/blog/2010/6/14/the-murder-of-khaled-said.html.

Elsisi, Hannah. "'They Threw Her in with the Prostitutes!' Negotiating Respectability between the Space of Prison and the Place of Woman in Egypt (1943–1959)." *Genre & Histoire*, no. 25 (2020). https://journals.openedition.org/genrehistoire/5213.

Epstein, Charlotte. *The Birth of the State: The Place of the Body in Crafting Modern Politics*. Oxford: Oxford University Press, 2021.

Foucault, Michael. *Discipline and Punish: The Birth of the Prison*. New York: Vintage Books, 1977.

Freedom Initiative. *No One Is Safe: Sexual Violence throughout the Life Cycle of Detention in Egypt 2015–2022*. 2022. https://egyptianfront.org/wp-content/uploads/2022/04/Fi_NoOneIsSafe_03-22_v6.pdf.

Ghiglia, Marianna. "Journalistes en quête d'eux-mêmes. Une socio-histoire des professionnels de l'information en Égypte (1941–nos jours)." Doctoral thesis, Aix-Marseille University, 2020.

Gramsci, Antonio. *Prison Notebooks*. Vols. 1–3. New York: Columbia University Press, 2011.

Griffiths, Arthur. "Egyptian Prisons." *North American Review* 165, no. 490 (1897): 276–87.

Hafez, Sherine. "Bodies That Protest: The Girl in the Blue Bra, Sexuality, and State Violence in Revolutionary Egypt." *Signs: Journal of Women in Culture and Society* 40, no. 1 (2014): 20–28.

———. "The Revolution Shall Not Pass through Women's Bodies: Egypt, Uprising and Gender Politics." *Journal of North African Studies* 19, no. 2 (2014): 172–85.

———. *Women of the Midan: The Untold Stories of Egypt's Revolutionaries*. Bloomington: Indiana University Press, 2019.

Harlow, Barbara. *Resistance Literature*. London: Routledge, 1997.

Hilmy, Ahmed. *al-Sijun al-misriya fi 'ahd al-ihtilal al-'inglizi* [Egyptian Prisons during the British Occupation]. Cairo: Tab'a al-matba'a al-najah al-masr, 1911.

Hopkins, Nicholas S., ed. *Political and Social Protest in Egypt*. Cairo Papers in Social Sciences. Cairo: AUC Press, 2009.

Human Rights Watch. "'We Do Unreasonable Things Here': Torture and National Security in al-Sisi's Egypt." September 6, 2017. www.hrw.org/report/2017/09/05/we-do-unreasonable-things-here/torture-and-national-security-al-sisis-egypt.

Ibrahim, Saad Eddin. "Saad Eddin Ibrahim." *Journal of the International Institute* 12, no. 1 (Fall 2004). http://hdl.handle.net/2027/spo.4750978.0012.104.

Ippolito, Dario, and Patrizio Gonnella. *Bisogna aver visto. Il carcere nella riflessione degli antifascisti*. Rome: Edizioni dell'asinoa, 2019.

Khalil, Linda. "The Rise of Egypt's Prison Industrial Complex." The Century Foundation, June 20, 2014. https://tcf.org/content/commentary/the-rise-of-egypts-prison-industrial-complex/?agreed=1.

Levi, Primo. *The Drowned and the Saved.* Trans. Raymond Rosenthal. New York: Penguin, 1988.

———. *I sommersi e i salvati.* Torino: Einaudi, 1986.

LeVine, Mark. *We'll Play till We Die: Journeys across a Decade of Revolutionary Music in the Muslim World.* Berkeley: University of California Press, 2022.

Lockman, Zachary. "Notes on Egyptian Workers' History." *International Labor and Working Class History*, no. 18. (1980): 1–12.

Magdi, Amr. "Why Executions in Egypt Are Skyrocketing and Why They Should End." Middle East Eye, March 24, 2019. www.hrw.org/news/2019/03/25/why-executions-egypt-are-skyrocketing-and-why-they-should-end.

Magdy, Solafa. "Women in Egypt's Prisons: Tales of Oppression, Abuse and Human Rights Violations." Tahrir Institute for Middle East Policy, April 23, 2023. https://timep.org/2023/04/19/women-in-egypts-prisons-tales-of-oppression-abuse-and-human-rights-violations.

Mamdouh, Rana, and Salma Hindy. "President Abdel Fattah al-Sisi Re-elected until 2030." *Mada Masr*, December 18, 2023. https://www.madamasr.com/en/2023/12/18/news/u/president-abdel-fattah-al-sisi-re-elected-until-2030.

Mandour, Maged. "Egypt: Mega Prisons Deepen Sisi's Dystopian System of Repression." Middle East Eye, November 9, 2021. www.middleeasteye.net/opinion/egypt-repression-deepens-sisis-dystopian-vision.

Mansour, Thaer. "New Egyptian Law on Prison System Met with Widespread Satire on Social Media." *al-Araby*, March 10, 2022. https://english.alaraby.co.uk/news/egyptians-satirise-law-turning-prisoners-inmates.

Middle East Eye staff. "Egypt: Prisons Employ 'Systemic Sexual Violence' against Detainees." Middle East Eye, April 8, 2022. www.middleeasteye.net/news/egypt-sexual-violence-detainees-human-rights-report.

Mohamed, Mohsen. *No One Is on the Line.* Trans. Sherine Elbanhawi. Chapel Hill, NC: Laertes, 2023.

Norton, Augustus Richard, ed. *Civil Society in the Middle East.* Vol. 1. Leiden: Brill, 1994.

———. *Civil Society in the Middle East.* Vol. 2. Leiden: Brill, 1996.

Peters, Rudolph. "Egypt and the Age of the Triumphant Prison: Legal Punishment in Nineteenth Century Egypt." *Annales Islamologiques* 36 (2002): 253–85. https://acjr.org.za/resource-centre/copy_of_Triumphant%20prison%20AnnIsl.pdf.

Quijano, Anibal. "Coloniality of Power, Eurocentrism, and Latin America." *Nepantla: Views from the South* 1, no. 3 (2012): 533–80.

Rached, Tahani, dir. *Quatre femmes d'Égypte* [Four women of Egypt]. National Film Board Canada, 1997.

Revolutionary Socialist Movement. *Rayat al-idrab fi sama' misr* [Strike banners in the Egyptian sky]. Online history of the workers movement, published April 20, 2014. Available at https://revsoc.me/our-publications/22402.

Royle, Charles. *The Egyptian Campaigns, 1882–1885*. 1886. Gutenberg edition available at www.gutenberg.org/files/41744/41744-h/41744-h.htm.

Russell, Bertrand. *Autobiography*. London: Psychology Press, 1998.

Rutherford, Bruce K. "Egypt's New Authoritarianism under Sisi." *Middle East Journal* 72, no. 2 (2018): 185–208.

Sallam, Yara. "How We Got Used to the Screams of Those on Death Row." *Mada Masr*, October 10, 2017. www.madamasr.com/en/2017/10/10/opinion/u/blog-how-we-got-used-to-the-screams-of-those-on-death-row.

Sanders, Lewis, IV. "Egypt's Prisons: Not a Place for Humans." DW.com, May 28, 2020. www.dw.com/en/egypts-prisons-not-fit-for-humans/a-53585733.

Scott, James. *The Law Affecting Foreigners in Egypt: As the Result of the Capitulations, with an Account of Their Origin and Development*. Edinburgh: William Green and Sons, 1907. Available in Gale's online resource, *The Making of Modern Law: Foreign, Comparative, and International Law, 1600–1926*. www.gale.com/c/making-of-modern-law-foreign-comparative-and-international-law-1600-1926.

Sepúlveda, Luis. *La frontiera scomparsa*. Milan: Guanda, 1996. Originally published in Spanish as *La Frontera Extraviada*, 1994.

Shaker, Nadeen. "Cannot Be Contained." *Khabar Keslan*, April 1, 2018. www.khabarkeslan.com/articles/2018/3/30/cannot-be-contained.

Simon, Jonathan. "Rise of the Carceral State." *Social Research* 74, no. 2 (2007): 471–508.

Sorbera, Lucia. "Body Politics and Legitimacy: Towards a Feminist Epistemology of the Egyptian Revolution." *Global Discourse* 6, no. 3 (2016): 493–512. https://doi.org.10.1080/23269995.2016.1188461.

———. "Gender: Still a Useful Category to Analyse Middle East History? A View from Egypt (1919–2019)." In *The Routledge Handbook of Middle East Politics: Interdisciplinary Inscriptions*, ed. Larbi Sadiki, 362–76. London: Routledge, 2020.

Soyinka, Wole. *The Man Died: Prison Notes of Wole Soyinka*. London: Harper & Row, 1972.

Stacher, Joshua. *Watermelon Democracy: Egypt's Turbulent Transition*. New York: Syracuse University Press, 2020.

Stevenson, Tom. "Sisi's Way: Tom Stevenson on Egypt's Prisons." *London Review of Books* 37, no. 4 (February 19, 2015). www.lrb.co.uk/the-paper/v37/n04/tom-stevenson/sisi-s-way.

Taurasi, Giovanni. *Le nostre prigioni. Storie di dissidenti nelle carceri fasciste*. Sesto San Giovanni: Mimesis Edizioni, 2021.

Thiong'o, Ngũgĩ wa. *Devil on the Cross*. New York: Penguin Books, 2017.

———. *Wrestling with the Devil: A Prison Memoir*. New York: New Press, 2018.

US Department of State. "US Relations with Egypt." April 29, 2022. www.state.gov/u-s-relations-with-egypt.

Walsh, Ryan. "Shareholders in Repression: Economic Predation in Egypt's Prisons." Tahrir Institute for Middle East Policy, April 4, 2023. https://timep.org/2023/04/04/shareholders-in-repression-economic-predation-in-egypts-prisons.

World Prison Brief. "2022 Egypt Report." 2022. www.prisonstudies.org/country/egypt.

Yee, Vivian. "'A Slow Death': Egypt's Political Prisoners Recount Horrific Conditions." *New York Times*, August 8, 2022. www.nytimes.com/2022/08/08/world/middleeast/egypts-prisons-conditions.html.

Yee, Vivian, Allison McCann, and Josh Holder. "Egypt's Revolving Jailhouse Door: One Pretrial Detention after Another." *New York Times*, July 16, 2022. www.nytimes.com/interactive/2022/07/16/world/middleeast/egypt-prisoners.html.

Zaki, Patrick. *Sogni e illusioni di libertà. La mia storia*. Milan: La Nave di Teseo, 2023.

Founded in 1893,
UNIVERSITY OF CALIFORNIA PRESS
publishes bold, progressive books and journals
on topics in the arts, humanities, social sciences,
and natural sciences—with a focus on social
justice issues—that inspire thought and action
among readers worldwide.

The UC PRESS FOUNDATION
raises funds to uphold the press's vital role
as an independent, nonprofit publisher, and
receives philanthropic support from a wide
range of individuals and institutions—and from
committed readers like you. To learn more, visit
ucpress.edu/supportus.

Printed in the USA
CPSIA information can be obtained
at www.ICGtesting.com
JSHW021755291124
74518JS00001B/3